AMBIVALENT
AMERICA

AMBIVALENT AMERICA

A Psycho-political Dialogue

June L. Tapp
American Bar Foundation
University of Chicago

Fred Krinsky
University of Southern California

GLENCOE PRESS
A Division of The Macmillan Company
Beverly Hills, California
Collier-Macmillan Limited, London

Glencoe Press
A Division of The Macmillan Company
8701 Wilshire Boulevard
Beverly Hills, California 90211
Collier-Macmillan Canada, Ltd., Toronto, Canada

Library of Congress catalog number: 71-124866

First Printing, 1971

To Kami, Mara, and Bob,
   who helped me understand
   the authoritarian-democratic
   mixture in myself.

To Lyn, David, Bobby, Jeff, and Glenn,
   whose past and future have served
   as inspiration and motivation.

Contents

Preface

Many attempts have been made in the past by individual historians, psychologists, political scientists, and others to provide an explanatory thesis for American political and historical phenomena and development. It is not our purpose to take issue specifically with the conjectures of our predecessors. Rather we would justify our incursion into this area of thought by bringing an inter-disciplinary approach to the same questions, hopefully adding dimensions which have heretofore been either neglected or slighted.

However, there is a distinct attempt on our part to present an analysis of American political and ideological development which differs in one major aspect from previous ones. We reject the notion of a single norm—be it "progressivism," "libertarianism" or what will you—as *the* American pattern from which departures are merely deviations. We question the correctness of a single construct to describe attitudes and behavior surrounding historical phenomena in any polity. While we accept the designations of authoritarian and democratic as descriptive of political and personal styles, we question the false polarization of the world into essentially fixed typologies. Our hypothesis is not only more broadly-based but also the studied reflection of a wealth of recent contributions which afforded fresh insights. We believe that the findings and perspectives provided by contemporary social psychology, added to previous scholarly contributions, will provide our colleagues and students alike with the urge to continue where we temporarily stop.

We lay stress on the inter-disciplinary approach for, in the post-Freudian period, the social psychologists particularly have forced political scientists to reconstruct their concepts regarding the nature of political man. And it has become self-evident that "man" in mass society, and in his needs to adjust to it, is not the same "man" so neatly categorized by the sixteenth- to eighteenth-century rationalist philosophers.

The book, then, is divided into three sections. The first is a short essay by the editors in which the theory of psycho-political homeostatis and mixture is set forth. It is followed by selections from the behavioral sciences in support of the theoretical speculation that ambivalence is basic to personal and political phenomena. Lastly, there is a series of primary-source, historical readings which again give supportive evidence to this hypothesis of conflictive balance.

We want to thank our friends and critics, Peter Leigh, Felice Joan Levine, Kathleen McCourt, Ed Rancourt, Brenda Smith, and Roberta Tabor for their "supportive services," which contributed greatly to the evolution of this Psycho-Political Dialogue.

The Generation of
an Hypothesis*

I

The original impetus for this work derived from the climate of repression which prevailed in America during the early 1950's. The source of the attack on traditional democratic theory at that time seemed to emanate from a right-wing authoritarian base; the current attacks from the left and right have served as the catalyst for a re-examination of our views.

This introductory essay therefore presents the basic hypothesis upon which this book is built: that all of American political life, in theory and in practice, arises from a constant pull in two opposing directions: towards freedom, and towards authority.

---

*Many of the ideas in this essay appeared in somewhat altered form in *The Personalist*, Vol. 48, No. 1 (Winter 1967). The original piece developed as a result of continuous dialogue between the authors in the late 1950's.

In Western civilization there are strong cultural forces that foster both authoritarian and democratic characters, e.g., capitalism, nationalism, militarism, authoritarian education, the patriarchal family, etc., versus the Christian ideal, humanitarianism, socialism, cooperative movements, etc.   —Abraham H. Maslow

In the last two decades, American political writing, devoted to an attack on conventional democratic wisdom, has posed basic questions about the nature of democracy in America. What is the nature of democracy on the American scene? Has it changed? Are the authoritarian and near-anarchistic trends now present in American thought only a recent occurrence? Or is the problem deeper, related to the nature of man? Has there been an increase in the suppression or limitation of certain guaranteed freedoms? Are there particular processes or situations conducive to democratic or authoritarian choices? Are such choices simply different sides of the personality? A possible hypothesis for these dilemmas, suggested by Erich Fromm, is that man's unconscious motivation toward slavery accounts for a consistent and repetitive "escape from freedom."[1]

Posed, then, is the query: If conflicting dispositions affect behavior, is it sufficient to assert man's ideological choices as either democratic (free) or authoritarian (slave)? This forced dichotomy does not reflect the variety of the human personality; a more powerful and realistic model may be needed to demonstrate the ambivalence and combinations in individuals and societies.

For purposes of orientation and discussion, the designations "authoritarian" and "democratic" depict psychological styles which manifest themselves as either radical or conservative. Prototypically, the authoritarian is an absolutist who is dedicated to an immutable ideology and procedure. Single-minded about the rightness of his goals and means, the authoritarian operates as an inflexible, dogmatic personality with a rigidly established plan sanctioned by an authority, e.g., God, an elite, or a scientific method. The authoritarian sees the mass of mankind as manipulable creatures, incapable of reasoning, weak in leadership and decision-making, and filled with sentimental values that cloud political perception.

Theoretically a "democrat," though depicted as having certain content commitments (i.e., substantive beliefs such as equality, dignity of man, liberty, fraternity), more importantly has a commitment to the inquiry process as the means for achieving goals. For the democrat, meaning exists in the process itself. The democrat entertains alternative choices in addition to his own. He, too, may be politically radical or conservative. In contrast to the authoritarian, the democrat is flexible in his plans, if not his goals. He sees other men as cooperative and compromising creatures capable of reasoning, potentially skilled in leadership and decision-making, practiced in consenting and contracting, and dedicated to the preservation of an open society.

If these personality types are discrete, why are both authoritarian and democratic components frequently seen in the same men? If men are by nature thoroughly democratic, as some like Locke and Jefferson maintain, how could their choice of authoritarian leaders be explained? Many who see man's nature as opposite, like Adams, Cooper, Hamilton, or Hobbes, provide no answer. What makes for the contradictory impulses and ambivalent motives in man's attitudes and actions? For example, why are there both authoritarian and democratic episodes within a decade or century, as in France in the eighteenth century; Germany in the twentieth; or in both Jefferson and Hamilton as early revolutionaries?

Authoritarian and democratic psychological orientations and related political expressions may be conceptualized on a continuum. Rarely is an ideal or extreme type encountered. Most individuals are a mixture. Consequently, man experiences conflict and tension which engender change as he reacts to the demands of specific situations and seeks to maintain subtle balance. Although political expressions are in large part extensions of personality, the confounding of internal and external conditions may so affect attitudes and behaviors that it becomes exceedingly difficult to assess the true nature and relative proportions of the authoritarian-democratic mix.

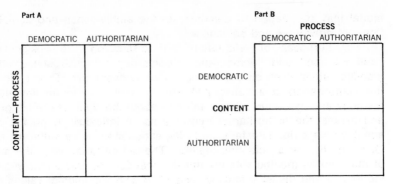

FIGURE 1. Simplistic—Discrete Models

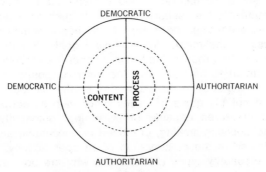

FIGURE 2. Continuous Model

Figure 1 illustrates the simplistic models. The dichotomization in Part A results if democratic and authoritarian are viewed as mutually exclusive constructs and if individuals are forced to describe themselves using only extremes. Part B shows that the terms democratic and authoritarian apply to both content and process but this model still does not adequately represent the subtle mixtures.

Figure 2 illustrates the democratic-authoritarian continuum we conceptualize here. Instead of the discrete cells of Figure 1, in Figure 2 individuals can be placed within any of the four quadrants, depicting their relative affinities to both the content and process axes. The center of the circle represents an equal mix of both tendencies on both axes. The model in Figure 2 permits a more inclusive and comprehensive description of man's psychological and political styles.

Dramatic evidence exists of man seeking both "escape to" and "escape from" freedom, and of man breaking from authoritarianism as well as pushing toward it, repeated almost reactively in the same personality, same decade, and same national entity. There is a continuing need for freedom, equality, fraternity in every personality, party, and nationality. There is also operative, at times simultaneously, a fear of freedom and a desire for protective security-providing authority. In selecting the democratic approach as good, just, and desirable, man elects the most rational choice by retaining the opportunity to be either the authoritarian or the democrat. It may be more useful to hypothesize that man is a dynamic, emergent organism fluctuating between authoritarian and democratic modes in his quest for balance.

The review of American history reveals supporting evidence of the ambivalent nature of man and conflicting ideological choices. From its inception the United States has had authoritarian and democratic influences in both personalities and policies; the present trend is simply evidence of the tension traditionally operative within American systems.

The authoritarian mode in American thought stems from Puritan times, perhaps our earliest period of paradox. The Puritan tradition was authoritarian in approach to man, church, and government, with seemingly contradictory commitments to rational analysis and individual choice. These commitments, democratic seeds in an authoritarian flowerbed, undoubtedly underlay the development of rational inquiry, the ultimate rejection of uninvestigated schemes, and the separation of church and state. Evident in the Puritan world by the late seventeenth century was the ambivalent devotion to security and to science, to the learned ministry and to such as Ann Hutchinson, to the theocratic state and to common law, to witchcraft—a reaction pattern—and to education—another reaction pattern. By the eighteenth century the Puritans sought both God and security and God and freedom.

Jonathan Edwards' success can be attributed to his role as a synthesizer of the authoritarian and democratic components of human personality. Edwards was able to placate both dimensions of man's nature: to make men feel, while guilty and humbled at the mercy of an angry God, capable of using will and making the correct choice.[2] Edwards also demanded from both individuals and congregations an intellectual and emotionally sober dedication in the search for God and security.

For the Puritans the conflicting forces of democratic-autocratic idealism and reality are recurrent themes. The Puritan, both autocrat and democrat, was continuously involved in playing out his ambivalences. The nature of man at this historical juncture reveals itself as mixed and moving, reacting and balancing, unsure of the authoritarian alternative offered by the "elect" Puritans while seeking the democratic option of investigation. American Puritanism is an important example of man in search of equilibrium, security, and synthesis. It exemplifies the duality of human existence and the pendulum sway of authoritarian-democratic components. The orthodox Christian who asserts man's crassness, demands his obedience, and proclaims his obligation to use "democratic" means is the twentieth-century descendant of the early Puritan.

Similar examples of mixture and conflict may be drawn from the Revolutionary period. Alexander Hamilton's background, ability, and personal struggles illustrate his strong drive for security, for a defined system and selected leadership, for an elitist administration of the general welfare.[3] Psychologically an authoritarian, he again demonstrates the mixed nature of man's personality in confronting situational alternatives. For example, though a political and social conservative, he was an economic radical.

Ironically it is the twentieth-century democrat who cries for the welfare state first projected on the American scene by the authoritarian Alexander Hamilton, who envisioned the people as a great beast. Evidently the question of the social costs of welfare and security plagued both centuries. The eighteenth century rejected Hamilton's supposed suppression of the common man and his democratic urge. The twentieth century, even in the 1970's, invites back general welfare albeit without the strong national structure previously suggested and now finally accepted by the common man. There are, of course, lingering echoes of the welfare debate still heard occasionally in an academic hall, and with strange persistence in some political campaigns. But the non-partisan acceptance of welfare can be noted in the campaign speech made by the Republican candidate Dwight D. Eisenhower, speaking in Boise, Idaho, in 1952:

> This middle way today starts off with certain very definite assumptions. We have accepted a moral obligation—the education of our young, decent housing, the rights of working men and working women to be productive, the rights of each of us to earn what he can and to save it as far as taxes will let him. We accept as part of these social gains the fact that Americans must have adequate insurance against disaster. No one counts that thing a political issue any more. That is part of America.[4]

In Hamilton, as in Edwards, the authoritarian-democratic synthesis is discernible in the movement toward personal and political goals. Hamilton fought for the Constitution while rejecting democratic participation for the masses. Despite his autocratic plans and leadership, he never compromised the democratic process. Hamilton perpetuated the Puritan concept of the elite and of man's selfish nature, but he also mirrored the demands of the masses for liberty and security. As an eighteenth-century man, he was ever reflective of the democratic spirit. Unfortunately, he never had enough "spirit" to convince the common man, and therefore remained, as did many authoritarian personalities in American history, a visionary rejected at the popular level.

Hamilton's life raises many questions about the role of the authoritarian personality and ideology in the forming and maintaining of American democracy. Why are elites and frequently structure-builders rejected by the common man? Perhaps a clear authoritarian choice frightens the average man and causes him to react and elect instead the rational synthesizer—the Jeffersons of the eighteenth century, or the Franklin D. Roosevelts of the twentieth. History may prove that the American leader who is authoritarian psychologically but dedicated politically to the substance of democracy (i.e., equality, liberty, fraternity, dignity) is rarely elected. Apparently the common man at times of choice seeks freedom and the promise of liberty and participation.

John Adams mirrors much that was said of Alexander Hamilton. Since he advocated rule by representatives chosen from the elite, Adams is best described as an authoritarian personality advocating an authority-laden democracy.[5] His political predilections are traceable to his living at a time when men were moving psychologically and politically from Alexander Hamilton to Thomas Jefferson.[6] Adams' success derived in part from America's ambivalence toward dreams of equality and realities of inequality—again contradictory forces reaching toward compromise.

Both Alexander Hamilton and John Adams display the Puritan ethos of "ought" and "elect" apparent also in James Fenimore Cooper. Cooper had no faith in man's ability to choose, decide, or lead. He was especially suspicious of the tyranny of the majority. Jefferson also was sensitive to the latter danger, but Cooper, unlike Jefferson, feared all but the intellectually trained elite and saw little possibility in the creativity or rationality of the masses.[7] He embodied the literary authoritarian-democrat, a totalitarian liberal, dedicated to the ideals of equality and freedom but skeptical of their achievement other than through a disciplined democratic elite—almost a contradiction in terms.

The libertarians cover a greater historical span but a shorter ideological one. William G. Sumner, a representative of this group, synthesized a political and social position that equated Christianity, capitalism, liberty, and individualism.[8] The influences of the Puritans, Federalists, English common law, *laissez-faire* capitalism, and, more importantly, a basic mistrust of the general populace, are evident in Sumner's views and in the views of other libertarian figures such as William Orton and Paul More. All three defined democracy in terms of a *particular* political, religious, and economic system. In demanding a particular system of democracy as their plan for society and by substituting a rigidly defined system, their suggestions lost the free choice of true democratic process.

Peculiarly tied by historical accident to Puritan theology, Lockean legal heritage, Darwinian social theory, and Smithian economics, these men expounded a potpourri of antithetical choices vacillating between democracy-authoritarianism, individualism-collectivism, secularism-religiosity, and conservatism-change. Their position is clearest in their desire to be described as libertarians and humanists rather than democrats and humanitarians. Furthermore, the libertarians restricted the growth of liberty and democracy by defining a particular systematic approach and actively discriminating against contrary views. Although Sumner, Orton, and More advocated different approaches to science, religion, social science, ethics, and even man, all of them dogmatically asserted the rightness of their own views, and even more subtly, man's inability to control the world.

Revealing the constant tensions between authoritarianism and democracy, More insisted upon a special "natural aristocracy" shepherding society among equalitarian democracy, oligarchy, and plutocracy.[9] In rejecting the welfare state as encompassing but accepting the orthodox church and advocating a particular religious approach, Orton exemplified the dilemma of an authoritarian in a democratically oriented environment.[10] The powerful presence of libertarians on the American scene reiterates the homage paid and the need met by the authoritarian alternative in man's nature. Movements toward and away from such views, whether in a short span or a century, attest to man's need to satisfy multiple, often contradictory, motives and continually reach satisfactory balance.

Over two decades ago Gabriel Almond recognized the popular rejection of the "natural aristocratic" elite.[11] However, he sought a resolution of democratic problems using expertise, and proposed a disciplined democratic elite of experts to save democracy for the masses. While Almond's process stance demanded an ordered, rigid, and defined system, his content position was assuredly democratic. The conflict between the two was resolved by a commitment to content democracy and the use of a manipulative elite. Perhaps Almond represented another mixture of the democratic and authoritarian modes on the content and process axes.

In the same vein and in response to what they refer to as the various and multiple exigencies of a mass society, a group of writers, aptly described as minimal democrats, have essayed a reformation of democratic theory. These men are impossible to place on a left-right political continuum. Eschewing any ideological base for their theoretical formulations, they argue that the changes they propose are due more often than not to the neutral force of accelerated technology. What these men have to say in common is that contemporary conditions call for a modification of traditional democratic theory. These minimal democrats argue that the average American citizen can no longer clearly play the role envisioned for him by early democratic theory, not only because of the citizen's imperfection of mind and will, but also because the issues have become so deep, so obscure, and the machinery for their resolution so complex, that an ordinary man is helpless before the onslaught of these ideas. What is worse, most average citizens recognize their helplessness and the limitations of their role and become estranged from the political order.

Arthur Schlesinger characterizes this estrangement as a divorce between theory and practice which in turn leads to a morbid and dangerous condition.[12] Disaster is imminent so long as the belief system demands a major role for the citizen and at the same time severely limits those who must rule from ruling. Therefore, the minimal democrats have begun to argue that in American society free men must learn to live with a new concept of democracy, one in which the citizen's role is confined to selecting heroic leaders who must then be left free to cope in some superior fashion with the grotesquely difficult problems of present times. Walter Lippmann summarizes this position in his *Public Philosophy*,[13] arguing that, in the tradition of civility, the special political competence of the people is to give their consent to being governed, to grant or to withhold approval of the measures taken by leadership, but that it is not within the competence of the average citizens to do more. Again, another spokesman for minimalist democracy, Robert Coulson, wrote an essay a decade ago, "Let's Not Get Out the Vote."[14] His thesis was, in effect, "Let's keep all these uninformed who don't know anything about the intracies of the political system *away* from the polls." To invite mass participation by incapable people is to invite disaster; therefore, society should once and for all cut itself apart from the notion that democracy demands participation by each and every individual. The minimalist democrats insist that contemporary politics have so progressed that the average man cannot take part in the decisions and the determinations of his society, and that the citizen's greatest role, in fact his major function, is to choose those leaders who can heroically perform the tasks of keeping society free, leaving the decision-making to the experts who can readily understand the nature of the task.

As a political philosophy the minimalist democratic position is reminiscent of the Platonic notion of the guardians. But as was the case with Plato's guardians, there are serious questions of who shall guard the guardians, and who shall know that the experts are indeed going to rule in the name of the people for the same goals that the people want to achieve.

The preponderance of historical evidence leaves little doubt of the presence of authoritarian-democratic mixture in man's private and public personality, which manifests itself in ambivalent psychological and political expressions. Environment, growth, and process define man's nature and way of life as he attempts to gain security—safety or balance—in personal, social, political, and legal settings. No ultimate declaration about essential democratic or authoritarian perversity is relevant; only a recognition that both components are in a continuous relationship dynamically competing and seeking resolution. The pendulum of man's private and public expressions subtly suggests an open-ended, process-oriented, pluralistic society, providing choices which he makes in terms of particular personal, social, political, and legal pressures.

In his *Power and Personality* Harold Lasswell, cognizant of man's nature, asserts:

> The appearance of a tyrant is an extreme sign of mass demands for the devalued self to depend upon someone else. So long as these dependency demands are generated in the lives of men, the masses will force themselves upon potential tyrants, even though at first glance it looks as though the tyrants were forcing themselves on the masses.[15]

Perhaps the greatest problem for the real democrat, both in terms of content and process, is utilization of the authoritarian and authoritarian-democrat in society. In American development, the presence and influence of such personalities act as a stimulant. The contributions of authoritarians and authoritarian-democrats, though varied, have always reflected a sizeable segment of public opinion and represent a larger proportion of American history and politics than previously acknowledged.

For example, both the Puritans and the Founding Fathers provided a basis for American political theory which was crucial in establishing the social environment in which subsequent personalities and systems emerged. As noted earlier, authoritarian personalities (Hamilton, Adams) and even movements have contributed many structural ideas. Sometimes these contributions are direct. At other times they are the function of reactions (Jefferson, Cooper) to their presence; at still other times the very reaction of an authoritarian (Roger Williams)[16] to an authoritarian resulted in an amazingly democratic occurrence. If the progressive democratization of society calls for amending social institutions to aid the development of democratic personality then it is reasonable to contend that past authoritarian personalities and institutions encouraged the development of an indigenous and potentially increasing authoritarian strain.

The very configuration of democracy insures the presence of authoritarians and authoritarian-democrats. Its pluralistic nature demands variety and open-endedness, permitting the heretic the most chance and choice. The content emphases, regardless of political coloration, remain equality, fraternity, liberty, and dignity. Its process counterparts designate a system of balance, cooperation, compromise, exchange, and competition. These characteristics of democracy encourage man to test himself in the arena of expanded choice. The only restriction on his choice is that he maintain respect for the freedom of others. Psychologically and politically, democracy's advantages are another chance, cooperative goals, and compromised or balanced means in a process that involves both the authoritarian and the democrat.

A democratic environment is conducive to the enhancement of the democratic side of man, for it does not demand a particular economic, political, or religious system—rather it emphasizes the production and protection of the values of dignity, equality, fraternity, and freedom of choice. Perhaps, almost perversely, because true democracy demands an open process, the democratic system and democracy may be vanquished. As man's dependency needs increase through technology, theology, or psychology, his choices become more authoritarian, for he feels safer, more secure, when he has "freedom from." If within the democratic system authoritarians increase their strength by responding to these needs in man's nature, it is conceivable that the democratic process will annihilate itself.

In part the Puritans' theological dependency reflected an authoritarian trend, but in the eighteenth century antithetical tendencies indicated they had adopted more scientific avenues. In part, twentieth-century man's reliance on material invention and technology builds his dependency. This dependency, coupled with a heritage that has authoritarian dimensions, explains the increase in authoritarian choices. The democratic alternative may be too demanding for the man who must resolve his own authoritarian-democratic ambivalence and who must also respond to a complex society. As democracy insists upon free choice in an arena of conflict and compromise, it may announce its own death knell.

If such an outcome is likely, it is crucial to understand the role of the authoritarian and authoritarian-democrat in political and social systems. As Edward Shils affirms:

> The tasks of liberal democratic society are many and many different kinds of personality structures are compatible with and necessary for its well being. Even authoritarian personalities are especially useful in some roles in democratic societies and in many other roles where they are not indispensable, they are at least harmless.[17]

Why the inevitability of authoritarian orientations in society? In part the answer derives from the mixed nature of man. But perhaps it is also perpetuated by its utility and even contributory position to democratic settings.

Man's need for both democratic and authoritarian alternatives and the presence of such personalities and options in the environment may explain the success of those who reflect both qualities, the "rationals." Who are some of these men on the American scene? Thomas Jefferson, Andrew Jackson, and Franklin D. Roosevelt responded both to the democratic and to the authoritarian in man's nature. They provided security with the appearance of choice, and conversely they insisted upon choice with the assumption of security. They were autocratic in their assumptions about man's abilities, duties, rights, and democratic in their means of effectuating them. Psychologically, and even politically, they have been described as dictators by some. Jefferson's demand for an agrarian society secured the rights of men but in a system with particular roles. Jackson promoted universal male suffrage while he inaugurated party politics and patronage. Roosevelt insured the future with social security, sought freedom from want and fear, and introduced a more inclusive governmental system. However, all three are really in the inner circle of the democratic quadrant in terms of both process and content (see Figure 2, page 4). This may be the appropriate position for the educated, dedicated democratic elite. The rationals strike such a balance. They differ from the extreme, pure democrats (see Figure 2, outer circle), who in their undisciplined search for openness and freedom may cause their own annihilation.

While accepting man's rights and abilities, the ambivalence of his needs, and the presence and utility of a variety of psycho-political ideologies, the rationals adopt a disciplined and calculated approach in a secular democracy. They are reflective and aware of the authoritarian strain and obtain the necessary mixture for the survival of humane society. This in part may account for the recent plethora of statements from all segments of the liberal establishment restating the need for a society based on law and defined rules of procedure by which changes are wrought.

It is not enough to degrade, denounce, or disclaim the authoritarian frame. It is imperative that description and understanding of its manifestations be available to illustrate its radical and conservative strains. We must recognize the roles that authoritarians, democrats, and the various mixtures play in the environment. Both man's ambivalent and his rational natures need to be recognized in order to enhance the possibilities of development through education, participation, and law. Such efforts are essential to the eventual "freeing of man's spirit" and movement toward a more democratic mean.

The dangers of any elite include the exercise of unsolicited power, the restrictions of choice and participation, the promulgation of totalitarian democracy—of content over process. This possibility was sharply noted in a recent statement by Sidney Hook analyzing some of the writings of a current ideological hero of the new left, Herbert Marcuse:

> The truth Marcuse antecedently knows is that the ideal society, the completely human society, is one in which there is no repression of human desire and no oppression of man by man. It is a society nowhere in existence today, but one whose outlines our reason can grasp as well as the general direction in which we must move toward it. . . . But [Marcuse says that] "tolerance cannot be indiscriminate

and equal with respect to the contents of expression, neither in word nor in deed...."

... Admitting that, within existing democracy, tolerance is widespread for Right and Left, for Communist and Fascist, for black and white, for Marcuse and his critics—he then denounces it as false because it is impartial....

Marcuse, not a man of half measures, continues:

"Moreover, the restoration of freedom of thought may necessitate new and rigid restrictions on teaching and practices in the educational institutions which by their very methods and concepts, serve to enclose the mind within the established universe of discourse and behavior—thereby precluding *a priori* a rational evaluation of the alternatives."[18]

To the extent that they are unyielding to the importance of pluralistic education, ideological variety, and citizen participation, the disciplined and educated democratic elites, possibly authoritarian-democratic in approach, may push man's development mentally and materially to the point of compelling a democratic choice. Apparently this can only occur when man has redirected his dependent survival needs sufficiently to gain security and liberty simultaneously in various environments. Perhaps it will be the irony of history that the authoritarian element, by forcing the democratic alternative, will help man maintain order and gain freedom.

FOOTNOTES

1. E. Fromm, *Escape from Freedom* (New York: Rinehart, 1941).

2. J. Edwards, "Sinners in the Hands of an Angry God," in C. H. Faust and T. Johnson, eds., *Jonathan Edwards* (New York: American Book Co., 1935) p. 155.

3. A. Hamilton, *The Federalist:* Nos. 33, 27. Also, N. Schachner, *Alexander Hamilton* (New York: Appleton-Century Co., 1946).

4. D. D. Eisenhower, *Vital Speeches,* Vol. XVIII (Sept. 1, 1952) p. 677.

5. G. A. Peek, *Political Writings of John Adams* (New York: Liberal Arts Press, 1954).

6. E. Dumbauld, *The Political Writings of Thomas Jefferson* (New York: Liberal Arts Press, 1955); S. K. Padover, *The Complete Jefferson* (New York: Duell, Sloan and Pearce, Inc., 1943).

7. J. F. Cooper, *The American Democrat* (New York: Knopf and Co., 1931).

8. W. G. Sumner, *Forgotten and other Essays* (New Haven: Yale University Press, 1918).

9. P. More, *Aristocracy and Justice* (Boston: Houghton-Mifflin, 1915).

10. W. Orton, *Liberal Tradition: A Study of the Social and Spiritual Conditions of Freedom* (New Haven: Yale University Press, 1945).

11. G. Almond, *American People and Foreign Policy* (New York: Harcourt Brace Co., 1950).

12. F. M. Carney and H. F. Way, Jr., *Politics, 1964* (Belmont, Calif.: Wadsworth Publishing Co., 1964) pp. 5–6.

13. W. Lippmann, *Essays in the Public Philosophy* (Boston: Little, Brown and Co., 1955).

14. R. E. Coulson, "Let's Not Get Out the Vote," *Harpers Magazine,* Vol. 211 (Nov., 1955).

15. H. Lasswell, *Power and Personality* (New York: W. W. Norton and Co., 1948) p. 163.

16. P. Miller, *Roger Williams: His Contribution to the American Tradition* (Indianapolis: Bobbs-Merrill, 1953).

17. E. Shils, "Authoritarianism: 'Right' and 'Left,' " in R. Christie and M. Jahoda, eds., *Studies in the Scope and Method of "The Authoritarian Personality"* (Glencoe, Ill.: The Free Press, 1954) p. 49.

18. S. Hook, "Barbarism, Virtue and The University," *The Public Interest,* Vol. 15 (Spring, 1969) pp. 36–37.

The Perspectives
of Social Science:
The Thesis as Inquiry

II

Having now presented our hypothesis, we turn to the social sciences to verify and test if, indeed, there is a body of *current research* which adds substance to our speculation. We do this because the social science perspective encourages development of an inquiring approach toward knowledge and theory. From our examination of the interrelated disciplines of psychology, sociology, political science, and law, we have brought together a cohesive set of empirical and theoretical studies, articles, and cases which indicate that we are not alone in describing the multi-dimensional, ambivalent aspects of man's private and public life.

Extremist groups are not new to the American community. But over the past thirty years the dangers of totalitarianism have received more public attention, and social-science research has verified the continued presence of authoritarian tendencies even in American democratic society. Recent domestic and international situations, while intensifying anxieties and perhaps also authoritarian tendencies, have again signaled the necessity for examining authoritarian and democratic components in American personality and politics. Alexis de Tocqueville, in his classic description, noted two antithetical, conflicting styles suggesting that Americans possess both democratic and authoritarian dimensions and maintain a subtle balance between them. The historian V. L. Parrington argued that a major dynamic in American institutional and intellectual development was the conflict and tension between the authoritarian and democratic orientations of man and society.

These views—that there are authoritarian components in democratic personalities and polities and democratic ones in authoritarian personalities and polities—had some currency in the theories of such psychologists as Abraham Maslow, Theodore Adorno, Else Frenkel-Brunswik, and Erich Fromm before World War II. However, the urgency of the times and the threat of potential fascism during the 1940s pushed the direction of systematic social psychological research toward unitary descriptions of authoritarian personalities and politics and less toward assessments of democratic character structures. This early work on authoritarian ideology almost obscured scholarly research about the contradictions and ambivalences in American political expressions and personality styles.

The search for understanding the style of the authoritarian, anti-authoritarian, and the intermediate, mixed types emerged in response to ideological and methodological criticisms. Acknowledgment of both authoritarian and democratic components in personality and politics stimulated social scientists to study the nature of these democratic-authoritarian relationships and to explore the conditions for compromise as well as the expressions in individual and group behavior. Our tasks include understanding the nature and function of authoritarian, democratic, and mixed types, describing the conditions that encourage the development of particular styles, and asking if an open, humane society needs all modes of expression. The pertinent content and process questions are twofold: What is the effect of authoritarian and democratic dispositions on individual and group behavior? What is the effect of authoritarian and democratic climates on personal, social, political, and legal actions?

The domain of public behavior is too complex to be readily dealt with in any single conceptual schema or by any single discipline. The determinate nature of the relationship between personality and politics, like the complexity suggested by the multiple meanings of democracy and autocracy, demands a conjoining of the behavioral and political sciences. As it became clearer that democratic and authoritarian had more than political connotation—also describing individual styles and group relations—so it became clearer that the study of democracy and authoritarianism must also be enlarged to embrace the nonpolitical realms.

Impetus for psycho-political research emanated from a growing awareness that past efforts describing the antecedents and nature of behavior in the polity inadequately recognized the influence of psychological factors in public affairs. This research perspective gained additional momentum as social scientists experienced theoretical, methodological, and data-gathering revolutions and increasingly questioned the validity and reliability of knowledge about public life acquired through unsystematic investigation. Also, more precise techniques for observation, classification, and measurement stimulated new directions in research and new partnerships in disciplines.

A psycho-political approach stresses the inextricable relationship between theory and research, and the inexorable necessity of an interdisciplinary tack for a fuller understanding of personality and ideology. One cannot understand the products of the interplay between organism and environment in political-legal systems without considering the nature of man (his psychological makeup) and the effect of society (the social structure). A psycho-political approach supplements the common goal of all social research: the description, explanation, and prediction of human phenomena with particular focus on attitudes and actions. It reflects the advances possible from a marriage of disciplines, theories, and methodologies. The behavioral science input enhances insight about ideological and nonideological behavior in political and nonpolitical milieus, encourages appropriate theoretical as well as empirical distinctions, and generates more refined hypotheses and analytical models. Psychology advances general propositions about human behavior; political science, about such behavior in the polity—the mutual relevance is apparent.

The selections in this section reflect the interests of social scientists, particularly psychologists, who have addressed themselves to the problems of authoritarian and democratic styles in personality and ideology, the impact of conflicting styles on individual and group behavior, and the expressions of authoritarian-democratic mixtures in personal, social, political, and legal systems. They are intended to be ideational tantalizers. None is so short as to miss the point of the original research, but none is so long as to discourage the reader from delving further.

These readings reflect the conjoining of behavioral and political sciences and, by the nature of their research and exposition as well as theoretical and empirical contributions, are intended to stimulate the reader's curiosity, as well as broaden his comprehension about interdisciplinary enterprises.

The selections are also intended to alert the future social scientist

and citizen to the important role of conflict and ambivalence in public
and private life. Far too little theoretical and empirical attention has
been paid to the effect of continuity and mixture in the social process;
far more attention has been accorded the concept of dichotomy.
Duality, mixture, and inconsistency are frequent experiences in psychological, political, and legal systems. In the twentieth century we must
learn to appreciate the conflicts and compromises congenial to change
and necessary in democratic societies.

Emergent Conceptualizations of Authoritarian and Democratic Personalities

1

Nevitt Sanford,
   The Approach of the Authoritarian Personality

Daniel J. Levinson,
   Politico-Economic Ideology and Group
   Memberships in Relation to Ethnocentrism

Edward A. Shils,
   Authoritarianism: "Right" and "Left"

Milton Rokeach,
   Personality, Ideology, and Cognitive Functioning

   Authority, Authoritarianism, and Conformity

Nevitt Sanford, one of the major authors of the *Authoritarian Personality* study, wrote an elegant, perceptive summary of the history, development, and findings of this classic Berkeley project. The *Authoritarian Personality* was a monumental attempt to relate personality and ideology that reached into the present era and expanded to more contemporary concerns about socialization in democratic climes. It provided a major impetus for the research explosion about authoritarianism. Even this early work considered the individual variations and multiple meanings of authoritarianism. Influenced by the psychoanalytic orientation and continental sociology, *Daniel Levinson* in the *Authoritarian Personality* study focused on hypotheses reflecting contemporary pressures. Although in retrospect the development of the F-Fascism scale was naive about the distribution of psychological types and the overall political structure of American society, the profound influence of this study on subsequent theory and research can hardly be estimated. As the readings reveal, its impact extended beyond the traditional boundaries of psychology and personality assessment; its authority stimulated other theoretical and empirical endeavors. The *Authoritarian Personality* was indirectly responsible for a burgeoning of instrumental and experimental work and cross-discipline thinking that enriched the American intellectual and scientific scenes.

The Approach of the Authoritarian Personality (1956)*

That "The Authoritarian Personality" should have a place in a book on theories of personality is a little surprising and very pleasing. . . . It is important to note at the outset that *The Authoritarian Personality* the book, and the authoritarian personality, the concept, are two different things. Authoritarian personality is the name for a "type" of personality or a personality syndrome that is, supposedly, fairly common in the world today. Different writers conceive of the "type" or syndrome somewhat differently, and the work of describing the organization that exists in fact is far from having been completed. Experience

---

*N. Sanford, in *Psychology of Personality: Six Modern Approaches,* J. L. McCary, ed. (New York: Lagos Press, 1956), pp. 255–319.

has shown that *The Authoritarian Personality* was not a very happy title for the book. It will be obvious to anyone who reads the volume that it has to do mainly with potential fascism, and that the title was not thought of until after the writing was virtually finished. This title was supposed to convey the idea that the main concern was with a pattern of personality organization, and to indicate the similarity of the work to that of Fromm (25) and of Maslow (38)* who had written about the "authoritarian character." But the title has led to misunderstandings. For example, since authoritarian personality has become almost a household term, it is not infrequently asked why, in such a large study of this personality type, a more systematic method of study was not used or why more of the common manifestations of this type in action were not covered. The answer, of course, is that we were not studying the authoritarian personality; we set out to study anti-Semitism, arrived eventually at the conception of potential fascism in the personality, and finally chose *The Authoritarian Personality* as a connotative title.

The Authoritarian Personality has no systematic position such as that presented by factor theory, psychoanalysis, field theory or even culture-personality theory; but it is not eclectic either. The "psychoanalytic bias" which so many reviewers have found in our work is readily admitted; yet it does seem fair to say that the current trend toward unification in theory finds expression in this work.

Unification is expressed in the backgrounds of the authors and in the very fact of their collaboration. European sociology and American social psychology, nonpsychoanalytic dynamic theory of personality, field theory, neo-Freudian theory, training in experimental, statistical and clinical methods were, in addition to classical psychoanalysis, well represented in the backgrounds of the research workers. . . .

The data to be presented consist mainly of what adult subjects had to say about their childhoods. Recognizing, however, that the childhood experiences of the subjects must have depended in considerable part upon the total social situation in which their parents lived, and noting variations in the incidence of authoritarianism from one culture or subculture to another, it becomes clear that an account of the origins of authoritarian personality must include attention to broad historical and cultural forces. Although one cannot go so far beyond the limits of his own discipline without trepidation, these larger determinants must be considered. . . .

---

*Numbers in parentheses refer to the bibliography in the original book.

The Authoritarian Personality has been called by highly responsible critics "monumental," "a classic," "a milestone" in social research. This can be interpreted as a rather severe criticism of social
psychology and personology. What have our people been doing then?
It ought not to be so difficult to produce a work like *The Authoritarian
Personality*. All that is really essential is a reasonably comprehensive
theoretical framework, curiosity, and freedom—freedom from hamper-
ing research conventions, from the conventional expectations of spon-
sors and from the aspiration to produce a monumental work. Then
one simply follows one's nose, so to speak. Instead of saying, "This
experiment raises more questions than it answers," and then turning
attention to something else, one proceeds to try to answer a few of
those questions—and later questions raised by this new effort. If the
pattern which emerges in the end has such coherence that it appears
to have been put in at the beginning, so much the better. There is no
good reason why work which proceeds in this way should not maintain
high standards in sampling, in generalization, in the collection and
analysis of data, but even so it is inevitable that much of it will have
to be followed up and checked by more exacting methods. There is a
difference between exploratory research as used here and the conventional hypothesis-testing research which is so common today. It is no
criticism of the latter to say that there is need for more "explorations
in personality."

The F Scale

Although the idea of constructing a scale for measuring potential
fascism in the personality appeared at a relatively late stage in these
explorations, it still came at a time when the focus of attention was
upon anti-Semitism and prejudice. A Likert-type scale for measuring
ethnocentrism (E) had been constructed and studied in relation to anti-
Semitism (A-S). This scale, which embraced hostility to various intra-
and extra-national outgroups as well as the tendency to overestimate
and to glorify the ingroup, correlated so highly with anti-Semitism, .80,
that it seemed reasonable to view this latter as, mainly, a manifestation
of general ethnocentrism. Ethnocentrism, in the group's thinking, had
become something very general indeed. Not only did it include generalized outgroup rejection and exaggerated ingroup loyalty but also such
defects in thinking as stereotypy, rigidity, and rationalization; it was a
way of looking at groups and group relations that was, in the long run

at least, maladaptive; it had begun to take on the aspect of a fundamental psychological problem.

The high correlation between A-S and E meant that it would be possible to go on studying anti-Semitism without having to rely on the original A-S scale itself. This scale had evoked protests both from a local chapter of the Anti-Defamation League, who considered that the instrument spread anti-Semitism, and from the dean of a graduate school, who objected to "the pro-Semitic bias" in this research. From whatever point of view it was seen, this scale did tend to bring the matter of prejudice painfully into the open and it was used with reluctance, particularly in groups that included Jews. But the same considerations held for members of other minority groups. The real need was for an instrument that would measure prejudice without appearing to have this aim and without mentioning the name of any minority group.

The idea of the F scale was a product of thinking about the A-S and E scales. An effort was being made to abstract from the A-S and E scale items the kinds of psychological dispositions—fears, anxieties, values, impulses—being expressed, the thought being that a systematic covering of this ground might suggest additional E items. There were certain general themes in the item content: e.g., Jews were "extravagant," or "sensual" or "lazy" or "soft"; or Jews were mysterious, strange, foreign, basically different; or minority groups generally failed to come up to ordinary standards of middle-class morality. It was as if the subject, in agreeing with these scale items, was not so much considering Jews or other minority group members as expressing concern lest other people "get away" with tendencies which he himself had to inhibit, or anxiety lest he be the victim of strange forces beyond his control, or lest his moral values, already somewhat unstable, be undermined. And since, apparently, items expressing these kinds of preoccupation were agreed with consistently by some subjects regardless of the minority groups involved, would not these subjects agree with such items even though no minority group were mentioned at all? In short, why not have a scale that covered the psychological content of the A-S and E scales but did not appear to be concerned with the familiar phenomena of prejudice? Certainly this fitted in with Leo Loewenthal's memorable if somewhat exaggerated dictum: "Anti-Semitism has nothing to do with Jews."

It cannot really be claimed that this notion came as the result of a deliberate quest for an instrument that would be less awkward to administer to groups of varied ethnic backgrounds, although it came at a time when the need for such an instrument was keenly felt and this implication of the new notion was more or less immediately seen. Furthermore, this notion was conceived at a time when the group was prepared to exploit it to the full. Interviews with subjects scoring high on A-S and E had suggested many psychological characteristics of the highly prejudiced subjects, and whereas many of these characteristics had not yet found a place in the A-S or E scales there was no reason why they should not. And now, since attention was going to be directed to items expressing the general outlook of the highly prejudiced individual, it was possible to make use of the vast literature on Nazism and Fascism and, particularly, the ideas represented by Dr. Adorno and the Institute for Social Research. Finally, it was possible to make explicit a theoretical assumption which, actually, had been a guide to the group's thinking for some time.

The essence of this assumption was that some of the deeper needs of the personality were being expressed by agreement with prejudiced statements. If this were true, then these needs should express themselves in other ways as well. If, for example, a subject's tendency to attribute weakness to Jews sprang from his own underlying fear of weakness, that fear might also express itself in an over-accent upon his own strength and toughness. Thus, scale items having to do with the supposed weakness of Jews or of other people and items expressing exaggerated strength and toughness would correlate positively in a population of men because agreement with both kinds of items commonly sprang from the same underlying source, fear of weakness. All of us were accustomed to this kind of thinking in terms of levels of functioning in the personality; it had loomed large in earlier work of Frenkel-Brunswik (20) and of Sanford (52). It is, of course, essentially psychoanalytic.

Given this way of looking at things, the task became one of imagining what personality needs were commonly expressed in overt prejudice, and then thinking of other suface manifestations of these same needs. The intention was, of course, to gain access to those other manifestations by means of scale items. Here it was possible to make good use of the existing literature on anti-Semitism and Fascism. Fromm (25), Erikson (16), Maslow (38), Chisholm (7), Reich (42), Stagner (59) were among the writers who influenced us the most, although heaviest reliance was on the group's own earlier explorations. The central personality trends which were expected to be most significant were those which emerged from the analysis of clinical material and those which, as hypothetical constructs, seemed best to explain the consistency of response to the A-S and E scales.

Content of the F Scale

For every item of the F scale there was a hypothesis or, more usually, several hypotheses stating the nature of its supposed connection with prejudice. And there were hypotheses concerning the relations of these items one to another, theorizing having led the group more and more toward the conceptualization of a *pattern* of personality that predisposed the individual to prejudice and fascism.

Here it seems worthwhile to go into some detail, for progress in an understanding of authoritarianism will come from the closest involvement with the subtle workings of this and similar trends in the personality.

Conventionalism

First consider the idea of *conventionalism*. It was observed in our conversations with anti-Semitic subjects that most of their accusations against Jews were couched in conventionally moralistic terms. This theme was also pronounced in the original A-S scale items. It may be recalled that Hitler made this same type of accusation when addressing middle-class audiences. Our thought here was that we were dealing not so much with bad experiences with Jews or with adaptation to a general climate of opinion as with a need to adhere strictly to conventional, middle-class values, a disposition to feel anxious at the sight of or the thought of any violation of these values—something that could be attributed to instability in the individual's own value system. It is important to note that conventionalism refers not merely to conformity with middle-class values but to *rigid* adherence to such values, to an *over*accent upon them and to responsiveness to contemporary *external* social pressure. Items expressive of this trend invited the subject to go *all-out* in his support of conventional values, e.g., "A person who has bad manners, habits, and breeding can hardly expect to get along with decent people."

Authoritarian Submission

Submission to authority, desire for a strong leader, subservience of the individual to the state, had for some time been put forward as important aspects of the Nazi creed. It was thus natural that these themes should be taken into account in a search for the correlates of prejudice. *Authoritarian submission*, as we termed the hypothetical generalized disposition of personality, was conceived of not as a balanced, realistic respect for valid authority but as an exaggerated, emotional need to submit. This seems well represented in the item: "Every person should have a deep faith in some supernatural force higher than himself to which he gives total allegiance and whose decisions he obeys without question." Here, as with conventionalism, the individual is assumed to be oriented toward external powers or agencies of control rather than under the direction of a conscience of his own.

Authoritarian Aggression

Authoritarian submission is closely related, conceptually, to *authoritarian aggression*. Both attitudes, according to theory, spring from underlying hostility toward ingroup authorities, originally the parents. The individual strives to keep this hostility in check by overdoing in the direction of respect, obedience, gratitude toward the ingroup authorities and by displacing the underlying hostility toward these authorities onto outgroups. This is the most essential connection between authoritarian submission and ethnocentrism. But it appears that the tendency to displace hostility is more general than that seen in the common forms of prejudice; the greatest variety of people and actions are likely to become the objects of condemnation. The connection of this hostility and its original source is seen in the fact that the kinds of things for which the individual would punish other peoples are the same as those for which he was punished or for which he feels in his heart he deserves to be punished. But he has identified himself with the ingroup authorities of his childhood, and found in the tendency to punish wrongdoing in others a safe, and fairly well-sanctioned, outlet for his aggression. The items chosen to represent authoritarian aggression offer the subject a chance to favor condemnation, total rejection, stern discipline or severe punishment as ways for dealing with a variety of people and forms of behavior; e.g., "Sex crimes, such as rape and attacks on children, deserve more than mere imprisonment; such criminals ought to be publicly whipped, or worse."

Anti-intraception

It was common to note in the interviews of more prejudiced subjects, and in some of the A-S and E scale items with which they heartily agreed, disapproval of a free emotional life, of the intellectual or theoretical, of the impractical. These were things they tended to attribute to their outgroups. And there was theory at hand to explain the relations of these attitudes to prejudice and to the personality trends just discussed. The individual who had been forced to repress hostility against his parents and others who appeared to be strong, and who was thus forced into submissiveness which impaired his self-respect, would naturally be required to maintain a narrow range of consciousness. Self-awareness might threaten his whole scheme of adjustment. He would be afraid of genuine feeling because his emotions might get out of control, afraid of thinking about human phenomena because he might, as it were, think the wrong thoughts. The term *anti-intraception* was borrowed from Murray *et al.* (41). It stands for a general attitude of impatience with and opposition to feelings, fantasies, speculations and other subjective or "tender-minded" phenomena. A sample item: "When a person has a problem or worry, it is best for him not to think about it, but to keep busy with more cheerful things."

Superstition and Stereotypy

The narrowness of consciousness just referred to appeared also to be a major source of both *superstition* and *stereotypy*, two tendencies which loomed large in our early clinical studies of highly prejudiced individuals. Superstitiousness indicates a tendency to shift responsibility from within the individual onto outside forces beyond one's control. It suggests a narrow area within which there is a conscious sense of self-determination, a broad area of unconscious forces which are projected onto the external world, to appear to the individual as mystical or fantastic determinants of his fate. Stereotypy is the tendency to think in rigid, oversimplified categories, in unambiguous terms of black and white, particularly in the realm of psychological or social matters. It was hypothesized that one reason why people, even those who are otherwise "intelligent," resort to primitive explanations of human events is that so many of the ideas and observations needed for an adequate account are not allowed to enter into the calculations: because they are affect-laden and potentially anxiety-producing they could not be included in the conscious scheme of things. The assumption here is, of course, that many of the common phenomena of prejudice were superstitions or stereotypes. The present task was to devise scale items that would express these tendencies without reference to minority groups, e.g., "It is entirely possible that this series of wars and conflicts will be ended once and for all by a world-destroying earthquake, flood, or other catastrophe."

Power and Toughness

As suggested above, the state of affairs in which the individual has to submit to powers or agencies with which he is not fully in sympathy leaves him with a nagging sense of weakness. Since to admit such weakness is to damage self-respect, every effort is made to deny it. These include the projection of weakness onto outgroups according to the formula "I am not weak, they are," and the use of the mechanism of overcompensation, according to which the individual seeks to present to the world an aspect of *power and toughness*. Accent on the strong-weak, dominant-submissive, leader-follower dimension in human relations is, of course, a familiar feature of the Nazi outlook. In our experience it appeared that the "power complex" contained elements that were essentially contradictory. Whereas the power-centered individual wants to have power, he is at the same time afraid to seize it and wield it. He also admires power in others and is inclined to submit to it, but is at the same time afraid of the weakness thus implied. A common solution for such a person is to align himself with power figures, thus gratifying both his need to have power and his need to submit. By submitting to power he can still somehow participate in it. The following is a sample of the items designed to represent this theme: "Too many people today are living in an unnatural, soft way; we should return to the fundamentals, to a more red-blooded, active way of life."

Destructiveness and Cynicism

Although authoritarian aggression provides a very broad channel for the expression of underlying hostile impulses, it seemed that this might not be enough for many of the prejudiced subjects. We supposed that they harbored, as a result of numerous externally imposed restrictions upon the satisfaction of their needs, a great deal of resentment and generalized hostility, and that this would come into the open when it could be justified or rationalized. *Destructiveness and cynicism* was the term for rationalized, ego-accepted aggression, not including authoritarian aggression. Cynicism was regarded as a form of rationalized aggression: one can the more freely be aggressive when he believes that everybody is doing it and, hence, if he wants to be aggressive he is disposed to believe that everybody is similarly motivated, e.g., that it is "human nature" to exploit and to make war on one's neighbors. It seemed a fairly safe assumption that such undifferentiated aggressiveness could be directed against minority groups with a minimum of external stimulation.

Projectivity

The mechanism just described is, of course, a form of projection. And it will have been noted that this unconscious defensive device has had an important place in our earlier related theory-making, particularly in the discussion of authoritarian aggression and of superstition. Indeed, projection has a crucial role in the whole theory of prejudice as a means for keeping the individual's psychological household in some sort of order. The most essential notion is that impulses which cannot be admitted to the conscious ego tend to be projected onto minority groups—convenient objects. In constructing the F scale, the concern was with a readiness to project, with *projectivity* as a general feature of the personality, considered independently of the object onto which the projection was made. Hence, the items expressive of this tendency were designed to tap any preoccupation with "evil forces" in the world, with plots and conspiracies, germs, sexual excesses.

Sex

Concern with *sex* seemed to deserve a certain amount of special consideration. Inhibitions in this sphere, and moral indignation with respect to the sexual behavior of other people, had been noted in the interviews with our prejudiced subjects; sexual immorality was one of the many violations of conventional values which they attributed to minority groups. Ego-alien sexuality was conceived then as a part of the picture of the typical prejudiced person, and included in the F scale were several items having to do with belief in the existence of "sex orgies" and with the punishment of violators of sex mores.

In summary, there were nine major personality variables which, by hypothesis, were dynamically related to overt prejudice.

1. *Conventionalism.* Rigid adherence to conventional middle-class values.

2. *Authoritarian Submission.* Submissive, uncritical attitude toward idealized moral authorities of the ingroup.

3. *Authoritarian Aggression.* Tendency to be on the lookout for, and to condemn, reject and punish people who violate conventional values.

4. *Anti-intraception.* Opposition to the subjective, the imaginative, the tender-minded.

5. *Superstition and Stereotypy.* The belief in mystical determinants of the individual's fate; the disposition to think in rigid categories.

6. *Power and Toughness.* Preoccupation with the dominance-submission, strong-weak, leader-follower dimension; identifica-

tion with power figures; exaggerated assertion of strength and toughness.

7. *Destructiveness and Cynicism.* Generalized hostility, vilification of the human.

8. *Projectivity.* The disposition to believe that wild and dangerous things go on in the world; the projection outward of unconscious emotional impulses.

9. *Sex.* Ego-alien sexuality; exaggerated concern with sexual "goings on," and punitiveness toward violators of sex mores.

Theory Underlying the F Scale

In their theoretical work on the F scale the research group leaned heavily upon the concepts of superego, ego, and id. It was considered that these features of the personality have characteristic modes of functioning in the ethnocentric subject. As a first approximation, one might say that in the highly ethnocentric person the superego is strict, rigid and relatively externalized, the id is strong, primitive and ego-alien, while the ego is weak and can manage the superego-id conflicts only by resorting to rather desperate defenses. But this general formulation would hold for a very large segment of the population and, thus, it is necessary to look more closely at the functioning of these parts of the person in the authoritarian syndrome.

In considering the variables which entered into the theory underlying the F scale, it may be seen that the first three—Conventionalism, Authoritarian Submission, and Authoritarian Aggression—all have to do with superego functioning. The accent is upon external reinforcements of strict superego demands, and upon punishment in the name of those authorities to whom the subject has submitted.

Anti-intraception, Superstition and Stereotypy, and Projectivity may be regarded as manifestations of a relatively weak ego. Anti-intraception involves the primitive defensive mechanisms of repression, denial, keeping things ego-alien. Superstition shows an inclination to shift responsibility onto the external world, as if the ego were giving up its attempts to predict and control, while Stereotypy is an attempt to deal with complex events by means of oversimplified categories. Projectivity is the consistent use of another relatively primitive mechanism of defense.

Power and Toughness is another manifestation of ego weakness, involving as it does an over-accent upon the conventionalized aspects of the ego, e.g., the emphasis on "will power"; but this variable, like Destructiveness and Cynicism, and Sex, also expresses with a minimum of indirectness the activity of id tendencies.

However, superego, ego and id can be separated in this fashion only arbitrarily. In actuality, the functioning of any one of these agencies depends at any moment upon the activities of the other two; and everyday behavior, expressed attitudes and values, are not readily classifiable as manifestations of superego, ego or id but are to be understood as expressions of the relationships among these agencies. This, at any rate, was the thinking that went into the F scale. Consider the item: "He is indeed contemptible who does not feel an undying love, gratitude, and respect for his parents." On the surface, this item expresses authoritarian aggression and authoritarian submission and, hence, might be classified as primarily a superego item. But the theory was that agreement with this extreme statement might well mask an underlying hostility toward the parents. To put this differently, it was hypothesized that unconscious hostility toward the parents was a distinguishing feature of the highly ethnocentric person, and the problem was to determine how this tendency might give itself away in an attitude scale. One answer was through signs of a reaction formation, this mechanism being a common one in the highly ethnocentric person. Thus the present item has to do with an interplay of superego, ego and id: an underlying unconscious, ego-alien tendency, coming mainly from the id, has led to anxiety of punishment (superego) which the ego seeks to ward off or reduce by transforming the forbidden tendency into its opposite. But this is not all. This is merely the authoritarian submission expressed in the item. "He is indeed contemptible" is authoritarian aggression. The ego must, so to speak, be doubly sure that punishment is avoided and it must see to it that the original id tendency finds some sort of gratification; hence, it joins forces with the punitive agency, imputes the "badness" to other people who may then be freely aggressed against in good conscience.

Or consider the item: "The wild sex life of the old Greeks and Romans was tame compared to some of the goings on in this country, even in places where people might least expect it." Here it is assumed that underlying sexual tendencies, inhibited because of a strict superego, have found through the ego's work some expression in fantasies, which, however, can be enjoyed or tolerated only when other people, and not the self, are the actors and when the fantasies are accompanied by moral indignation.

Now it is not suggested that the whole authoritarian personality structure is somehow embedded in each F scale item. But it is fair to say that theory of the kind just indicated lay behind the writing of each item, and that, according to this theory, the F pattern is a structure whose features are so closely interrelated that a clear expression of one permits quite reasonable inferences concerning the activity of the others. Perhaps the items just used are among the best for making this point, but all the F scale items should be viewed from this standpoint.

The F scale works as if the superego, ego, id theory were correct, and there is no doubt but that without this theory the scale would not have been constructed. On the other hand, it cannot be claimed that such results as have been obtained could not be explained as well in other terms.

Clinical Studies of the F Pattern

In trying to understand the inner workings of the F-syndrome one is not, of course, limited to consideration of the F scale. The interviews and projective techniques which yielded the hypotheses underlying the F scale also yielded some of the most convincing evidence concerning the truth of those hypotheses. To consider an example, the interviews, like some questionnaire material, showed unmistakably that the tendency to glorify his parents was a distinguishing feature of the highly ethnocentric subject. And the interviews also gave evidence of ambivalence in this subject's relationship with his parents. It was usually not long after the statements of glorification that a note of complaint or self-pity began to creep into the interview. How might one demonstrate that overt glorification of the parents is functionally related to underlying hostility toward them? One way would be to use a projective technique to obtain an independent measure of the latter and see if the two vary together. Unfortunately, this is not simple. What are the TAT signs of repressed aggression? Certainly not the frequency and intensity of aggressive actions by heroes of the stories. These seem to be, for the most part, indications of aggression that is accepted by the ego; it is more pronounced in the low scorers than in the high scorers on the F scale. But Betty Aron (2) did conclude that there was more *ego-alien* aggression against the parents in the stories of high scorers, the indications being such things as the frequency with which parent figures were the victims of affliction or death and the frequency and intensity of aggression against parental figures on the part of characters with whom the storyteller was not identified. Thus, to arrive at diagnoses of deep-lying tendencies on the basis of the TAT requires *interpretation*. Although Aron's work goes a long way toward the objectification of such interpretation, and although it argues persuasively for a functional relationship between overt glorification and underlying hostility, it remains in need of independent validation.

The same considerations hold for the Projective Questions. The material elicited by this procedure is for the most part on the same level of personality as the F scale. Responses to the open-ended questions could easily be—and they sometimes were—translated into F scale items. Thus the Projective Questions yielded a large amount of material that confirmed independently the F scale findings on the difference between ethnocentric and nonethnocentric subjects. But, more than this, the material from the Projective Questions called for interpretation, for the conceptualization of underlying trends that would explain the pattern of overt expression.

Two of the Projective Questions were as follows:

1. We all have times when we feel below par. What moods or feelings are the most unpleasant or disturbing to you?

2. There is hardly a person who hasn't said to himself: "If this keeps up I'll go nuts." What might drive a person nuts?

These two questions, like the six others used, brought out numerous differences between highs and lows on the E scale. The "lows" are disturbed by conscious conflict and guilt feelings, frustrations of love and dependence, consciousness of hostility toward loved objects, and they suppose that people are "driven nuts" by inner psychological states or by a dominating environment. The "highs," on the other hand, are more disturbed by violations of conventional values, by self or others or by a threatening or nonsupporting environment; they are also more disturbed by, and state that people are "driven nuts" by, what Levinson called "rumblings from below."

According to Levinson, "These responses refer to situations or bodily conditions which, by inference though not explicitly, tend to bring out ego-alien trends such as passivity, anxiety, and hostility." Examples, from the subjects' responses, are: "Quietness, boredom, inactivity"; "When at a party everything is quiet and dead as a morgue"; "Lack of work or anything to do, causing restlessness and lack of self-confidence." How does one know that such responses as these are signs that the subject is struggling with id tendencies, such as passivity and hostility, which might break into the open unless the anti-intraceptive defenses of keeping busy, having excitement, not thinking too much, are employed to the full? One does not *know*, of course, but this formulation seems to go a long way toward explaining why it is that the very same subjects who feel that they must keep busy are also most concerned about the dangers to mental health of "overwork," "too long hours," "mental fatigue," "undertaking too much." The very activities which ward off the bad impulses may, if persisted in too long, intensify those impulses and increase the danger of a breakthrough. The point to be emphasized is that, when one is working with a theory that postulates levels of personality, he need not suppose that his hypothetical "deeper tendencies" are, so to speak, things which he will one day get his hands on. Even in psychoanalytic practice these deeper tendencies are rarely revealed directly; they are the stuff of interpretations, not just those which the analyst offers the patient but those which he makes for himself. In other words, psycho-analysis, like the research reported in *The Authoritarian Personality*, makes maximum use of hypothetical constructs. The "correctness," or one might better say the usefulness, of the psychoanalytic formulation is gauged by its service in making sense of a great diversity of material and in predicting what a patient will do next. And it is the same in such research as this: does the formulation explain the relationships ob-served and does it permit the prediction of responses in particular types of situations? The truth of such formulations may rarely be demonstrated to the satisfaction of all, but one may hope to creep up on it.

The largest amount of clinical material in *The Authoritarian Per-sonality* was derived from interviews, the analysis of which is reported in great detail in chapters by Else Frenkel-Brunswik, William Morrow and Maria Levinson. As critics have pointed out the statistical relation-ships based on the analysis of interview material from the regular sam-ple of subjects are seriously in need of cross-validation. Criticisms of the methodology in Frenkel-Brunswik's chapters have often been severe, but these are precisely the chapters that most people turn to for an elucidation of the inner working of the potentially fascist pat-tern, for here they find richness, complexity and comprehensiveness. There is a paradox here. The interviews were not conducted with any thought to their later quantitative analysis. They were going to be used for exploratory purposes and, later, as the basis for case studies that would exemplify some of the patterns that emerged from the other pro-cedures. When it became apparent, however, that certain differences between "high" and "low" ethnocentric subjects appeared regularly in the interview material it seemed that comparisons in quantitative terms would be an aid to description. This, as it turned out, was asking for trouble, for what was essentially clinical work now became subject to the standards for criticism which hold for small sample statistical studies.

Morrow, in his study of prison inmates, used his interview material only for case studies and thus escaped such criticism as was directed toward Frenkel-Brunswik, while Levinson in her study of psychiatric clinic patients analyzed the regular intake interviewers in a way that was methodologically impeccable. The fact that all these approaches led to about the same conclusions concerning the structure and functioning of the F-syndrome probably has made more of an impression upon the authors than upon many readers, who have tended to take chapters or procedures or special studies one at a time and to ask whether they really showed what was claimed. Or perhaps the same general bias on the authors' part pervaded all of these investigations. At any rate, it was not suggested that the numerous findings concerning the dynamics of the F-syndrome did not need to be followed up by other workers.

The picture of potential fascism in the personality was considerably expanded by these clinical studies. All of the major variables of the F scale appeared in these studies. But there were many others besides. Although the procedure was to convert clinical findings into scale items whenever possible, many such findings were still to come in long after a place had been reached when it seemed wise to stop changing the F scale.

It may be well to mention briefly, on the basis of findings from the clinical procedures, some additional features of the potentially fascist pattern: relative inability to accept blame; a tendency to view interpersonal relations in terms of power and status rather than in terms of love and friendship; a manipulative attitude toward other people; the inability or the unwillingness to deal with the indefinite, the ambiguous or the merely probable; tendency to treat property as an extension of the self; tendency to see the real self and the ideal self as essentially the same, and signs of self-contempt underlying this self-overestimation; self-pity; rigidity in adjustment; constriction of fantasy; concreteness of thinking; less differentiated emotional experience; undifferentiated conception of the opposite sex; relative absence of a value for achievement for its own sake; ego-alien dependency; tendency in emotional crises to emphasize somatic rather than psychological complaints.

Perhaps some of these characteristics overlap, or might be reduced to, some of the variables of which the F scale took account. Perhaps not. What, indeed, *are* the essential or "basic" elements of the pattern under consideration? The chief point here is that the F scale does not pretend to cover all the facets of the potentially fascist pattern. . . .

It is not proper to speak of an individual as "an authoritarian personality," thus implying that this is all one needs to know about him. . . .

. . . And one may speak of types of authoritarianism. Authoritarianism may vary from one individual to another according to which of the constituent variables are relatively pronounced, a matter which may depend upon what other factors are at work in the personality. Some of these variations in authoritarianism may be common in large populations. . . .

. . . [O]ne of the most promising leads for further research . . . would concern the suggested "types" or subvarieties of high and low authoritarianism. . . .

It may be well to review briefly here the typology of authoritarianism and nonauthoritarianism which appears in *The Authoritarian Personality*. There is still hope that further research in this area may yet be stimulated. This typology is largely the work of Adorno, and is based upon clinical observation and analysis. . . .

High-authoritarianism

The varieties of high-authoritarianism were labeled, by Adorno, *Surface Resentment, Conventional, "Authoritarian," Tough Guy, Crank,* and *Manipulative.*

Surface Resentment

Surface Resentment is not on the same logical level as the other high patterns. It refers not so much to any deep-lying tendency in the personality as to a state of affairs in which the individual is provoked to prejudiced and authoritarian modes of behavior by externally imposed frustrations.

The Conventional

The Conventional pattern emphasizes conventional values and determination by external representatives of the superego. Individuals exhibiting this pattern would be very slow to engage in any of the more violent expressions of prejudice; they would be equally slow to oppose or to condemn such expressions if this meant "to be different."

The "Authoritarian"

The "Authoritarian" pattern is probably the purest instance of potential fascism as that picture emerged from the research. It is also very similar to Erich Fromm's conception of the "sado-masochistic character." The subject achieves his social adjustment by taking pleasure in obedience and subordination, while remaining ambivalent toward his authorities. Part of the repressed hatred of authority is turned into masochism and part is displaced onto outgroups.

The Tough Guy

The Tough Guy pattern, as might be expected, has the accent on "power and toughness" and "destructiveness and cynicism." One may find at a deeper level either the type of structure described by Erikson (16), in which a successful insurrection against the hated father is made possible through adherence to the gang leader or "older brother," or, the true psychopathic organization in which there is a basic disturbance in object relations and failure in superego formation, the individual being prepared to do anything to protect himself against what he perceives to be a hostile world.

The Crank

The outstanding feature of the Crank is "projectivity," with the "superstition and stereotypy" also looming large. According to theory, individuals exhibiting this pattern have reacted to early frustrations by withdrawing into an inner world, one that has been built in considerable part upon denials of reality. They concentrate upon self-aggrandizement and the protection of their self-conception by projective formulas.

The Manipulative

In the Manipulative pattern "anti-intraception" is extreme. There is a marked deficiency of object-cathexis and of emotional ties. In the extreme case people become objects to be handled, administered, manipulated in accordance with the subject's theoretical or practical schemes.

Low-authoritarianism

The patterns found among subjects low in potential fascism were labeled *Rigid, Protesting, Impulsive, Easygoing* and *Genuine Liberal.*

The Rigid

The *Rigid* Low appeared to have most in common with the over-all High pattern. The main idea here is that the absence of prejudice, instead of being based on concrete experience and integrated within the personality, is derived from some general external, ideological pattern. To quote Adorno, "The latter kind of low scorers are definitely disposed toward totalitarianism in their thinking; what is accidental up to a certain degree is the particular brand of ideological world formula that they chance to come into contact with. We encountered a few subjects who had been identified ideologically with some progressive movement, such as the struggle for minority rights, for a long time, but with whom such ideas contained features of compulsiveness, even of paranoid obsession, and who, with respect to many of our variables, especially rigidity and total thinking, could hardly be distinguished from some of our high extremes."

The Protesting

In the *Protesting* Low-authoritarian the decisive feature is opposition to whatever appears to be tyranny. The subject is out to protect the weak from the strong. One might say that he is still fixated at the level of the normal Oedipus Complex. Here, perhaps, belong those individuals who can lead or at least be effective in revolts but who can find nothing to do once the revolt has met with success.

The Impulsive

In the *Impulsive* Low-authoritarian unconventionality is the outstanding theme. Here the subject is able not only to be different but to sympathize with what is different, to look upon it as if it promised some new kind of gratification. For whatever reason, it appears that id impulses, with the exception of destructive ones, are allowed rather free expression. In some cases it seems that the rational ego is lined up with the id, in others that the individual is driven to gratify id impulses in order to gain proof that this may be done without catastrophic consequences.

The Easygoing

The *Easygoing* pattern is the opposite of the Manipulative high-authoritarian one. It is marked by imagination, capacity for enjoyment and a sense of humor that often assumes the form of self-irony. The subject in whom this pattern stands out is reluctant to make decisions or to commit himself and extremely unwilling to do violence to any person or thing. He seems to be governed by the idea of "live and let live." Theory concerning the etiology of this pattern puts the accent on the absence of traumatic experiences and upon pleasant relations with the mother and other females.

The Genuine Liberal

The *Genuine Liberal* is close to the psychoanalytic ideal, representing a balance of superego, ego and id. This pattern has features in common with those just described. As in the Impulsive pattern, there is relatively little repression, the subject sometimes having difficulty in controlling himself, but his emotionality is directed toward other people as individuals. As in the Protesting nonauthoritarian, there is identification with the underdog, but this is not compulsive or overcompensatory. And like the Easygoing type the Genuine Liberal is close to reality and relatively free of stereotypy, but he lacks the element of hesitation and indecision. Since his opinions and values are most essentially his own, in the sense of being integral to the personality, he stands rather in contrast to the Rigid Low scorer, although there may well be an element of rigidity in the firmness of his convictions. Perhaps the outstanding features of this pattern are ethical sensitivity and value for independence. The subject in whom it is highly developed cannot "keep silent" in the face of something wrong; he resists any interference with his personal convictions and beliefs, and he does not want to interfere with those of others.

There is a question as to the existence of a pattern of nonauthoritarianism in which liberal values and opposition to prejudice are aspects of a well internalized religious conscience. A major conclusion from our study of ethnocentrism in relation to religious attitudes and group memberships was that the "genuinely" religious, as opposed to conventionally religious, person tended to be low on ethnocentrism. According to the present typology a genuinely religious person might exhibit the Protesting or even the Genuine Liberal pattern. It might well be, however, that neither of these patterns does justice to the person in whom nonauthoritarianism is mainly the expression of a superego that insists upon values and standards of Christianity.

This typology deserves a great deal of study and empirical testing. As far as the present work goes, there is the most empirical support for the differentiation between the Conventional and the Tough Guy types of authoritarianism. The differences found by this study between the sample of authoritarian prison inmates and those of authoritarian college and professional people were quite obvious, though they were by no means great enough to obscure the common features.

Closely related to this matter of differentiation within the extremes is the question of possible similarities between one extreme and the other. This question has aroused very considerable interest in recent years. Other workers have been quick to grasp the significance of our conclusion that in authoritarianism one deals with a way of thinking, a way of looking at the world, that can vary independently of the content of ingroups or outgroups. This means that authoritarianism might cut across any existing dimension of political ideology, a matter that certainly invites investigation. . . .

It is noteworthy that these similarities of extreme rightists and extreme leftists, and other similarities that have been mentioned, i.e., Rigidity and Stereotypy—and still others that might well be hypothesized, e.g., Anti-intraception and Manipulativeness—lie mainly in formal traits rather than in the contents of imagery or in broad motivational directions. This seems to be in keeping with the fact that, in the tendency to equate fascism and communism, the accent has been on similarities in method, and on the fact that means tend to be substituted for ends. . . .

The need, of course, is for investigation of leftist zealots by methods as comprehensive as those that have been employed with potential fascists.

Authoritarianism as a Determinant of Behavior

. . . It is important to note that the authoritarian structure is a structure of *personality*, and that personality is by no means the same thing as behavior. Authoritarianism in personality is a matter of dispositions, readinesses, potentialities; whether or not it is expressed in behavior will depend upon numerous other factors including those of the social situation. . . .

. . . As a central structure of personality, authoritarianism may be expected to influence behavior in a wide variety of situations; or, more correctly, as a system of response readiness more or less ingrained in the person, authoritarianism may be expected to express itself somehow in most of the individual's behavior. . . .

. . . To quote from a recent paper by Milton Rokeach (47), ". . . authoritarianism may well be observed within the context of any ideological orientation, and in areas of human endeavor relatively removed from the political or religious arena . . . authoritarianism can be recognized as a problem in such areas as science, art, literature and philosophy . . ."

. . . The stress upon personality *structure* has not been intended to suggest something fixed and solid and impregnable to influence from outside. Not only is authoritarianism in personality conceived of as more or less normally distributed; it is further believed that almost anyone is capable of having his authoritarianism evoked by sufficiently strong stimuli. . . .

Conclusion

The Authoritarian Personality was an effort to bring to bear upon the problem of social discrimination an approach that combined psychoanalytic theory of personality, clinical methods for the diagnosis of personality, and modern social-psychological devices for opinion and attitude measurement. The major contribution of the work was the empirical elucidation of the F or Authoritarian personality syndrome. It was shown that prejudice and other social attitudes and ideological trends were functionally related one to another and to this central structure. The conclusion was that these manifestations cannot be fully understood apart from the total personality of the individual who exhibits them. The elucidation of the F-syndrome involved not only the discovery of the major elements or factors that comprise it but the application of a variety of concepts for formulating the way in which personality is organized. Of particular importance was the conceptualization of levels of personality and of the conditions of communication among the levels. These, and other concepts from psychoanalytic, dynamic psychology, were not tested in any crucial way; but so consistent were the findings with them, that one could be left with little doubt as to their power and productivity.

Research that has used *The Authoritarian Personality* as its point of departure has tended, on the whole, to confirm the findings reported there. This research has both sharpened and expanded the picture of the content of the syndrome, and it has demonstrated the relations of this structure to behavior in a wide variety of situations. It has not, unfortunately, *deepened* knowledge of authoritarianism in personality. The accent has been upon quantitative studies of large groups of subjects and a few variables at a time. Such studies are important and economical; but sooner or later one must get back to the individual. A pressing need at this moment is for systematic, comprehensive and carefully conducted interviews with subjects representing the total range of scores on F, and for a method of analysis sufficiently rigorous to provide crucial checks on some of the very numerous propositions concerning the genesis and inner workings of the authoritarian personality syndrome. Such interviews, combined with a variety of projective techniques, would undoubtedly turn up additional variables and provide new insight into the dynamics of authoritarianism. Finally, one might hope that the method of approach exemplified in *The Authoritarian Personality* might be employed in the discovery and elucidation of other patterns of personality.

Politico-Economic Ideology and Group Memberships in Relation to Ethnocentrism (1950)*

While fascist and socialist-communist (Marxist) ideologies represent the extreme right and left, respectively, with regard to political economy and group relations, neither point of view has as yet found much active, open support on the American political scene. The focus of the present study was, therefore, on liberalism and conservatism, the currently prevalent left- and right-wing political ideologies—with an eye, to be sure, on their potential polarization to the more extreme left and right. . . .

The right-left dimension (reactionary-fascist, conservative, liberal, socialist-communist) is, of course, an extremely complex one. Crucial qualitative differences can be found not only among various degrees of left-ness or right-ness, but also among various ideological camps falling at approximately the same point on the right or left. Furthermore, there exists today a great deal of ideological heterodoxy, not to speak of simple confusion, so that a cutting across of formal political categories may be expected in many individuals.

---

*D. Levinson, in T. Adorno, E. Frenkel-Brunswik, D. Levinson, and R. N. Sanford, *The Authoritarian Personality* (New York: Harper & Row, 1950), p. 152.

Edward A. Shils, as a fellow social scientist, recognized the singular contribution of *The Authoritarian Personality*, but he issued a critical and influential commentary that dominated subsequent theory and empirical research. He queried the unidimensional approach and noted its naiveté about left and right authoritarianism. Agreeing that the task for social research was clarification of the approximate relationship between personality and ideology, Shils maintained that the ideology of the investigators affected their approach and interpretations. He recommended clearer distinction between attitude and behavior assessments, recognition that personality is not always prime in political behavior, and awareness that both authoritarianism and democracy are necessary components in society.

Authoritarianism: "Right" and "Left" (1954)*

Fascism and Bolshevism, only a few decades ago thought of as worlds apart, have now been recognized increasingly as sharing many very important features. Their common hostility towards civil liberties, political democracy, their common antipathy for parliamentary institutions, individualism, private enterprise, their image of the political world as a struggle between morally irreconcilable forces, their belief that all their opponents are secretly leagued against them and their own predilection for a secrecy, their conviction that all forms of power are in a hostile world concentrated in a few hands and their own aspirations for concentrated and total power—all of these showed that the two extremes had much in common. . . .

The obsolete belief that all political, social and economic philosophies can be classified on the Right-Left continuum however dies very hard. A recent and very instructive instance of this steadfast adherence to the Right-Left polarity is the monumental investigation into *The Authoritarian Personality*. An examination of the manner in which political preconceptions enter into one of the most elaborate social-psychological investigations hitherto undertaken illuminates important problems of procedure in social research and offers opportu-

---

*E. A. Shils, reprinted with the permission of The Macmillan Company from *Studies in the Scope and Method of The Authoritarian Personality* by R. Christie and M. Jahoda (Editors), Copyright 1954 by The Free Press, a Corporation, pp. 27–49.

nities for the further interpretation of a body of rich data. The left-right dichotomy is present not only in the general interpretive chapters written by Professor Adorno but even in the severely empirical chapters written by Professor Levinson and Dr. Sanford. The entire team of investigators proceeds as if there were an unilinear scale of political and social attitudes at the extreme right of which stands the Fascist— the product and proponent of monopoly-capitalism and at the other end what the authors call the complete democrat who—as I shall presently demonstrate—actually holds the views of the non Stalinist Leninist.* . . .

. . . The questionnaire, concerned as it legitimately was to distinguish nativists and fundamentalists from others put all those rejecting the nativistic-fundamentalist view expressed in each questionnaire item into the same category—distinguishing them only with respect to the strength of their disagreement. This failure to discriminate the substantially different types of outlook which could be called liberal, liberal collectivist, radical, Marxist, etc., is not just the outcome of the deficiency of the questionnaire technique in general nor does it arise from carelessness. It flows from the authors' failure to perceive the distinctions between totalitarian Leninism (particularly in a period of Peoples Front maneuvers), humanitarianism and New Deal interventionism. . . .

The Berkeley group have emphasized, among others, the following deeper tendencies of the authoritarian of the Right:

    a) Extreme hostility towards "outgroups";

    b) Extreme submissiveness towards the "ingroups";

    c) The establishment of sharp boundaries between the group of which one is a member and all other groups;

    d) The tendency to categorize persons with respect to certain particular qualities and make "all or none" judgments;

    e) A vision of the world as a realm of conflict;

    f) Disdain for purely theoretical or contemplative activities;

    g) A repugnance for the expression of sentiments, particularly sentiments of affection;

---

*The authors themselves occasionally sense the difficulties of their position and seek to remedy them by the introduction of *ad hoc* concepts such as "pseudo-conservative" and "pseudo-democrat." These categories are not however introduced in a systematic way into either their quantitative or their clinical analyses.

h) Belief that oneself and one's group are the objects of manipulative designs and that oneself and one's group can survive only by the manipulation of others;

i) The ideal of a conflictless wholly harmonious society in contrast with an environing or antecedent conflictful chaos. There are other properties as well but these will serve for illustrative purposes.

Anyone well acquainted with the works of Lenin and Stalin*, or with European and American Communists of recent decades, will immediately recognize that the cognitive and emotional orientations enumerated above correspond very closely to the central features of the Bolshevik *Weltanschauung*. . . .

The authors of *The Authoritarian Personality* have demonstrated in a more plausible manner than any previous investigators that there is a determinate relationship between particular attitudes towards public objects and symbols and "deeper" cognitive and emotional attitudes or dispositions.† . . .

. . . Movements and institutions, even if they are authoritarian, require both more and less than authoritarian personality structures. On the other hand, a liberal democratic society itself could probably not function satisfactorily with only "democratic liberal personalities"‡ to fill all its roles. . . .

The tasks of a liberal democratic society are many and many different kinds of personality structures are compatible with and necessary for its well being. Even authoritarian personalities are especially useful in some roles in democratic societies and in many other roles where they are not indispensable, they are at least harmless.

The fact that there is no point to point correspondence of personality and social role does not however mean that they have no approximate relationship to one another. The task of social research in this field is to clarify and make more determinate the scope of this relation-

---

*For a very useful collection of excerpts from the writings of Lenin and Stalin arranged in categories similar to those used in the present analysis, c.f. Nathan, Leites, *A Study of Bolshevism* (Glencoe, Ill.: Free Press, 1953).

†The evidence concerning the operation of the mechanisms of repression and reaction-formation is much less convincing than the evidences about the deeper dispositions but it is plausible. The operation of these mechanisms must be adduced in order to bring systematic coherence into the data gathered in the clinical interviews.

‡From which the "leftist Authoritarians" have been separated.

ship. *The Authoritarian Personality* both by its very solid achievement and its very significant deficiencies has contributed towards our progress in the solution of this task.

> **Milton Rokeach's** attention to the ahistorical nature of authoritarianism provided another dimension to the study of authoritarianism. Concerned with the general properties of authoritarianism and its applicability to all history through alternative forms, he reinforced his theory by distinguishing between "dogmatism" and "opinionation." Rokeach's refinements provided clarification about the structure and content of ideological systems. These distinctions enabled him to advance researchable hypotheses about reactions to authority and to distinguish between authority and authoritarianism. Development of such an empirically-based theory verifying the continuous nature of all belief systems is important and relevant for the mixed culture and personality styles in the American context.

Personality, Ideology, and Cognitive Functioning (1960)*

. . . Our goal . . . is to conceive of authoritarianism in an ahistorical way so that it will be equally applicable to all stages of history and to alternative forms of authoritarianism within a given historical stage. . . .

. . . [I]f our interest is in the scientific study of authoritarianism, we should proceed from right authoritarianism not to a re-focus on left authoritarianism but to the general properties held in common by all forms of authoritarianism. Authoritarianism can be observed at any one time in history in a variety of human activities, and we should think that it would have similar properties regardless of whether it is exhibited under Caesar, Napoleon, Hitler, Stalin, Khrushchev, Roosevelt, or Eisenhower. What is needed is therefore a deliberate turning

---

*Excerpts from "Personality, Ideology, and Cognitive Functioning" (pp. 9, 14, 392-393) by Milton Rokeach, in *The Open and Closed Mind* (New York: Basic Books, 1960).

away from a concern with the one or two kinds of authoritarianism that may happen to be predominant at a given time. Instead, we should pursue a more theoretical ahistorical analysis of the properties held in common by all forms of authoritarianism regardless of specific ideological, theological, philosophic, or scientific content. . . .

. . . From the literature on prejudice and authoritarianism, one would expect that those who are intolerant, or authoritarian, or closed, characteristically show either-or, black-white categorizations of people. But the data we have presented on disbelief systems show that this is not so. Disbeliefs are seen to be arranged by virtually everyone in terms of a continuum of similarity.

Authority, Authoritarianism, and Conformity (1961)*

While the concepts of authoritarianism and the authoritarian personality have been, and continue to be, widely employed in contemporary thought and research,† thus far they have not been explicitly defined in a satisfactory conceptual way. In the most widely known work by Adorno, Frenkel-Brunswik, Levinson, and Sanford (1950) on the authoritarian personality, the closest thing to a conceptual definition is a listing of various traits or personality characteristics, like authoritarian aggression and submission, conventionality, anti-intraception, rigidity, and projectivity which, on psychoanalytic grounds, are thought to characterize persons judged to be high on authoritarianism. But the concept itself, as far as I can tell, has not been explicitly defined in a formal way.

To my mind, there is sufficient empirical evidence now available from a variety of sources to support the hypotheses put forward by the authors of *The Authoritarian Personality* regarding at least the

---

*Excerpts from "Authority, Authoritarianism, and Conformity" (pp. 230–239, 242–246, and 254–255) by Milton Rokeach in *Conformity and Deviation*, edited by Irwin A. Berg and Bernard M. Bass, Copyright© 1961 by Irwin A. Berg and Bernard M. Bass. Reprinted by permission of Harper & Row, Publishers, Inc.

†Christie and Cook (1958) cite over two hundred publications through 1956 stemming from the work by Adorno *et al.* (1950).

major personality characteristics differentiating those scoring high and
low on the F scale. But I would like to raise for discussion and scrutiny
a number of implicit assumptions widely held about the nature of
authoritarianism which to one degree or another underlie or inhere
in current conceptualizations, and which for the most part antedate
the work of Adorno *et al.* These assumptions, I will argue, have pro-
foundly influenced the direction taken by current theory and research,
and are therefore worth examining in a critical way in the hope that
they might lead to fresh insights and fresh directions in future research.

In Defense of Authority

One assumption which is widespread is that authoritarianism is
rooted in a reliance on authority while its opposite, antiauthoritarianism, is characterized by a rejection of authority and, in its place, a
reliance on reason. Reasonable as this assumption may appear to be
at first glance, there are grounds for assuming otherwise. It is incon-
ceivable that we could get to know as much as we do about the world
we live in if we were not able to rely on authority and if we had only
ourselves and our own powers of reason to rely on.

This idea, namely, the idea that all men *need* authority, may sound
strange coming from a psychologist who, along with many others, has
viewed with alarm the phenomenon of authoritarianism and the social
psychological processes underlying it. But it is an idea which has been
long accepted by philosophers of religion, philosophers of politics, and
political scientists. Thus, Trueblood reminds us that it is a popular
error to believe that "authority and reason are somehow rival ways
of coming to the truth" (1942, p. 72). Charles Hendel writes: "This
question of the apparent opposition of authority and freedom has long
been the chief concern of political and social philosophy" (1958, p. 18).
He elaborates this view at somewhat greater length as follows:

> We are further confused by an uncritical general philosophy unfavorable
> to authority in any form. . . . The free, responsible, self-governing indi-
> vidual is thought of as self-sufficient. . . . We fail to realize that man can
> enjoy the desired freedom and self-sufficiency only in a social order
> where there is an effective authority. But in popular philosophy there is
> no room for this truth.
>   The mind is also closed to the need and value of authority in society
> by a long-prevalent optimistic notion of history. . . . The harshness as
> well as the crudity of primitive human existence is seen happily left
> behind, and authority is one of the antiquated relics of the past. . . . His-

tory is "the story of freedom" and the goal of it is a state of freedom without authority [Hendel, 1958 pp. 5–6].

Another contemporary political scientist, Carl J. Friedrich, expresses a similar view when he asks: "But are reasoning and authority so antithetical? Does authority have no basis in reason? The following analysis seeks to elucidate the proposition that authority and reason are closely linked, indeed that authority rests upon the ability to issue communications which are capable of reasoned elaboration" (1958, p. 29).

Similar views have recently been expressed by Hannah Arendt (1958) and also by Catlin who writes: "For the purposes of political science, authority is neither in itself good or bad. It carries no poison necessarily, whatever may be the warnings of psychologists and others . . ." (1958, p. 128).

Erich Fromm (1941) clearly sees the difference between authority and authoritarianism when he makes a distinction between rational authority and inhibiting authority. To compare the two he gives as examples the relation between teacher and student on the one hand, and slave and owner on the other. In the former, the aim of the relationship is to decrease the psychological distance between one and the other in order to make them more like each other. In the latter case, the aim is to increase psychological distance, one at the expense of the other.

If we had only our own reason to rely on and not authority, all of history would be forever beyond our ken; we would have no knowledge of current affairs in places we ourselves have not been; we would know nothing of advances in science and technology beyond those we have made or discovered for ourselves; and there would be no point in consulting the *Encyclopedia Britannica*.

Authority and Authoritarianism

The widespread failure to make a distinction between authority and authoritarianism, which rests on the equally widespread insistence on the distinction between authority and reason, have led to a variety of ramifications, a few of which are worth mentioning briefly in passing. For example, it has led to the view that the therapist should not speak his mind to his patient, that teachers should not teach their students, and that leaders should not lead, because these all involve authoritarian relationships. Instead, it is suggested students will learn for themselves and from each other when they are ready for it, and so also with patients. And a really democratic group is a leaderless group.

There is really nothing so ugly about authority, only certain kinds of authority. And there need be no inherent contradiction between reliance on authority and reliance on reason, so long as we use independent reason to guide us in selecting the authorities we choose to influence us and so long as we use reason to tell us when to throw overboard one authority in favor of another. A person is said to be high in authoritarianism because he relies on authority while another does not. Rather, the difference lies in different notions about the *nature* of authority, different theories, if you will, about the way to employ authority as a cognitive liaison system to mediate between the person and the world he is trying to understand and adapt to.

Definition of Authority

I will now define authority as any source whatsoever to which we look for information, or to which we turn to verify information already possessed about any aspect of the universe. We all look to authority in order to serve our cognitive needs to know, and to guide action designed to serve other needs. The student looks to his teacher and the concentration camp prisoner looks to his Nazi guard for information. In the former case, in order to satisfy curiosity and in the latter case in order to find out precisely what must be done and what must not be done in order to avoid being beaten or shot. Even a mathematician who has just proven a theorem by deductive logic must somewhere along the line submit the product of his thought to the scrutiny of another mathematician, if for no other reason than to make sure that he didn't make a mistake.

It is with considerations such as these in mind that the proposal has been advanced elsewhere in some detail (Rokeach, 1960) that authoritarianism and antiauthoritarianism be conceived in terms of opposing orientation in modes of reliance on authority, ranging from open orientations to authority at one extreme to closed orientations at the other.

Crucial to this analysis is what is meant by open and closed. By *open* I mean that the power of authority rests solely upon the perception of the source's cognitive correctness, accuracy, and consistency with other information, as obtained by other means—that is, from one's own cognitions, and from other information obtained from other sources. Authority which gives information in conflict with one's own cognitions will be judged unreliable and will be rejected, in order to be replaced by other authority judged to be more correct, accurate, or consistent. In *closed* authoritarian orientations to authority, however, the power of authority does not at all hinge upon cognitive correctness but solely on the ability of authority to mete out arbitrary rewards and punishments.

Content and Prestige of Communication Sources

It is assumed that every communication received from an external authority source contains two kinds of information. It contains information of a substantive nature and it contains information about the authority source itself. Substantive information is typically obtained from the sheer content of the message. The prestige aspects of the source are obtained from the expressive and evaluative aspects of the message. And the *way* in which the communication is delivered, such as tone of voice, facial expression, the social conditions under which the message is delivered, and so on. The more open one's orientation toward authority, the more will the two kinds of information be clearly distinguished from each other and the more will each be evaluated and responded to on their respective merits. That is, the person has freedom to choose or not to choose to be influenced in a direction desired by the source, depending on his own assessment of both sets of information. However, the more closed one's orientation toward authority the more difficult it will be, by virtue of the authority's effective capability to mete out reward and punishment, to discriminate the two qualitatively different kinds of information, and consequently, to assess and act on them on their respective merits. What the external authority says is true about the world will become cognitively indiscriminable from what the external authority wants us to believe is true, and wants us to do about it. The person in such a closed state of mind will thus be forced to evaluate and to act in ways desired by the source rather than in terms of what Kohler (1938) has called "inner requiredness" and what Katz and Stotland (1959) have called "appropriateness."

From this basic distinction between the two extreme kinds of orientations to authority, it is possible to derive quite a number of other cognitive characteristics which are hypothesized to distinguish open from closed belief systems. For example, given a person incapable of distinguishing substantive information from information about the source, the parts within his belief system will be more segregated or isolated from each other, there will be less differentiation within and between various parts of the belief and disbelief system, and he will be characterized by a narrower time perspective. This is not the place to enter into a detailed discussion of why this is so. The interested reader is referred elsewhere (Rokeach, 1960) for fuller treatment of the topic and for a systematic discussion of the many cognitive variables which are conceived to differentiate open from closed belief systems or open and closed orientations toward authority.

Ideological Content vs. Ideological Structure

All of the preceding leads me now to a second, closely related issue which has strongly influenced thinking and research on the nature of authoritarianism. Should we, in assessing the degree to which a person is authoritarian, that is, has a closed orientation toward authority, pay attention to the *content* or to the *structure* of his belief system? In the formulations of the California group, and in the construction of the F Scale, it was ideological content rather than ideological structure which was emphasized. Consider, for example, the F Scale item: "People can be divided into two distinct classes: the weak and the strong." This item is compatible in its content with fascist ideology but not with communist ideology. I have already had occasion elsewhere (1956; 1960) to point out that the California research, by virtue of the fact that it was content-oriented, dealt only, or at least primarily, with rightist or fascistic forms of authoritarianism and not with all forms of authoritarianism. A general theory of authoritarianism has to be structure- rather than content-oriented.

How does one get at the structure of an ideology rather than at its content? Here I have found the concepts of such psychologists as Lewin (1951), Krech (1949) and, to a somewhat lesser extent, Tolman (1948) most helpful. The variables which they employ to describe the life space, the psychological field, and the cognitive map are precisely the kinds of variables which seem to get at structure rather than content. Where the content-oriented F Scale deals with such variables as conventionalism, authoritarian aggression and submission, superstition and a belief in the supernatural, the structure-oriented Dogmatism Scale deals with such variables as isolation, differentiation, time perspective, various formal aspects of the central-peripheral dimension of beliefs, and so on. In short, the items on the Dogmatism Scale are deliberately worded to avoid specific ideological content so that the structural attributes of authoritarianism being measured may apply equally well to all ideologies.

Already discussed elsewhere (Rokeach, 1956; Rokeach, 1960) so that the specifics need not be repeated here, are the individual items of the Dogmatism Scale, the structural attributes these items try to measure, and the extent to which the total scale has turned out to be successful as a measure of general authoritarianism. It will perhaps suffice here to say that even though the Dogmatism and F Scales are highly correlated, communists in England score lower than other political groups on the F Scale but higher than the same political groups on the Dogmatism Scale. Also, in contrast to the F Scale, which is significantly associated with political conservatism, the Dogmatism Scale is found to be relatively independent of liberalism-conservatism, that is, it is found with relatively equal frequency along all positions of the political spectrum.*

The Ingroup-Outgroup Dichotomy

Psychologists and sociologists have long been accustomed to think in terms of ingroups and outgroups when addressing themselves to certain aspects of intergroup relations, social attitudes, and prejudice. A person is said to be a member of one or more ingroups, and whatever is left over are conceived to be the person's outgroups, without any further articulation of the latter concept. Similar distinctions are made between positive and negative authority, positive and negative reference groups, and between belief and disbelief. In line with such dichotomic conceptions authoritarianism has been assumed to imply an absolute acceptance, or overglorification, of the ingroup and at the same time an absolute rejection, or villification, of the outgroup.

Continuum of Outgroups

Our own conceptualizations and findings with regard to the organization of belief systems suggest that this way of thinking is inadequate to deal with certain observable facts and is therefore in need of reformulation. We find that arrayed against the ingroup is not a global, undifferentiated cluster of outgroups but rather a series of outgroups organized along a continuum of similarity to the ingroup. Furthermore, the extent to which one accepts or rejects various outgroups is, at least in part, a function of the degree of belief congruence of outgroup to ingroup. In other words, represented within the cognitive structure of all persons is a belief system and series of disbelief subsystems arranged along a gradient of congruence to the belief sys-

---

*In addition to the main references already cited, see also the factorial studies by Rokeach and Fruchter (1956) and Fruchter, Rokeach, and Novak (1958).

tem. Consider, for example, the cognitive organization we typically find for a group of Catholic college students and also, of Catholic priests. When they are asked to rank various Christian denominations in terms of similarity (belief congruence), we get the following order: Catholic, then Episcopalian, then Lutheran, then Presbyterian, then Methodist, and last, Baptist. If a group of Baptists are asked to rank these same religions for similarity, we get exactly the reverse order: Baptist, Methodist, Presbyterian, Lutheran, Episcopalian, and Catholic. The similarity continuum for Episcopalians is the same as that for Catholics, with the exception, of course, that Episcopalians judge Catholics as most similar to themselves. The similarity continua for the major religious groupings within Christianity are basically the same, with each group merely judging the other groups from the standpoint of its own position along the similarity continuum. The similarity data obtained from college students of various denominations are generally in good agreement with those obtained for clergymen of the same denomination. . . .

Authoritarianism As a Determinant of Social Discrimination

I come now to a fourth assumption about the nature of authoritarianism which needs to be re-examined. It is widely assumed that individual differences in prejudice or social discrimination are in large part a function of individual differences in authoritarianism. There are various kinds of evidence available from a variety of sources which do indeed seem to support this view. Recall, for example, the rather sizable correlations found in the California research between authoritarianism and ethnocentrism. However, the research I have just referred to on the relation between similarity and rejection clearly suggests that this is not the whole story. We actually find two variables which are significantly associated with the degree of rejection of a particular outgroup. One is authoritarianism. Groups scoring above the mean on the Dogmatism Scale almost always show higher mean rejection scores of various religious outgroups. The second variable, however, is sheer cognitive similarity or congruence between belief and disbelief systems. Our data clearly show that even if the individual differences in authoritarianism were altogether eliminated from the picture there would still be considerable discrimination against various outgroups on the basis of cognitive similarity alone. In fact, we find that far more of the variance is attributable to cognitive similarity than to authoritarianism as a source of attitudinal rejection and as a basis for differential preference and conflict in every-day life.

Belief Congruence vs. Ethnic or Race Congruence As the Basis of Intolerance

Another assumption widely held is that authoritarianism involves a greater tendency to cognitively categorize the world of people in terms of ethnic and racial groupings and to discriminate on this basis. A major weakness in this conception is that it is difficult to deal with certain manifestations of authoritarianism which are not at all associated with ethnic or racial discrimination, or which are indeed associated with its opposite—extreme tolerance toward ethnic or racial groups. For example, how are we to account for our finding that communists in England score higher than other political groups on authoritarianism, as measured by the Dogmatism Scale, but score lowest of all groups on a measure of ethnic and racial intolerance? And again, the phenomenon of authoritarianism may be observed in the academic world and in other areas of human activity where there is not necessarily a concomitant manifestation of ethnic or racial intolerance.

In my own view, the difficulties posed seem to arise once again from the fact that we have long been accustomed to define prejudice in terms of ideological content rather than structure. Prejudice against the Jew and Negro seem compatible with certain kinds of ideologies—for example, Fascism or the dominant ideology of the South—but not with others—for example, Marxism, socialism, or democracy. Does this mean that no instances of prejudice are to be found associated with the last-mentioned ideologies? Obviously not. The problem then becomes: how can the problem of man's intolerance to man be reformulated so that all forms of intolerance, regardless of specific ideological content, will gracefully fall under scrutiny?

In an attempt to answer this question I have previously proposed that we redefine prejudice (or intolerance or bigotry) in terms of structure rather than content, a proposal parallel to the one made in redefining authoritarianism. Prejudice is redefined in terms of the way we feel and act toward those who agree and disagree with us on specific issues we care about. In other words, the criterion is a belief criterion rather than a racial or ethnic one. The Opinionation Scale tries to get at this belief criterion. The basic idea underlying this scale is very simple. How often and to what degree will persons agree with belief statements preceded by such opinionated phrases as: "Anyone who is intelligent knows that . . . ," "Only a simple-minded fool would believe that . . . ," "Anyone with an ounce of common sense knows perfectly well that . . . ," and so on. The more such statements are endorsed by a person the more the assumed rejection of others *because* they disagree, and the more the assumed acceptance of others *because* they agree.

The results obtained with the Opinionation Scale differ from those obtained with traditional tests of prejudice, which as has already been mentioned, contain references to ethnic and racial groups. English communists who score relatively low on the California Ethnocentrism Scale score high on the Opinionation Scale. Other groups which score high on the Ethnocentrism Scale also score high on the Opinionation Scale. These results, as well as a variety of other results presented elsewhere (Rokeach, 1956, 1960) suggest that at most, only the rightist form of authoritarian categorizes and discriminates in terms of ethnic and racial groups. But such categorizations cannot be considered a general attribute of authoritarianism.

In fact, we have gone one step further to suggest that even those social discriminations which at first glance appear to be based on racial and ethnic considerations may, from a psychological standpoint turn out to be more due to belief than to racial or ethnic discrimination. Our subjects—white college students at Michigan State University—seem to prefer more as friends Negroes who agree with them on various issues than whites who disagree with them on the same issues. For example, 42 out of 65 white subjects—two out of three—rated more favorably on a friendship scale a Negro who agrees with them on the desegregation issue than a white who disagrees with them on desegregation. Fifty-five out of the 65 subjects—11 out of 13—preferred friendship with a Negro who believes in God to a white atheist. Our findings for Southern college students are very similar. On the issue of desegregation in education, 92 out of 136—again 2 out of 3—preferred friendship with a Negro who agrees than with a white who disagrees; 110 out of 136—again 11 out of 13—preferred friendship with a Negro who believes in God to a white atheist. Similar results are obtained with Jewish children between the ages of 7 and 16. We find that they overwhelmingly prefer friendship with Gentiles who agree with them on various issues than with Jews who disagree with them.

Belief Congruence Is Basic

All these findings indicate that a basic principle of organization and categorization, for authoritarian and nonauthoritarian alike, is belief congruence rather than racial or ethnic congruence. We find that when belief is held constant, there are relatively small differences in preferences of white over Negro, and, in the Jewish children, in preferences of Jew over Gentile. But when race or ethnic group is held constant, we find enormous differences in preference for those who agree over those who disagree with the subject's views. These differences are greater for those who are authoritarian than for those who are less so, suggesting that authoritarians differ from nonauthoritarians not so much in terms of a greater tendency toward ethnic or racial categorizations as in the extent to which authoritarians categorize and discriminate more sharply those who agree from those who disagree with their views.

Overidealization of Ingroup and Vilification of Outgroups

A sixth assumption about the nature of authoritarianism is that the authoritarian vilifies the outgroup but overidealizes the ingroup. If this assumption is correct, we should find, in a white population, that the greater the rejection of the Negro, the greater the acceptance of the white. In the research to which I have just referred, we were able to get independent measures of the extent to which each subject rejects Negroes and whites. We find, in our Northern sample, that the greater the rejection of the Negro, the greater also the rejection of the white. The correlation is .80. A similar finding is obtained for our Southern sample, with the exception that the correlation is lower—a +.43 correlation between rejection of the Negro and rejection of the white. In the study with Jewish children, those who express a dislike of Gentiles also express a dislike of Jews. These results, when considered alongside such other findings as those by Adorno *et al.* (1950), Campbell and McCandless (1951), Rokeach (1952), and Sullivan and Adelson (1954) would suggest that the authoritarian overidealizes the ingroup only when there is fear of retaliation. When given the opportunity, without fear of retaliation, the authoritarian seems quite capable of expressing his negative feelings toward the ingroup, no less than toward various outgroups. . . .

Summary

While authoritarianism has not been explicitly defined in a satisfactory conceptual way, one can discern many implicit assumptions about its nature which are widely accepted. I have had occasion here to consider six of these assumptions and to call for their reconsideration. First, the dichotomy between reliance on authority versus reliance on reason is suggested to be a false one since everyone has to rely on authority in order to know the world he lives in. Instead, I have proposed that we think in terms of open versus closed orientations to authority. Second, we should bear in mind the distinction between ideological content and ideological structure. A person may adhere to an ideology democratic in content but his mode of adherence may be authoritarian. Third, authoritarianism does not seem to imply an absolute rejection of negative authority. Instead, it seems more fruitful to conceive of a gradation of negative authority arranged on a continuum of similarity to positive authority, with rejection becoming increasingly greater as a function of dissimilarity. Fourth, the rejection of a particular outgroup is often traceable to the degree of cognitive similarity between outgroup and ingroup which is to a large extent independent of authoritarianism as such. Fifth, authoritarianism involves an exaggerated categorization of people in terms of belief congruence rather than in terms of racial or ethnic congruence. And, sixth, authoritarianism seems to involve a fear of the ingroup no less than a fear of the outgroup.

REFERENCES

Adorno, T. W., Else Frenkel-Brunswik, D. J. Levison, R. N. Sanford, *The Authoritarian Personality* (New York: Harper & Bros., 1950).

Arendt, Hannah, "What Was Authority?" in C. J. Friedrich, ed., *Authority* (Cambridge: Harvard University Press, 1958).

Campbell, D. T. and B. McCandless, "Ethnocentrism, Xenophobia, and Personality," *Human Relations*, Vol. 4 (1951), pp. 185–92.

Catlin, G. E. G., "Authority and its Critics," in C. J. Friedrich, ed., *Authority* (Cambridge: Harvard University Press, 1958).

Friedrich, C. J., "Authority, Reason, and Discretion," in C. J. Friedrich, ed., *Authority* (Cambridge: Harvard University Press, 1958).

Fromm, E., *Escape From Freedom* (New York: Farrar & Rinehart, 1941).

Fruchter, B., M. Rokeach, and E. G. Novak, "A Factorial Study of Dogmatism, Opinionation, and Related Scales," *Psychological Reports,* Vol. 4 (1958), pp. 19–22.

Hendel, C., "An Exploration of the Nature of Authority," in C. J. Friedrich, ed., *Authority* (Cambridge: Harvard University Press, 1958).

Katz, D., and E. Stotland, "A Preliminary Statement to a Theory of Attitude Structure and Change" in S. Koch, ed. *Psychology: A Study of Science,* Vol. 3 (New York: McGraw-Hill, 1959).

Kohler, W., *The Place of Value in a World of Facts* (New York: Liverright, 1938).

Krech, D., "Notes Toward a Psychological Theory," *Journal of Personality,* Vol. 18 (1949), pp. 66–87.

Lewin, K., *Field Theory in Social Science* (New York: Harper, 1951).

Rokeach, M., "Attitude as a Determinant of Distortion in Recall," *Journal of Abnormal and Social Psychology,* Vol. 47 (1952), pp. 482–88.

Rokeach, M., "Political and Religious Dogmatism: An Alternative to the Authoritarian Personality," *Psychological Monographs,* No. 18 (Whole No. 425), (1956), p. 70.

Rokeach, M., *The Open and Closed Mind: Investigations into the Nature of Relief Systems and Personality Systems* (New York: Basic Books, 1960).

Rokeach, M., and B. Fruchter, "A Factorial Study of Dogmatism and Related Concepts," *Journal of Abnormal and Social Psychology,* Vol. 53 (1956), pp. 356–60.

Sullivan, P. L., and J. Adelson, "Ethnocentrism and Misanthropy," *Journal of Abnormal and Social Psychology,* Vol. 49 (1954), pp. 246–50.

Tolman, E. C., "Cognitive Maps in Rats and Men," *Psychological Review,* Vol. 55 (1948), pp. 189–208.

Trueblood, D. E., *The Logic of Belief* (New York: Harper, 1942).

The Interdependence of Personality and Environment on Individual and Group Behavior

2

Ronald Lippitt and Ralph K. White,
How Satisfying Is Democracy?

An Experimental Study of Leadership and Group Life

Alan C. Elms and Stanley Milgram,
Personality Characteristics Associated with Obedience
and Defiance Toward Authoritative Command

The research of Ronald Lippitt and Ralph K. White, and then Alan Elms and Stanley Milgram, though from different historical periods, is illustrative of the work of investigators who, using experimental designs, observed and measured actual behavior in realistic situations. Their work assessed authoritarian and democratic behavior in order to describe what determines authoritarian and democratic preferences. Neither group of researchers reported a strict authoritarian-democratic dichotomy, but rather a binary mixture without a single consistent personality pattern dominating actions or attitudes. Apparently personality and situational determinants influenced behavioral responses, and the incidence of mixed expressions was more prevalent than anticipated.

How Satisfying Is Democracy? (1960)*

Erich Fromm's phrase "escape from freedom" sums up one of the more frightening aspects of dictatorship in the modern world: the frequent tendency of human beings to relapse into a passive, dependent, irresponsible acceptance of a slavish role, without resentment and often even with relief. People have often put chains on themselves voluntarily, or at least have acquiesced without a murmur when others put chains upon them. It would be sheer wishful thinking, then, to generalize too far on the basis of the fact that certain groups of eleven-year-old children, in certain specific circumstances, preferred democracy to autocracy. Even their preference had definite limitations. . . . Actually, history and everyday experience, as well as a number of systematic experiments, have shown that both reactions are possible and frequent—that some people, in some circumstances, prefer democracy, while other people in the same circumstances, or the same people in other circumstances, prefer autocracy. What is needed, evidently, is not to demonstrate once again this much-demonstrated fact, but to attempt the more analytical task of trying to discover more about what kinds of people, in what kinds of circumstances, find their needs satisfied in a more or a less democratic type of organization.

---

*R. K. White and R. Lippitt, *Autocracy and Democracy* (New York: Harper & Bros., 1960), p. 258.

An Experimental Study of Leadership and Group Life (1958)*

The study here reported, conducted in 1939 and 1940, attempted in an exploratory way to discover the extent to which various aspects of leadership behavior and of total group life could be fruitfully studied by experimental procedures of controlled matching and planned variation in conditions. The study had as its objectives:

1. To study the effects on group and individual behavior of three experimental variations in adult leadership in four clubs of eleven-year-old children. These three styles may be roughly labeled as "democratic," "authoritarian" and "laissez-faire."

2. To study the group and individual reactions to shifts from one type of leadership to another within the same group.

3. To seek relationships between the nature and content of other group memberships, particularly the classroom and family, and the reactions to the experimental social climates.

4. To explore the methodological problems of setting up comparative "group test situations," to develop adequate techniques of group process recording, and to discover the degree to which experimental conditions could be controlled and manipulated within the range of acceptance by the group members.

---

*R. Lippitt and R. K. White, in Eleanor E. Maccoby, Theodore M. Newcomb, and Eugene L. Hartley, eds., *Readings in Social Psychology* (3d Ed.; New York: Holt, Rinehart & Winston, 1958), pp. 496–511. Prepared by the authors from data more fully reported in (1) Kurt Lewin, Ronald Lippitt, and Ralph K. White, "Patterns of Aggressive Behavior in Experimentally Created 'Social Climates,'" *Journal of Social Psychology*, Vol. 10 (1939), pp. 271–99; (2) Ronald Lippitt, "An Experimental Study of Authoritarian and Democratic Group Atmospheres," in *Studies in Topological and Vector Psychology I, University of Iowa Studies in Child Welfare*, No. 16, 1940; (3) Ronald Lippitt, "An Analysis of Group Reactions to Three Types of Experimentally Created Social Climates," (unpublished doctoral thesis, State University of Iowa, 1940); (4) Ronald Lippitt, "Field Theory and Experiment in Social Psychology: Authoritarian and Democratic Group Atmospheres," *American Journal of Sociology*, Vol. 45 (1939), pp. 26–49; (5) Ronald Lippitt, "The Morale of Youth Groups," in Goodwin Watson, ed., *Civilian Morale* (Boston: Houghton Mifflin Co. for Reynal & Hitchcock, 1942); and (6) Ronald Lippitt and Ralph K. White, "The 'Social Climate' of Children's Groups," in Roger Barker, Jacob Kounin, and Herbert Wright, *Child Development and Behavior* (New York: McGraw-Hill Book Co., 1943).

The major experimental controls may be described briefly as follows:

1. *Personal characteristics of group members.* Because a large group of volunteers were available from which to select each of the small clubs, it was possible to arrange for comparability of group members on such characteristics as intelligence, and on such social behaviors (measured by teachers' ratings) as obedience, amount of social participation, leadership, frequency of quarreling, amount of physical energy, etc.

2. *The interrelationship pattern of each club.* In each group, by the use of a sociometric questionnaire in each classroom, it was possible to select groups which were very closely matched in terms of patterns of rejection, friendship, mutuality of relationship, and leadership position.

3. *Physical setting and equipment.* All clubs met in the same clubroom setting, two at a time in adjacent meeting spaces, with a common equipment box.

4. *Activity interests.* It was important to know the extent to which initial interest in the planned activities might be responsible for differences in degree of involvement in activity during the experiment. Therefore it was ascertained in the beginning that all groups of boys were comparably interested in the range of craft and recreational activities in which they would later be engaged.

5. *Activity content.* It is clear that the structure and content of an activity often exerts a powerful influence on the patterns of interdependence, cooperation, competition, etc. in group life. Therefore, it was important that activity content should be equated in these three types of leadership situations. In order to insure this, the clubs under democratic leadership met first in time during the week, and the activities which were selected by those clubs were automatically assigned to the parallel clubs under authoritarian leadership. In the laissez-faire situation, there were a number of potential activities of the same type as that selected by the "democratic clubs."

6. *The same group under different leadership.* The experimental design also made it possible to have a perfect matching of club personnel on the same analysis by comparing the same club with itself under three different leaders.

	Period 1 (7 weeks)	Period 2 (7 weeks)	Period 3 (7 weeks)
Treatment ... Club .... Leader	Autocracy Sherlock Holmes I	Autocracy Sherlock Holmes IV	Democracy Sherlock Holmes II
Treatment ... Club .... Leader	Autocracy Dick Tracy II	Democracy Dick Tracy III	Autocracy Dick Tracy I
Treatment ... Club .... Leader	Democracy Secret Agents III	Autocracy Secret Agents II	Democracy Secret Agents IV
Treatment ... Club .... Leader	Democracy Charlie Chan IV	Democracy Charlie Chan I	Autocracy Charlie Chan III

Experimental Variations

In the beginning the experimenters had planned for only two major variations in adult leader behavior: an authoritarian pattern and a democratic pattern. Later it was decided that it would be more fruitful to add a third variation of "laissez-faire" adult behavior, although with the four available clubs it would make the experimental design less rigorous. The method of systematic rotation can be noted in the above chart, which refers to the earlier experiment (the same method was followed in the later experiment).

The three types of planned variation were as follows:

1. *The sequence of social climates.* A number of the hypotheses focused upon the effect of a particular type of group history in determining the reactions of a group to a present pattern of leadership. The chart indicates the variety of group history sequences which were selected for exploratory study.

2. *"Leader role" and "leader personality."* There was a question as to the extent to which certain basic personality characteristics of the adult leaders would be important determinants in the individual and group behavior patterns which resulted. To study this variable, four adults with very different personality patterns were selected as leaders and all of them after proper indoctrination took two or three different leadership roles with different groups during the course of the experiment as indicated on the chart. This made it possible to discover whether

certain of the leaders induced common reaction patterns which could be traced to their "personality" as contrasted to their "leadership role."

3. *The three planned leadership roles.* The three variations in leader role which were worked through in careful detail by the four club leaders may be summarized as follows:

Plan for Authoritarian Leadership Role

Practically all policies as regards club activities and procedures should be determined by the leader. The techniques and activity steps should be communicated by the authority, one unit at a time, so that future steps are in the dark to a large degree. The adult should take considerable responsibility for assigning the activity tasks and companions of each group member. The dominator should keep his standards of praise and criticism to himself in evaluating individual and group activities. He should also remain fairly aloof from active group participation except in demonstrating.

Plan for the Democratic Leadership Role

Wherever possible, policies should be a matter of group decision and discussion with active encouragement and assistance by the adult leader. The leader should attempt to see that activity perspective emerges during the discussion period with the general steps to the group goal becoming clarified. Wherever technical advice is needed, the leader should try to suggest two or more alternative procedures from which choice can be made by the group members. Everyone should be free to work with whomever he chooses, and the divisions of responsibility should be left up to the group. The leader should attempt to communicate in an objective, fact-minded way the bases for his praise and criticism of individual and group activities. He should try to be a regular group member in spirit but not do much of the work (so that comparisons of group productivity can be made between the groups).

Plan for Laissez-Faire Leadership Role

In this situation, the adult should play a rather passive role in social participation and leave complete freedom for group or individual decisions in relation to activity and group procedure. The leader should make clear the various materials which are available and be sure it is understood that he will supply information and help when asked. He should do a minimum of taking the initiative in making suggestions. He should make no attempt to evaluate negatively or positively the behavior or productions of the individuals or the group as a group, although he should be friendly rather than "stand-offish" at all times.

The data below will indicate the extent to which these planned variations were carried out and the pattern of social stimulation which was represented by the leader behavior in each of the clubs.

The Three Patterns of Leader Behavior

From the great variety of observations recorded on the behavior of each leader it was possible to compute quantitative profiles of leader performance which could be compared to see the extent to which the three different types of leadership role were different and the degree to which the adults carrying out the same role were comparable in their behavior patterns. Figure 1 illustrates some of the major differences in the patterns of behavior of the three leadership roles. Most of the comparisons on the graph meet the test of statistical significance. The "average leader" comparisons are based on four democratic, four authoritarian, and two laissez-faire leader roles. The first three classifications of behavior, "leader orders," "disrupting commands" and "nonconstructive criticism," may be thought of as representing adult behavior which has a limiting effect upon the scope and spontaneity of child activity. About 60 percent of all of the behavior of the average authoritarian leader was of these types as compared to 5 percent for the democratic and laissez-faire leaders. The data show that the authoritarian leader usually initiated individual or group activity with an order, often disrupted on-going activity by an order which started things off in the new direction not spontaneously chosen, and fairly frequently criticized work in a manner which carried the meaning, "It is a bad job because I say it is a bad job" rather than, "It is a poor job because those nails are bent over instead of driven in."

The next three behavior classifications, "guiding suggestions," "extending knowledge," "stimulating self-guidance," may be thought of as extending individual and group freedom and abilities. We note here some of the major differences between the democratic and the laissez-faire leadership role. Whereas the democratic leader took the initiative (where he felt it was needed in making guiding suggestions) much more frequently than the laissez-faire leader, a major proportion of the latter leadership role was giving out information when it was

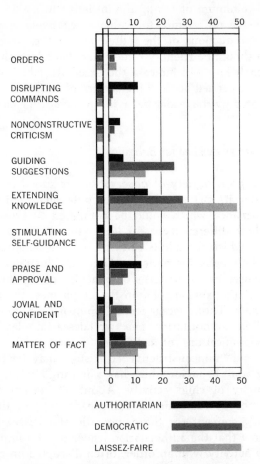

Fig. 1. Comparison of behavior of average authoritarian, democratic, and laissez-faire leader.

asked for. It is clear, however, that the democratic leader did not take initiative for action away from the group as indicated by the fact that the average democratic leader showed a greater proportion of "stimulating self-guidance" than even the laissez-faire leader. The category of "stimulating self-guidance" was made up of three main items: "leader's requests for child's opinions on individual and group plans," "use of child judgment as criterion," and "taking consensus of opinion." The data indicate that the democratic leaders stimulated child independence eight times as often as the authoritarian leader and about twice as often as the laissez-faire leader, although the latter two types of adults showed about the same proportion of this behavior in their total pattern of activity.

The classification on the graph entitled, "praise and approval" is made up of such behavior items as "praising," "giving credit," "giving O.K.s," etc. It indicates largely the functioning of the adult as a dispenser of social recognition. The authoritarian adult was significantly more active in this regard than either of the other two types of leaders.

The extent to which the adult discussed personal matters unrelated to the club situation (home, school, etc.), and also joked on a friendly basis with the club members, is indicated by the "jovial and confident" classification. The democratic leader had social interactions of this type with the group members about eight times as often as either the authoritarian or laissez-faire leaders. This is perhaps one of the best indices of the extent to which the democratic leaders were "on the same level" as the club members.

The last classification on Figure 1, "matter of fact," indicates one measurement of the extent to which the various social atmospheres were "fact-minded" as compared to "personal-minded" as far as the behavior of the adults was concerned.

The degree to which all the adult leaders, delegated to assume a given leadership role, behaved in a comparable fashion on these major aspects of leadership role is indicated by the fact that, on all comparisons differentiating major characteristics of the three roles, there is no overlapping of the behavior of any representative of one role with any representative of a different role. Thus it is possible to conclude that three clearly different leadership patterns were created with a much smaller range of individual differences in leader behavior within each pattern than between the patterns.

Leadership Role and Personality Style

An examination of the behavior patterns of the different leadership roles by the same individuals (see chart on page 68) reveals that on the items of leader behavior there is no greater similarity between the different performance patterns of the same individual than between those of different individuals. If we turn to the data of the three interviews with each club member in which at each transition stage in their club life they compared their leaders and talked very fully about them, we find again that there is no evidence of any adult personalities being rated favorably or unfavorably independently of their particular leadership role (i.e., authoritarian, democratic, laissez-faire). All leaders stood high as well as low for one group or another and all the comments about their "personalities" were concerned with attributes of their leadership roles which had been measured.

The following excerpts from interviews of club members who had just completed six months of club life which included an authoritarian, a laissez-faire, and a democratic leader (in that sequence) indicate rather clearly the aspects of "leadership personality" which were perceived as important.

"RW (democratic) was the best leader and DA (laissez-faire) was the poorest. RW has good ideas and goes right to the point of everything ... and always asked us what to do next time the club met, which was very nice. . . . DA gave us no suggestions like RW did, and didn't help us out at all, though he was very nice to us . . . but let us figure things out too much. I liked RL (authoritarian) pretty well for that kind of work."

"RL (authoritarian) was best, and then RW (democratic) and DA (laissez-faire). RL was the strictest and I like that a lot. DA and RW let us go ahead and fight, and that isn't good, though RW didn't do it as much as DA did. DA just didn't give us much to do. RW was OK, but he didn't have so many ideas as RL did. RW wanted to do what we did; RL didn't want to go with us lots of times, and he decided what we were to do."

"I liked RW (democratic) best, then DA (laissez-faire) and then RL (authoritarian). RW was a good sport, works along with us and helps us a lot; he thinks of things just like we do and was just one of us—he never did try to be the boss, and wasn't strict at all, but we always had plenty to do (the golden mean). DA didn't do much, just sat and watched; there wasn't much I didn't like about him, but he didn't help us much . . . not like with RW when we had regular meetings and that was very good. RL was all right mostly; he was sort of dictator like, and we had to do what he said pretty nearly; he helped us work but he was sort of bossy."

"I liked RW (democratic) the best and RL (authoritarian) the least. RW was in between DA and RL, I like everything about him. I once said I didn't want to change from DA but I'm glad we changed. We could do what we pleased with DA but he was too easy going, not hard enough nearly, but he's a real nice person. With RL, we always had something to do, and we did get a lot of things done, but I didn't like anything about him; he was much too strict. He was not cross, but very direct."

"I'd take RW (democratic) for a club leader, and DA (laissez-faire) was the worst. RW is just the right sort of combination; RL (authoritarian) was just about as good as RW, but he was kind of cross once in a while. RW had interesting things to do, he was just about right in everything. DA was too easy; he didn't know anything about the club—didn't know about its ways. He didn't understand us boys at all. . . . I didn't like him as well as RL because he had too few things for us to do."*

Another indirect indication that individual personality characteristics were not of any great significance in influencing group life in this study might be inferred from the finding that the total patterns of group reactions of different clubs to the same atmosphere tend to be remarkably homogeneous in spite of differences in adult leadership.

Data Collection and Analysis

Before continuing to summarize the individual and group behaviors which resulted from these three variations in leadership role, we will indicate briefly the types of data collection and analysis in the total study.

Eight types of club records were kept on each group, of which the four most important were kept by four different observers as follows.

1. A quantitative running account of the social interactions of the five children and the leader, in terms of symbols for directive, compliant, and objective (fact-minded) approaches and responses, including a category of purposeful refusal to respond to a social approach.

2. A minute-by-minute group structure analysis giving a record of activity subgroupings, the activity goal of each subgroup, whether the goal was initiated by the leader or spontaneously formed by the children, and rating on degree of unity of each subgrouping.

3. An interpretive running account of strikingly significant member actions and changes in the atmosphere of the group as a whole.

4. Continuous stenographic records of all conversation.

---

*Beside indicating the leadership characteristics perceived as important by the boys, the reader will note that one boy in this club (an army officer's son) preferred his authoritarian leader and that the other four split in that two preferred their authoritarian leader second best and two liked their laissez-faire leader second best.

These data were synchronized at minute intervals so that placed side by side they furnished quite a complete and integrated picture of the on-going life of the group.

Five other types of data covering the lives of the club members were collected, the three most important being:

1. Interviews with each child by a friendly "non-club" person during each transition period from one kind of group atmosphere and leader to another. These interviews elicited comparisons of the various club leaders with one another, with the teacher and with parents as well as other data about how the club could be run better, who were the best and poorest types of club members, what an ideal club leader would be like, etc.

2. Interviews with the parents, concentrating on kinds of discipline used in the home, status of the child in the family group, personality ratings on the same scales used by the teachers, discussion of the child's attitude toward the club, school and other group activities.

3. Talks with the teachers concerning the transfer to the school-room of behavior patterns acquired in the club and vice versa.

The reliability of the eleven trained observers ranged from .78 to .95 with an average reliability of .84. Another reliability computation on the coding of three thousand units of conversation into twenty-three categories of behavior showed a percent agreement of .86. The analyses of what constituted a "group life unit" showed reliabilities ranging from .90 to .98. A number of methodological researches carried on since the date of this study seem to suggest that it is possible to get much more meaningful and reliable observation data than has been generally believed if much more time and effort are spent on a careful "calibration" of psychologically well-trained observers.

Comparative Group Test Situations

The experimenters also postulated that a fruitful way to discover some of the major differences between the three types of group atmosphere would be to arrange comparable "test episodes" in each club. So at regular intervals the following situations occurred:

1. Leader arrives late.

2. Leader called away for indeterminate time.

3. Stranger ("janitor" or "electrician") arrives while leader out and carries on critical attack of work of individual group member, then of group as a whole.

The Four Resultant Styles of Group Life

Some of the major findings, summarized from stenographic records and other case material which are elsewhere reproduced, are as follows: Two distinct types of reaction were shown to the same pattern of authoritarian leadership. All of the data, including the documentary films, indicate that three of the clubs responded with a dependent leaning on the adult leader, relatively low levels of frustration tension, and practically no capacity for initiating group action, while the fourth club demonstrated considerable frustration and some degree of channelized aggression toward the authoritarian leader. (This latter pattern is much more comparable to the behavior of the club under authoritarian leadership in a previous experimental study of two clubs.)

Figure 2 indicates the major differences in the relations which developed between the group members and the adult leaders in the four resultant social atmospheres. In both types of authoritarian atmosphere the members were markedly more dependent upon the leader than in either the democratic or laissez-faire situations, dependence being somewhat greater in the more passive clubs. All other clubs showed a somewhat greater feeling of discontent in their relations with the adult leader than did the members of the democratic clubs, members of the "aggressive autocracy" being outstanding in their expression of rebellious feelings. There is evidence from other sources that the actual "felt discontent" in the "apathetic autocracies" was somewhat higher than indicated by the conversation which was considerably more restricted than was that of the democratic and laissez-faire club members.

In both types of authoritarian situations the demands for attention from the adult were greater than in the other atmospheres. It seemed clear that getting the attention of the adult represented one of the few paths to more satisfactory social status in the authoritarian situation where all of the "central functions" of group life were in the hands of the dominator.

The category "friendly, confiding" indicates that the members of the democratic and laissez-faire clubs initiated more "personal" and

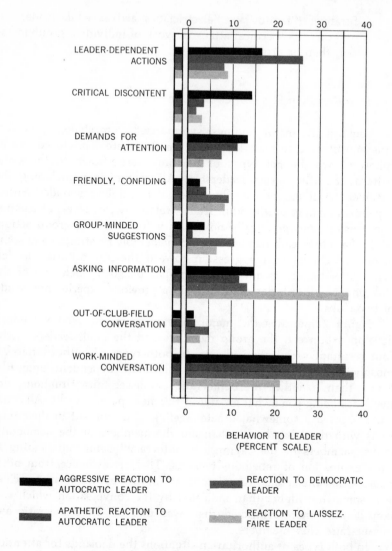

Fig. 2. Four patterns of group reaction to the three different types of leadership.

friendly approaches to their adult leaders, and the data on "out-of-club-field conversation" further indicate the more spontaneous exchanging of confidences about other parts of one's life experience in the democratic club atmosphere.

The data on "group-minded suggestions" to the leader show that the members in the democratic atmosphere felt much freer and more inclined to make suggestions on matters of group policy than in the other three group atmospheres. It is clear from other data that the lower level of suggestions in the laissez-faire situation is not because of any feeling of restricted freedom but because of a lack of a cooperative working relationship between the adult and the other group members.

The much greater responsibility of the members of the laissez-faire clubs to get their own information is shown by the fact that about 37 percent of their behavior toward their leader consisted of asking for information, as compared to about 15 percent in the other three club situations.

The final category in Figure 2, "work-minded conversation," indicates that a considerably larger proportion of the initiated approaches of the club members to their leaders were related to on-going club activity in the democratic and in the apathetic authoritarian situations than in the other two types of social climate.

Resultant Relationships of Club Members

The relationships between the club members also developed along quite different lines in the four social climates. Expressions of irritability and aggressiveness toward fellow members occurred more frequently in both the authoritarian atmospheres and the laissez-faire situation than in the democratic social climates. Unlike the relationships of high interpersonal tension and scapegoating which developed in the previous aggressive autocracy the club in this experiment seemed to focus its aggression sufficiently in other channels (toward the leader and toward the out-group) so that in-group tension did not rise to a dangerously high point.

There were more requests for attention and approval from fellow club members to each other in the democratic and laissez-faire situations than in the two authoritarian climates. It seems clear that the child members depended upon each other to a great extent for social recognition and were more ready to give recognition to each other in the democratic and laissez-faire situations.

It is interesting to find nearly as high a level of interpersonal friendliness in the authoritarian situations as in the democratic and laissez-faire atmospheres. The underlying spirit of rebellion toward the leader and cooperation in out-group aggression seem to be the "cohesive forces" in aggressive autocracy, while in apathetic autocracy with its much lower level of felt frustration, the shared submissiveness seemed to do away with all incentive to competition for social status.

Intermember suggestions for group action and group policy were significantly lower in both types of autocracy than in the laissez-faire and democratic atmospheres. The dissatisfactions arising from any lack of feeling of real progress in the laissez-faire situation led to a high frequency of expression of ideas about "something we might do." Contrary to the democratic situation, these suggestions seldom became reality because of the lack of the social techniques necessary for group decision and cooperative planning. The group achievement level, as contrasted to the "wish level," was far lower in laissez-faire than in any of the other three atmospheres.

Other Differences

By having the leaders arrive a few minutes late at regular intervals in each club life, it was possible to discover that in the five authoritarian situations no group initiative to start new work or to continue with work already under way developed, as contrasted with the democratic situations where leaders who arrived late found their groups already active in a productive fashion. The groups under the laissez-faire leaders were active but not productive. Figure 3 shows the percentage of total club time in each of the four social atmospheres which was spent in giving major attention to some planned club project. For each atmosphere there is a comparison between the time when the leader was in the room, the time when the leader had been called out for planned experimental periods, and the unit of time just after the leader returned. The data here give striking evidence of the extent to which work motivation was leader-induced in the two types of authoritarian situation. "Working time" dropped to a minimum with the leader out, and most of what was done was in the minutes just after the leader had left the room. We see that in the democratic atmosphere the absence or presence of the leader had practically no effect. The apparent increase in group productive time with the laissez-faire leader out of the room may or may not be a meaningful result. Two or three times it was noted that when the adult left, one of the boys exerted a more powerful leadership and achieved a more coordinated group activity than when the relatively passive adult was present.

The behavior of the groups under authoritarian domination after their transition to a freer social atmosphere provided a very interest-

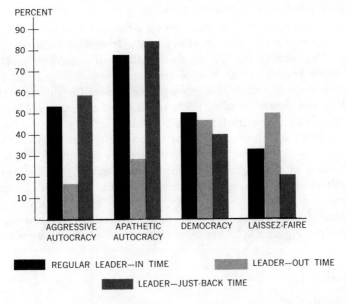

Fig. 3. Percent of time spent in high activity involvement.

ing index of unexpressed group tension. In Figure 4 it can be noted that both of these apathetic authoritarian clubs showed great outbursts

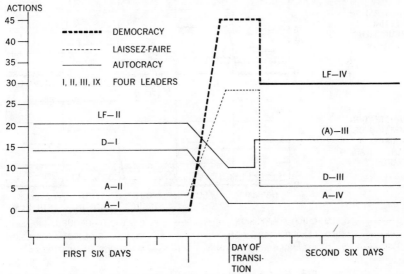

Fig. 4. Horseplay.

of horseplay between the members on the first day of their transitions to a laissez-faire and a democratic group situation. This need to "blow off" disappeared with more meetings in the freer atmosphere.

It will be recalled that in certain situations all groups were subject to the same frustration of hostile criticism by a strange adult (e.g., "janitor") while the adult leader was gone. Under the different types of leaders, the groups handled these frustrations differently. Members of the apathetic authoritarian clubs tended to accept individually and to internalize the unjust criticism or, in one or two cases, they "blew off steam" in aggressive advances toward an out-group (the other club meeting in the adjacent clubroom; see Figure 5). In the aggressive authoritarian situation, the frustration was typically channeled in aggression toward the out-group, although in several cases there was some direct reaction to the source of frustration, the hostile stranger (see Figure 5). In the democratic atmospheres there was evi-

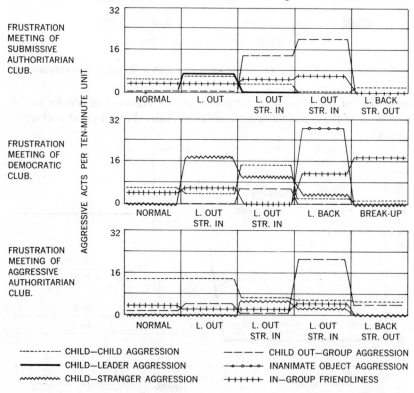

Fig. 5. Channels of group tension release in clubs of eleven-year-old boys under different types of leadership.

dence of a greater readiness to unite in rejection of the real source of frustration, the stranger, and to resist out-group aggression. Figure 5 shows an interesting case of a democratic club which first expressed its aggression directly against the stranger, then showed a slight rise in intermember tension, followed by an aggressive outburst against a sheet of three-ply wood with hammer and chisels accompanied by a striking rise in ingroup friendliness and a quick return to cooperative harmony. It was particularly interesting to discover that the clubs under democratic leaders resisted scapegoating as a channel of aggressive release.

The data indicate that the democratic type of adult role resulted in the greatest expression of individual differences, and that some type of uniformity-producing forces brought about a slightly lessened individual variability in the laissez-faire situation, and a much reduced range of individuality in the authoritarian clubs. Figure 6 gives an example of this analysis for the same group of individuals under three different leaders.

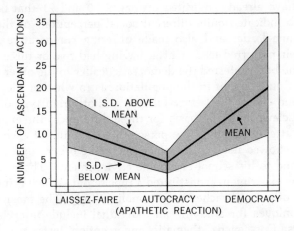

Fig. 6. The effect of changed atmosphere upon the range of individual differences within the same group.

Individual Differences and The Group Atmospheres

We now come to the question of to what extent it is correct to report the data as though all individuals and all groups under the same type of adult leadership role reacted with a high degree of uniformity to the induced social climate. Before turning to the final section of interpretation of individual differences in reaction to the same social climate, it will be interesting to look at the various club lives and see the extent to which the personalities making up each club or the different social atmospheres in which they lived seemed to be the most determining influence in the resulting behavior patterns. Two of the clubs had all three types of leadership. For these two groups it was possible by the techniques of analysis of variance to compare the effects of differences in child personnel and differences in all three experimental treatments. All four clubs were compared in the same way on various items of behavior for the two treatments of autocracy and democracy. It can be reported that in nearly all cases differences in club behavior could be attributed to differences in the induced social climate rather than to constant characteristics of the club personnel. One club showed a consistent variation from the rest through all atmospheres in level of friendliness between members, and one group showed a consistently lower level of social interaction which was not related wholly to their particular club environment.

We have already indicated on pages 70 and 71 that boys in the same club indicated quite different social perceptions of the behavior of the same leader and also made differing comparative judgments about their preferred leaders after having had two or three. Although all but one boy preferred the democratic leader to the other two types, there was quite a split in the population as to whether they preferred as a second choice the laissez-faire or authoritarian type of adult. To get some clews as to the basis for these differences the experimenters made an attempt to study the personality structure of each individual boy as it showed itself in his reactions to the other boys, to his adult leaders, and to his school and home environments. The records taken during the experiments constituted a type of data which is infrequently found in other approaches to personality study. The most commonly used techniques for studying an individual include interviews, questionnaires, Rorschachs, thematic apperception tests, psychoanalytic free association, and the social case history, consisting of interviews with parents and relatives, but not direct observations of social behavior.

It is not felt, of course, that such records are more useful than interviews, social case histories, or other customary techniques, but only that *when combined* with other techniques they are a valuable part of the total picture and are an extremely useful addition to the toolchest of the clinical psychologist, the educator, the vocational counselor, and others who want to understand and to help a particular individual.

To show this concretely, one condensed case study is summarized below. Like our other case studies, it is based primarily upon club behavior data with much less interview material and home study data than would be found in a first class clinical analysis, but with enough of these data to suggest how the club behavior data can be combined with other sorts in the building of an integrated personality structure.

The case chosen is one of two extremes, not in a single trait only, but in the large structure of intercorrelated traits, which has been found to be more important than any other trait cluster in our data. This cluster includes such variables as not being aggressive, not demanding attention, high work-mindedness, contentment in the strict but orderly atmosphere of autocracy, discontent in the free but disorderly atmosphere of laissez-faire, consistency of discipline in the home, and warmth of emotional relationship to parents.* These variables are statistically correlated to a marked degree; that is, the boys who show one of them usually show most of the others also. The reader can form his own judgment as to an appropriate name for the cluster. The boys who stand low in the cluster as a whole would often be called "bad" by the exasperated adults who have to deal with them, while those who stand high in it would be called "good." Goodness, then, or conscientiousness, might be as good a name as any. It should be noticed, though, that the cluster includes some things, such as liking autocracy better than laissez-faire, which are not included in the ordinary connotations of the word "conscientious." It should be noticed too that the boys who stand low in the cluster—boys like Reilly† who is described here—are not necessarily "bad" or antagonistic to adult values and requirements; they may be only heedless and relatively indifferent to those values. In groups such as ours which contain only healthy "normal" children, with no actual delinquents, it would do violence to common usage to call any of the boys "bad."‡ For these and other reasons the rather cumbersome term "adult-value-centeredness" seems more accurate than "conscientiousness" as a name for the cluster.

---

*A factor-analysis of the data will be published elsewhere; its technical character makes it unsuitable for this brief report.

†Names and other identifying data have been changed here.

‡The Freudian concept of the "super-ego" is relevant here; a "weak super-ego" does not necessarily mean active "badness" or antisocial tendencies. It may be noticed also that the cluster found in our data is similar to one which seems to have been discovered independently by a number of other investigators. It closely resembles Webb's "w" factor, which Thurstone renamed "conscientiousness."

Reilly: Club Personality

Reilly was the most talkative, the most conspicuous, and the most popular member of the Charlie Chan club. He was also one of the most irritating to those of his adult leaders who found themselves unable to cope with him. It was Reilly, for instance, who gleefully shouted, "Let's make war!" at the beginning of the first big water battle with the Secret Agents; it was Reilly whose vociferousness, as much as Fred's and Leonard's more aggressive horseplay, led to the complete disintegration of the group under laissez-faire leadership; and it was Reilly who led the "sitdown strike" against the autocratic leader, which was the one instance in any of the clubs of more or less organized rebellion against authority.

While he was so heedless of adult values and adult wishes, he was at the same time very popular with the other boys. He was the best-liked boy in his schoolroom, as determined by a sociometric questionnaire, and he had been elected president of his class. Yet he asserted his personality as vigorously in competition with other boys as in competition with adults. His personality contrasts sharply with that of Eddie, who was the best-liked boy in the other schoolroom from which our club members were selected. Where Eddie was conscientious, quiet, unassuming, and genuinely friendly with everyone, Reilly was exuberant, self-advertising, constantly bombarding the eyes and ears of others with his demands for attention, and, as the statistics showed, relatively low in both friendly and group-minded conversation. He was not actually a leader in the sense that he showed any planning or organizing ability; he was too impatient and too lacking in time-perspective for that. He was a leader only in the sense that he was liked, and also, perhaps, in the sense that his head-long, self-centered activity was imitated by others in the group.

It is interesting to find that, unlike the other two boys who stood with him at the bottom of the total group in the trait-cluster of "conscientiousness," he was never sullen, hostile, or maliciously mischievous. His scores in aggression were only about average, and his aggression (i.e., criticisms of other boys and playful collective aggression) was never really hostile in character. Even toward adults he was competitive rather than hostile. He ranked highest among the seventeen boys* in the proportion of his adult-contacts which had an attention-

---

*All statistics are based on a population of 17 rather than 20, since there were three boys about whom there was not an adequate amount of home background information.

demanding character. Characteristically, he would loudly interrupt when the adult was talking to some other club member, and vociferously demand that the adult pay attention to him rather than to the other boy. The absolute frequency of this behavior was also very high, as evidenced by the fact that he also ranked highest, out of 17, in the absolute volume of his verbal contacts with the adult leader, in both autocracy and democracy. (The motivation behind these contacts, to be sure, was probably rather different in the two atmospheres. In autocracy it seems to have been almost entirely an expression of competition for power—perhaps in order to win boy-admiration—while in democracy it was also an expression of genuine man-to-man friendliness.) It would seem, then, that his somewhat paradoxical popularity was not due to the kind of warm liking which drew other boys to the quiet and unassuming Eddie. Rather, it seems to have been due to the fact that he was so successful in getting a rather gullible public to accept him at his own valuation, while at the same time the absence of malice in his self-assertion kept it from arousing hostility in others. In spite of his competitiveness and essential self-centeredness, the group accorded him a sort of hero worship, perhaps largely because each of them would have liked to be the sort of vital and self-confident person—completely uncowed by adults—which he unquestionably was.

The statistical club-behavior data and interview data support this impressionistic picture. In addition to the quantitative data already mentioned, we find that he had unusually high scores in volume of conversation (with boys as well as with the adult leader), and in percent of "out-of-field" conversation, which in his case represented such things as bragging about his father's hardware store, his own chemistry set at home, etc. In the interviews he expressed a preference for his laissez-faire leader as compared with his autocratic leader, indicating, probably, that his need for orderliness was less than his need for free self-assertion. He also showed unusual frankness in his avowed preference for the boy-valued activity of "fighting," as compared with the adult-valued activity of working. In describing his autocratic leader he said, "We didn't have any fun then—we didn't have any fights."

Summarizing his club personality, we can say first that he was not noticeably motivated by any of the adult-sponsored values which were conspicuous in the conscientious boys—obedience, respectfulness, nonaggression, order, self-control, hard work; second, that his primary goal in the club situation was apparently competition, or *superiority* in the eyes of the other boys; and third, that he tended to perceive adults, not as objects of obedience, respect, or hostility, but as equals, with whom he could compete (or be friendly, as he was with his democratic leader) on very much the same basis as with any of the other boys. These more basic characteristics of his present personality-structure, and not the peripheral behavior-traits of talkativeness, attention-demanding, etc., are what must be especially taken into account, whether our interest is the practical interest of the adult group-leader who has to cope with him, or the scientific interest of the clinical investigator who wants to trace the origins of his present personality-structure in his home background and the behavior of his parents.

Home Background

His indifference to adult-sponsored values becomes intelligible when we discover that neither of his parents seems to have given him any incentive—neither fear of punishment nor hope of loving approval—to develop these values. His indulgent father apparently enjoyed his company (in a man-to-man relationship which offers a clew to his warm reaction to his democratic club leader), but his father was extremely busy and apparently accepted little or no responsibility for his training. His mother apparently disliked him, but felt helpless in relation to him; in the constant feud between them, there was neither the warmth which might have made him want to win her love by being "good," nor the firmness which might have made him fear her restrictions when he was "bad." These two attitudes, rejection and a feeling of helplessness, repeatedly came out in the interview with his mother. According to her, he is impudent, he is irresponsible, he is lazy, he is impatient and unable to stay long at one thing, he continually quarrels with his older brother and teases his younger brother. She blurted out these criticisms in a weary but almost defiant way. According to her, "punishment doesn't do him any good. I used to lose my temper and whip him; I was pretty mean, I guess," but he would be just as bad or worse afterward, so that now she doesn't ever punish him. "He sasses me back, and I can't stand a sassy child." Sometimes he argues for hours at a time; "maybe it's because I've given in to him several times," and he knows it's a good way to get things. For a while he had an allowance, but "he'd borrow on the next week's allowance and then expected to get it just the same," so the plan was discontinued. He now gets money for movies at least twice a week; if she tells him he can't go, he often goes to his father and gets the money from him.

Not only his indifference to adult values, but also his desire for superiority and his tendency to perceive adults as equals now seem more intelligible. Since his father does not try to exert much authority, and his mother lets the authority situation become a feud in which he often gets the upper hand, he naturally tends to look upon adults as equals. Since his father's affection is always present and his mother's never is, his life is not geared to the winning of affection; the goal of superiority, first of all in relation to his mother and his brothers, has tended to take its place. And, finally, his exuberant vitality and absence of hostility, which were noted as major reasons for his popularity, now make sense in the light of the fact that his home life contains no major frustrations, and no repressed hostilities. Though his personality-structure may bring him trouble later in life, his existence at the moment is full of affection from his father, triumph over his mother, and exciting, successful competition with other boys.

Interpretive Summary

The foregoing condensed and highly selective research report has attempted to show some of the interdependencies of leadership role, group composition, group history, and membership personality structure in this study of four experimental clubs of preadolescent boys.

The leader-induced social atmosphere of the group, together with the group history (the preceding club atmospheres), established a hierarchy of channels of expression of response to frustration. Whereas the "aggressive autocracy" club was more ready to express its frustrations in interclub wars, the "apathetic autocracies" were more prone to internalize the aggression, and the "democratic" and "laissez-faire" groups to react against the source of frustration.

Passive acceptance by the group of the socially induced frustrations of authoritarian leadership was found in some cases to mean a nonfrustrated acceptance of a dependent relationship, and in other cases to mean a frustrated hopelessness in the face of overwhelming power. When a transition to a freer atmosphere occurred these latter cases gave evidence by their "blow-off" behavior of their previous frustrations.

The adult restrictiveness of the benevolent authoritarian role and the environmental unstructuredness of the laissez-faire situation were both found to inhibit greatly genuine "psychological freedom" as contrasted to "objective freedom."

The adult-leader role was found to be a very strong determiner of the pattern of social interaction and emotional development of the group. Four clear-cut types of social atmosphere emerged, in spite of great member differences in social expectation and reaction tendency due to previous adult-leader (parent, teacher) relationships.

It was clear that previous group history (i.e., preceding social climates) had an important effect in determining the social perception of leader behavior and reaction to it by club members. A club which had passively accepted an authoritarian leader in the beginning of its club history, for example, was much more frustrated and resistive to a second authoritarian leader after it had experienced a democratic leader than a club without such a history. There seem to be some suggestive implications here for educational practice.

It was found in this exploratory study that the process of small-group life could be experimentally manipulated in a satisfactory way for scientific study and could be recorded adequately for meaningful quantitative analysis. There emerged a variety of meaningful clusters of correlations between member case history, member social perception of the group situation, member and group behavior, and leader behavior.

Personality Characteristics Associated with Obedience and Defiance Toward Authoritative Command (1966)*

Through variations in situational factors, Milgram (1965) has elicited sharply different amounts of obedience to authoritative command. Subjects thought they were administering electric shocks to a fellow volunteer in a "learning experiment." As many as 65% and as few as 30% of Ss in different conditions were willing to obey completely an "experimenter's" commands to deliver increasingly high levels of "shock" to a helpless victim (actually an experimental confederate), depending upon the victim's proximity.

---

*A. C. Elms and S. Milgram, *Journal of Experimental Research in Personality*, Vol. 1 (1966), pp. 282–89.

Milgram has stressed the situational determinants of varying levels of obedience in different experimental conditions. But within any one condition, the situation faced by each subject is quite similar. Some Ss choose to continue obeying the E's orders, even though they display signs of conflict (Milgram, 1963, 1965). Others, in the same situation and showing similar conflict, refuse at some point to obey further. Additionally, some Ss disobey E's commands under conditions where the victim cannot be seen or even heard (except for a few raps on the wall); other Ss continue to obey when the victim is sitting near them, or even when they must personally force the resisting victim's hand down onto a shock plate.

These differences in response suggest strongly that personality variables, as well as situational determinants, influence the degree of willingness to obey authoritative command. The present study was undertaken to gain information on a variety of personality variables relevant to behavior in the obedience experiments, and to indicate areas for more extensive exploration.

Method

Forty Ss were selected from 160 Ss who had participated in Milgram's four-part "Proximity Series" (1965). In the Remote and Voice Feedback conditions, only aural cues from the "shock victim" were available to S; in the Proximity and Touch Proximity conditions, visual cues were present as well. So that the personality data would be minimally influenced by "borderline" Ss (Ss who might have shifted from obedience to defiance or vice versa with only slight modifications in the experimental procedure), the 20 fully obedient Ss were chosen from the 28 obedient Ss in the latter two conditions, where the pressures for defiance were greatest; while the 20 defiant Ss were chosen from the 29 defiant Ss in the first two conditions, where the pressures for obedience were greatest. The Ss were selected on no other basis, since Milgram had matched experimental groups on age and occupational category; all Ss were males. The Ss were essentially self-selected within each experimental group, by their own obedient or defiant behavior.

The Ss were contacted for the present study in the approximate temporal order of their participation in the original experiments until 20 defiant Ss and 20 obedient Ss were obtained. The subject pools from conditions 1 and 4 were purposely exhausted first, since they represented the extremes in amount of cues for obedience or defiance.

Recruitment was by letter and subsequent telephone call, offering $6.00 for a 2-hour interview dealing with Ss' "opinions, experiences, and so forth" in connection with the original experiment. Out of 46 persons contacted, five declined to be interviewed, all of them "obedient" Ss. Four of these gave adequate reasons for not participating further (e.g., having moved out of town since the previous study); the fifth gave no reason for declining. The Ss were interviewed individually, and were paid at the beginning of the interview.*

Procedure

The Ss were first administered the MMPI card form, which had been shortened approximately 25% because of time limitations. Only items not involved in the standard personality or validity scales, or in two more recently developed scales (Do, Re), were omitted. The California F Scale (forms 40–45; Adorno et al., 1950)† was included with the MMPI, typed on cards shaped and numbered like those of the MMPI cards. The standard MMPI card-form instructions were used for the combined questionnaires, so that the California F items were categorized as "yes," "no," or "cannot say," rather than on the usual Likert scale.

The card form was followed by an oral questionnaire. Although the interviewer was frequently aware of the group from which S had been selected, the questionnaire was highly structured and was read verbatim for each S. The first question was an open-ended request to "tell me the most important things about yourself," without further probing questions. The S's responses, as for the questions asked subsequently, were noted in abbreviated word form and were typed out in full immediately after the interview. Additional questions involved attitudes as a child toward parents, nature of punishment in childhood, descriptions of personality of father, mother, and self, S's treatment of own children, experiences in combat duty, descriptions of Experimenter's and Learner's ("victim's") personalities, and attitudes toward the obedience experiment.

---

*These interviews are not to be confused with those conducted by a psychiatrist and discussed in Milgram (1964), or with the initial interview carried out for each S. The present interviews constituted a supplementary inquiry and were conducted by the first author several months after the S's participation in the experiment.

†Twenty-nine of the original items were used, plus a thirtieth topically revised item which replaced the "pre-war authorities" item.

After this questionnaire, S was given a series of concepts to be rated by means of semantic differential scales, with instructions slightly simplified from those suggested by Osgood, Suci, and Tannenbaum (1957). The concepts, each one printed at the top of a separate page, were: Father, Yale University, Conscience, Boss, Myself, Federal Government, Adolf Eichmann, Leader, Justice, Obedience, God, Follower, Defiance, "Learner" in Memory Project, Son, Command, Hate, Experimenter in Memory Project, Law, Mother. The rating scales, chosen from those which seemed to correlate highly and relatively specifically with certain factors in the several factor rotations reported by Osgood *et al.*, were: for the evaluative factor, *good-bad, kind-cruel, pleasant-unpleasant;* for the power factor, *hard-soft, strong-weak, severe-lenient;* for the activity factor, *active-passive, fast-slow, excitable-calm;* and a separate scale which seemed appropriate to the present study, *aggressive-defensive*. The ten scales were presented in the same order on each page, balanced in direction and ungrouped as to principal factor.

Finally, S was read ten hypothetical situations, each one dealing with problems of obedience or disobedience to authority, punishment or mercy toward others, indulgence in or refraining from cruel behavior.* The interviewer then assured S that his assistance had been valuable, told him a summary of the research project would be mailed to participants, and otherwise attempted to diminish any anxiety or other unfavorable effect which might have been aroused by the interview. . . .

Discussion

Previous researchers have identified various personality characteristics associated with apparent tendencies toward submission to authority (e.g., Adorno *et al.*, 1950; Rokeach, 1960). But submission to authority and similar characteristics in these studies were usually measured in the same way as the personality characteristics with which they were correlated. As a result, certain forms of response set common to the measures both of authoritarian tendencies and of personality characteristics may have elevated whatever relationships existed, and may have "created" relationships which did not exist. In the present research, the basic measure of submission to authoritative

---

*All differences between obedient and defiant Ss on this measure could easily have occurred through chance variation, and they are not discussed further.

command is an observation of actual behavior in a realistic situation. Thus, although it now seems clear that response sets contribute to scores on the California F Scale, for instance, it is unlikely that the same kind of response set determined Ss' responses in a situation calling for their actual obedience to commands to administer shocks to an innocent person, ultimately against that other person's will.

With this in mind, the significant difference between obedient and defiant Ss on the California F Scale remains meaningful even when educational level is not factored out. (As noted, the difference between obedient and defiant Ss' scores still approaches significance even with educational level controlled statistically.) Less-educated Ss may score higher on the F Scale because they are more willing to agree to blanket statements than are well-educated Ss, or because clichés and commonplaces appeal to them; but behavior in the experimental obedience situation requires more than acceptance of cliches or broad generalizations. Low education may be associated with authoritarian verbalizations or authoritarian behavior not only because of flaws in the measuring instrument, but because degree of education is itself in some way related to incidence of authoritarian personality characteristics. Whether the educative process itself diminishes authoritarianism in some way, or whether some other independent variable influences the two dependent variables of educational achievement and authoritarianism, is not evident from the present data.

Other similarities to findings reported in *The Authoritarian Personality* are found in obedient Ss' feelings of the father's lack of closeness when S was a child, and the relative glorification of the E and downgrading of the Learner. The authoritarian tendency toward stereotyped glorification of the father is not observed in obedients— quite the contrary—but this may be partly the result of the interviewer's negative ratings of "stern" and other authoritarian adjectives describing the father, in the blind categorization of descriptions. Additionally, the generally older Ss in the present study may find it easier to express critical attitudes toward their fathers than the young adults who composed a large proportion of Adorno *et al.*'s samples.

The reporting of less severe childhood punishment by obedients is also atypical of the "authoritarian personality." Lack of differences between obedients and defiants in attitudes toward mother, toward Adolph Eichmann, and in several other categories where differences might be expected if a strictly authoritarian-unauthoritarian dichotomy were present, may have resulted in part from extreme elevations or depressions of judgments by all Ss, which did not allow for real differentiation on a 5- or 7-point scale.

Obedient Ss' praising of the power figure (E) and denigration of the weak figure (Learner) may derive more directly from features of the experiment itself than do other characteristics of obedients. Self-justification for one's experimental behavior may have come *ex post facto* from recalling the E as more benevolent and the Learner as less worthy: the Good Scientist deserved to be followed, while the stupid, excitable, weak Learner deserved to be given a lesson. It is impossible to derive from the present data an indication of the direction of causality—whether the subject behaved as he did because he entered the experiment with potential stereotyped responses to power and weakness, or whether he later gave these stereotyped responses to power or weakness because of what he had done in the experiment, or both. Whichever pattern of causation is more accurate, obedients and defiants did respond differentially at the time of the original experiment, and such differences indicate probable initial differences in the two groups.

The response to the question "Did you ever shoot at a man in combat?" indicates a difference in attitude toward infliction of pain or harm. Obedient Ss may or may not have shot at men more frequently than defiant Ss have; if so, they may have felt less conflict over merely shocking a man. The reliability of their self-reports is unknown, but we can at least assume that obedient Ss more easily accept the idea of injuring others under certain circumstances. Eighty percent of obedient Ss with combat experience admit without qualification to having shot at people, while even the 25% of defiant combat-experienced Ss who had shot a gun in battle deny having shot at an individual person within seeing distance. The ability or lack of ability to accept such behavior could have (and may well have had) important consequences in an experimental situation in which an authority figure demands aggressive action against another person. The similarity to the authoritarian personality is again apparent; for instance, Adorno *et al.* (p. 386) report that

[W]e often find in our high-scoring subjects both overconformity and underlying destructiveness toward established authority, customs, and institutions. A person possessed by such ambivalence may easily be kept in check and may even behave in an exemplary fashion in following those external authorities who take over the function of the superego—and partly even those of the ego. On the other hand, if permitted to do so by outside authority, the same person may be induced very easily to uncontrolled release of his instinctual tendencies, especially those of destructiveness.

The semantic differential ratings lend additional detail to this picture of the obedient S as authoritarian personality. For instance, obedient Ss attribute more "goodness" to the two authority figures in the experimental situation, Yale University and the E himself; less goodness to the weak Learner; and apparently view the command-obedience situation more positively even in the abstract. At the same time, they see the E and Yale University as more aggressive, like themselves; and, consonant with their own actions, they impute more aggressiveness to obedience itself.

The absence of differences between groups on the MMPI scales is not altogether surprising. The scales may be able to detect certain pathological or "normal" personality patterns, but none of these patterns fits, in a clear majority of particulars, the qualities which might be expected of an obedient or defiant S. Even the description of the reference groups for the social responsibility scale (Gough *et al.,* 1952), which showed the only significant difference, contains conflicting characteristics from the viewpoint of the present study. The socially responsible person "shows a ready willingness to accept the consequences of his own behavior," a "sense of obligation to the [peer] group," and "greater concern for social and moral issues," as one might expect of the higher-scoring defiant Ss; but he also shows "dependability" and "trustworthiness" and is "more compliant and acquiescent," "less rebellious and recalcitrant," as one might expect of obedient Ss.

Various other differences appear between the two groups on the several parts of the interview, but among the multiplicity of questions it might be misleading to try to gather together the differences which do not approach statistically significant levels. Even significant differences may sometimes be deceptive. For instance, although in a number of instances obedient Ss displayed characteristics similar to those of high scorers in *The Authoritarian Personality,* several obedient Ss appeared to have warm relationships with family and with associates. One of these, otherwise apparently kind and sensitive to an extreme, seemed to have taken as a model for public behavior a grandfather who he said "believed one should take and carry out an order whether one believed it was right or wrong, as long as the person giving it was in authority to give it." Likewise, defiant Ss did not consistently show themselves in the interviews to be warmly humanitarian; one, a liberal and humanist by principle, displayed considerable bitterness toward his fellow man, including "a generally low opinion of the intellectual level of mankind."

The experimental obedience situation allows the *S* to express himself in binary fashion. He may continue to obey the *E* or he may break off the experiment. Behind this simple behavioral possibility may lie highly complex and possibly idiosyncratic motive structures. There may be only a functional equivalence of motive structures, in that different combinations of motives may lead to the same behavioral outcome. For example, a highly compliant *S* who is low in aggressive needs may obey the *E* to the very end. The same effect could be produced in a person whose submissive needs are low, but who possesses a strong need to release aggressive tensions. Because of the complexity of motives which subjects bring to the experimental situation, it is not possible to reduce twenty individuals to a statistically average "obedient subject" or "defiant subject." The results of this study suggest certain broad personality differences which relate to obedience or defiance in the experimental obedience situation; but they do not reveal a single personality pattern which is inevitably expressed in one behavior or the other.

Authoritarian-Democratic Expressions in Political and Legal Systems

3

Gabriel Almond and Sidney Verba,
 An Approach to Political Culture

 The Civic Culture and Democratic Stability

U.S. Supreme Court decision:
 Korematsu v. United States

Gabriel Almond and **Sidney Verba,** in considering the characteristics of *The Civic Culture,* addressed themselves to the crucial question of techniques for political socialization of elites and nonelites in democratic societies where individuals pursue conflicting citizen goals and roles. Although these two men are political scientists, they are included in this section because they utilize a social-psychological model in their analysis. Their five-nation study on politics was a multi-dimensional and multi-disciplinary attempt to explore the relationship between attitude, motivation, and performance. Employing survey-research techniques, the investigators systematically interviewed a thousand subjects in five nations to determine motivational bases of political attitudes and behaviors. The investigators discussed their intellectual commitment to the theories and methodologies of psychology, sociology, and anthropology, as well as history and political science. Their findings verified the heterogeneity of political culture and the mutual impact of democratic and authoritarian models. They also confirmed the notion that the democratic citizen accepts contradictory goals and incorporates certain inconsistencies to allow for the contradictions in himself and society. Almond and Verba found that civic culture, with its contradictory political attitudes, seems to be consistent with democratic political systems which also are a mixture of contradictions.

An Approach to Political Culture (1963)*

This is a study of the political culture of democracy and of the social structures and processes that sustain it. The faith of the Enlightenment in the inevitable triumph of human reason and liberty has been twice shaken in recent decades. The development of Fascism and Communism after World War I raised serious doubts about the inevitability of democracy in the West; and we still cannot

---

*Gabriel A. Almond and Sidney Verba, *The Civic Culture: Political Attitudes and Democracy in Five Nations,* Princeton University Press for the Center of International Studies, copyright 1963, pp. 3-35. Reprinted by permission of Princeton University Press.

be certain that the continental European nations will discover a stable form of democratic process suitable to their particular cultures and social institutions; nor can we more than hope that together they will discover a European democracy.

Without having first resolved these doubts, the events since World War II have raised questions of the future of democracy on a world scale. The "national explosions" in Asia and Africa and the almost universal pressure by previously subjected and isolated peoples for admission into the modern world put this more special political question into the broader context of the future character of the world's culture. Culture change has acquired a new significance in world history. The groping toward enlightenment and control over nature that acquired momentum three or four centuries ago in the West has become a world-wide process, and its tempo has shifted from centuries to decades. . . .

What is problematical about the content of the emerging world culture is its political character. . . .

. . . The emerging nations are presented with two different models of the modern participatory state, the democratic and the totalitarian. The democratic state offers the ordinary man the opportunity to take part in the political decision-making process as an influential citizen; the totalitarian offers him the role of the "participant subject."* . . .

If the democratic model of the participatory state is to develop in these new nations, it will require more than the formal institutions of democracy—universal suffrage, the political party, the elective legislature. These in fact are also part of the totalitarian participation pattern, in a formal if not functional sense. . . .

The Civic Culture

It is as an answer to this ambivalence that the civic culture recommends itself. For the civic culture is not a modern culture, but a mixed modernizing-traditional one. . . .

The civic culture and the open polity . . . represent the great and problematic gifts of the West. The technology and science of the West have now already passed out of her unique possession and everywhere are destroying and transforming traditional societies and cul-

---

*See F. C. Barghoorn, "Soviet Political Culture," a paper prepared for the Summer Institute on Political Culture, sponsored by the Committee on Comparative Politics, Social Science Research Council, Summer 1962.

tures. Can the open polity and the civic culture—man's discovery of a humane and conservative way to handle social change and partici-pation—spread as well? . . .

. . . Rather than inferring the properties of democratic culture from political institutions or social conditions, we have attempted to specify its content by examining attitudes in a number of operating democratic systems. And rather than deriving the social-psychological pre-condi-tions of democracy from psychological theory, we have sought to determine whether and to what extent these relations actually exist in functioning democratic systems. . . .

In our comparison of the political cultures of five contemporary democracies . . . we have included, in addition to our own country, Britain, Germany, Italy, and Mexico. . . . Our five-country study offers us the opportunity . . . to discover whether relations found in the American data are also encountered in democratic countries whose historical experiences and political and social structures differ from one another.

Types of Political Culture

We employ the term political culture for two reasons. First, if we are to ascertain the relations between political and nonpolitical atti-tudes and developmental patterns, we have to separate the former from the latter even though the boundary between them is not as sharp as our terminology would suggest. The term political culture thus refers to the specifically political orientations—attitudes toward the political system and its various parts, and attitudes toward the role of the self in the system. We speak of a political culture just as we can speak of an economic culture or a religious culture. It is a set of orientations toward a special set of social objects and processes.

But we also choose political *culture,* rather than some other special concept, because it enables us to utilize the conceptual frameworks and approaches of anthropology, sociology, and psychology.

. . . Here we can only stress that we employ the concept of culture in only one of its many meanings: that of *psychological orientation toward social objects.* When we speak of the political culture of a society, we refer to the political system as internalized in the cogni-tions, feelings, and evaluations of its population. People are inducted into it just as they are socialized into nonpolitical roles and social systems. . . .

The political culture of a nation is the particular distribution of patterns of orientation toward political objects among the members of the nation. . . . Orientation refers to the internalized aspects of objects and relationships. It includes (1) "cognitive orientation," that is, knowledge of and belief about the political system, its roles and the incumbents of these roles, its inputs, and its outputs; (2) "affective orientation," or feelings about the political system, its roles, personnel, and performance, and (3) "evaluational orientation," the judgments and opinions about political objects that typically involve the combination of value standards and criteria with information and feelings. . . .

. . . The political culture becomes the frequency of different kinds of cognitive, affective, and evaluative orientations toward the political system in general, its input and output aspects, and the self as political actor.

Parochial Political Culture

. . . The political cultures of African tribal societies and autonomous local communities . . . would fall into this category. In these societies, there are no specialized political roles: headmanship, chieftainship, "shamanship" are diffuse political-economic-religious roles, and for members of these societies the political orientations to these roles are not separated from their religious and social orientations. A parochial orientation also implies the comparative absence of expectations of change initiated by the political system. The parochial expects nothing from the political system. . . .

In this kind of polity the specialized agencies of central government might hardly touch the consciousness of townsmen, villagers, and tribesmen. Their orientations would tend to be unspecialized political-economic-religious ones, congruently related to the similarly unspecialized structures and operations of their tribal, religious, occupational, and local communities.

What we have been describing is extreme or pure parochialism that occurs in simpler traditional systems where political specialization is minimal. Parochialism in more differentiated political systems is likely to be affective and normative rather than cognitive. That is to say, the remote tribesman in Nigeria or Ghana may be aware in a dim sort of way of the existence of a central political regime. But his feelings toward it are uncertain or negative, and he has not internalized any norms to regulate his relations to it.

The Subject Political Culture

. . . The subject is aware of specialized government authority; he is affectively oriented to it, perhaps taking pride in it, perhaps disliking it; and he evaluates it either as legitimate or not. But the relationship is toward the system on the general level, and toward the output, administrative, or "downward flow" side of the political system; it is essentially a passive relationship, although there is . . . a limited form of competence that is appropriate in a subject culture.

Again we are speaking of the pure subject orientation that is likely to exist in a society where there is no differentiated input structure. The subject orientation in political systems that have developed democratic institutions is likely to be affective and normative rather than cognitive. Thus a French royalist is aware of democratic institutions; he simply does not accord legitimacy to them.

The Participant Political Culture

The third major type of political culture, the participant culture, is one in which the members of the society tend to be explicitly oriented to the system as a whole and to both the political and administrative structures and processes: in other words, to both the input and output aspects of the political system. Individual members of the participant polity may be favorably or unfavorably oriented to the various classes of political objects. They tend to be oriented toward an "activist" role of the self in the polity, though their feelings and evaluations of such a role may vary from acceptance to rejection. . . .

This threefold classification of political cultures does not assume that one orientation replaces the others. The subject culture does not eliminate diffuse orientations to the primary and intimate structures of community. To the diffuse orientations to lineage groups, religious community, and village it adds a specialized subject orientation to the governmental institutions. Similarly, the participant culture does not supplant the subject and parochial patterns of orientation. The participant culture is an additional stratum that may be added to and combined with the subject and parochial cultures. Thus the citizen of a participant polity is not only oriented toward active participation in politics, but is subject to law and authority and is a member of more diffuse primary groups.

To be sure, adding participant orientations to subject and parochial orientations does not leave these "earlier" orientations unchanged. The parochial orientations must adapt when new and more specialized orientations enter into the picture, just as both parochial and subject orientations change when participant orientations are acquired. Actually, some of the most significant differences in the political cultures of the five democracies included in our study turn on the extent and the way that parochial, subject, and participant orientations have combined, fused, or meshed together within the individuals of the polity.

Another caution is necessary. Our classification does not imply homogeneity or uniformity of political cultures. Thus political systems with predominantly participant cultures will, even in the limiting case, include both subjects and parochials. The imperfections of the processes of political socialization, personal preferences, and limitations in intelligence or in opportunities to learn will continue to produce subjects and parochials, even in well-established and stable democracies. Similarly, parochials will continue to exist even in "high" subject cultures.

Thus there are two aspects of cultural heterogeneity or cultural "mix." The "citizen" is a particular mix of participant, subject, and parochial orientations, and the civic culture is a particular mix of citizens, subjects, and parochials. For the citizen we need concepts of proportions, thresholds, and congruence to handle the ways in which his constellation of participant, subject, and parochial attitudes is related to effective performance. For the civic culture, . . . we need the same concepts of proportions, thresholds, and congruence to handle the problem of what "mix" of citizens, subjects, and parochials is related to the effective performance of democratic systems. . . .

Political cultures may or may not be congruent with the structures of the political system. A congruent political structure would be one appropriate for the culture: in other words, where political cognition in the population would tend to be accurate and where affect and evaluation would tend to be favorable. In general, a parochial, subject, or participant culture would be most congruent with, respectively, a traditional political structure, a centralized authoritarian structure, and a democratic political structure. . . .

Political Subculture and Role Culture

We have already made the point that most political cultures are heterogeneous. Even the most fully developed participant cultures will contain surviving strata of subjects and parochials. And even within that part of the culture that is oriented toward participation there will be persistent and significant differences in political orientation. . . .

. . . [T]he kind of cleavage we are most interested in is that which occurs in systematically mixed systems. Thus in a mixed parochial-subject culture one part of the population would be oriented toward diffuse traditional authorities, and another toward the specialized structure of the central authoritarian system. . . .

The mixed subject-participant culture is a more familiar and even more contemporary problem in the West. A successful shift from a subject to a participant culture involves the diffusion of positive orientations toward a democratic infrastructure, the acceptance of norms of civic obligation, and the development of a sense of civic competence among a substantial proportion of the population. . . .

The Civic Culture: A Mixed Political Culture

. . . The civic culture is not the political culture that one finds described in civics textbooks, which prescribe the way in which citizens ought to act in a democracy. The norms of citizen behavior found in these texts stress the pertinent aspects of political culture. The democratic citizen is expected to be active in politics and to be involved. Furthermore, he is supposed to be rational in his approach to politics, guided by reason, not by emotion. He is supposed to be well informed and to make decisions—for instance, his decision on how to vote—on the basis of careful calculation as to the interests and the principles he would like to see furthered. This culture, with its stress on rational participation within the input structures of politics, we can label the "rationality-activist" model of political culture. The civic culture shares much with this rationality-activist model; it is, in fact, such a culture *plus something else.* It does stress the participation of individuals in the political input process. In the civic cultures described . . . we shall find high frequencies of political activity, of exposure to political communications, of political discussion, of concern with political affairs. But there is *something else.*

In the first place, the civic culture is an allegiant participant culture. Individuals are not only oriented to political input, they are oriented positively to the input structures and the input process. In other words, to use the terms introduced earlier, the civic culture is a participant political culture in which the political culture and political structure are congruent.

More important, in the civic culture participant political orientations combine with and do not replace subject and parochial political orientations. Individuals become participants in the political process, but they do not give up their orientations as subjects nor as parochials. Furthermore, not only are these earlier orientations maintained, alongside the participant political orientations, but the subject and parochial orientations are congruent with the participant political orientations. The nonparticipant, more traditional political orientations tend to limit the individual's commitment to politics and to make that commitment milder. In a sense, the subject and parochial orientations "manage" or keep in place the participant political orientations. Thus attitudes favorable to participation within the political system play a major role in the civic culture, but so do such nonpolitical attitudes as trust in other people and social participation in general. The maintenance of these more traditional attitudes *and their fusion* with the participant orientations lead to a balanced political culture in which political activity, involvement, and rationality exist but are balanced by passivity, traditionality, and commitment to parochial values. . . .

. . . Each kind of polity—traditional, authoritarian, and democratic—has one form of culture that is congruent with its own structure. Starting from the orientation and psychological requirements of different types of political structure, we are in a better position to formulate hypotheses about the kinds of personality tendencies and socialization practices that are likely to produce congruent political cultures and stable polities. Thus in the case of the civic culture, we may say that a pattern of socialization which enables the individual to manage the inevitable dissonances among his diffuse primary, his obedient output, and activist input roles supports a democratic polity. We can then look at socialization patterns and personality tendencies and ask just which of these qualities are crucial, to what extent they must be present, and what kinds of experience are most likely to produce this capacity for dissonant political role management. . . . The most productive research on political psychology in the future will treat childhood socialization, modal personality tendencies, political orientation, and political structure and process as separate variables in a complex, multidirectional system of causality.

The Civic Culture and Democratic
Stability (1963)*

Is there a democratic political culture—a pattern of political attitudes that fosters democratic stability, that in some way "fits" the
democratic political system? . . . Civics texts would have us believe that
the problem facing the citizen in a democracy is, to quote the title of a
recent book in the field, *How to Be an Active Citizen.*† . . . Recent studies of political behavior call the rationality-activist model into question,
for it is becoming clear that citizens in democracies rarely live up to
this model. . . . The characteristics of the rationality-activist model of
democratic citizenship are indeed components of the civic culture; but
the point to be stressed here is that they are only *part* of that culture.

The civic culture is a mixed political culture. In it many individuals
are active in politics, but there are also many who take the more passive role of subject. More important, even among those performing
the active political role of the citizen, the roles of subject and parochial
have not been displaced. . . .

. . . It is true that the rationality-activist model of the citizen does
not imply that participant orientations replace subject and parochial
ones; but by not mentioning the latter two roles explicitly, it does
imply that they are irrelevant to the democratic political culture.

Actually, these two orientations do more than persist: they play
an important part in the civic culture. In the first place, the parochial
and subject orientations modify the intensity of the individual's political involvement and activity. Political activity is but one part of the
citizen's concerns, and usually not a very important part at that. The
maintenance of other orientations limits the extent of his commitment
to political activity and keeps politics, as it were, in its place. Furthermore, not only do the parochial and subject orientations persist side
by side with the participant orientations, but they penetrate and
modify the participant orientations. Primary affiliations, for instance,
are important in the patterns of citizen influence. In addition, a diffuse
set of social attitudes and interpersonal attitudes tends to affect the
content of the political attitudes—to make them less intense and divi-

---

*Gabriel A. Almond and Sidney Verba, *op cit.*, pp. 473–505.

†Paul Douglas and Alice McMahon, *How to Be an Active Citizen* (Gainesville,
Fla.: University of Florida, 1960).

sive. Penetrated by primary group orientations and by general social and interpersonal attitudes, political attitudes are not solely the results of articulated principle and rational calculation.

How can we explain the discrepancy between the ideals of the rationality-activist model and the patterns of political attitudes we actually find, even in the more stable and successful democracies? One possible explanation, and the one most often found in the literature on civic education, is that this discrepancy is evidence for the malfunctioning of democracy. Insofar as people do not live up to the ideal of the active citizen, democracy is a failure. If one believes that the realities of political life should be molded to fit one's theories of politics, such an explanation is satisfactory. But if one holds to the view that theories of politics should be drawn from the realities of political life—a somewhat easier and probably more useful task—then this explanation of the gap between the rationality-activist model and democratic realities is less acceptable. From the latter point of view, one would probably argue that the gap exists because the standards have been set unreasonably high. Given the complexity of political affairs, given the other demands made upon an individual's time, and given the difficulty of obtaining information necessary for making rational political decisions, it is no wonder that the ordinary citizen is not the ideal citizen. In the light of an individual's nonpolitical interests, it might be quite irrational to invest in political activity the time and effort needed to live up to the rationality-activist model. It may just not be worth it to be that good a citizen.*

But though a completely activist political culture may be a utopian ideal, there may be other, more significant reasons why an intricately mixed civic culture is found in the more successful democracies. The civic culture, which sometimes contains apparently contradictory political attitudes, seems to be particularly appropriate for democratic political systems, for they, too, are mixtures of contradictions. Harry Eckstein has suggested that a democratic political system requires a blending of apparent contradictions—he calls them "balanced disparities"—if it is to function effectively. On the one hand, a democratic government must govern; it must have power and leadership and make decisions. On the other hand, it must be responsible to its citizens. For if democracy means anything, it means that in some way governmental elites must respond to the desires and demands of citi-

---

*It is interesting to compare these ideas with Thoreau's statement that he "came into this world not chiefly to make this a good place to live, but to live in it."

zens. The need to maintain this sort of balance between governmental power and governmental responsiveness, as well as the need to maintain other balances that derive from the power/responsiveness balance—balances between consensus and cleavage, between affectivity and affective neutrality—helps explain the way in which the more mixed patterns of political attitudes associated with the civic culture are appropriate for a democratic political system.*

Power and Responsiveness

The maintenance of a proper balance between governmental power and governmental responsiveness represents one of the most important and difficult tasks of a democracy. Unless there is some control of governmental elites by nonelites, it is hard to consider a political system democratic. On the other hand, nonelites cannot themselves rule. If a political system is to be effective—if it is to be able to initiate and carry out policies, adjust to new situations, meet internal and external challenges—there must be mechanisms whereby governmental officials are endowed with the power to make authoritative decisions. The tensions produced by the need to pursue the opposing goals of governmental power and governmental responsiveness become most apparent in times of crisis. Wars, for instance (hot or cold), have often shifted the balance so far in the direction of governmental power and authority as to cause concern about the preservation of democratic responsiveness. Yet if the balance is not so shifted, it is argued that democratic governments may succumb to external challenges.

Crises bring to the fore the problem of maintaining an adequate balance, but the problem exists in the day-to-day running of a democracy. How can a governmental system be constructed so that a balance is maintained between power and responsiveness? As E. E. Schattschneider has put it, "The problem is not how 180 million Aristotles

---

*The contradictory demands placed upon democratic political systems have been stressed in some as yet unpublished lectures by Professor Harry Eckstein, upon which this chapter draws. The authors are grateful for the opportunity to see his notes on this subject. That democratic systems are called upon to pursue apparently opposing goals is also stressed in Berelson, Lazarfeld, and McPhee, *Voting* (Chicago, Ill., University of Chicago, 1954), pp. 305–322, and in Parsons, "Voting and the Equilibrium of the American Political System," in Burdick and Brodbeck, eds., *American Voting Behavior* (Glencoe, Ill.: The Free Press, 1959).

can run a democracy, but how we can organize a community of 180 million ordinary people so that it remains sensitive to their needs. This is a problem of *leadership, organization, alternatives, and systems of responsibility and confidence.*"* . . .

. . . Can the set of attitudes held by citizens help to maintain the delicate balance between the contradictory demands placed on a democratic system? This concentration upon the political attitudes of ordinary citizens does not imply a rejection of the important role of political structures or of elite attitudes and behavior. . . .

. . . Certain things are demanded of the ordinary citizen if elites are to be responsive to him: the ordinary citizen must express his point of view so that elites can know what he wants; he must be involved in politics so that he will know and care whether or not elites are being responsive, and he must be influential so as to enforce responsive behavior by the elites. In other words, elite responsiveness requires that the ordinary citizen act according to the rationality-activist model of citizenship. But if the alternate pole of elite power is to be achieved, quite contradictory attitudes and behavior are to be expected of the ordinary man. If elites are to be powerful and make authoritative decisions, then the involvement, activity, and influence of the ordinary man must be limited. The ordinary citizen must turn power over to elites and let them rule. The need for elite power requires that the ordinary citizen be relatively passive, uninvolved, and deferential to elites. Thus the democratic citizen is called on to pursue contradictory goals: he must be active, yet passive; involved, yet not too involved; influential, yet deferential.†

---

*E. E. Schattschneider, *The Semisovereign People* (New York: Holt, Rinehart and Winston, Inc., 1960), p. 138. Italics in original.

†It should be clear that the tension described here is not the same as that between the obligations of the citizen and the obligations of the subject, as discussed in chap. i. There we dealt with the fact that the democratic citizen has a set of role expectations within the input structure of the political system. He is expected to participate in some ways in decisions. At the same time he has "subject" obligations toward the output aspects of the political system. He is expected to abide by decisions once they are made. This mixture, too, is part of the civic culture. But the tension described in this section is not between an individual's role in relation to the input structure (i.e., as citizen) and his role in relation to the output structure (i.e., as subject)—a tension that at least in theory appears fairly easy to resolve. Rather, the tension described here is between two modes of relating to the input structures. The citizen has both to be influential and to affect the course of policy; at the same time he must be noninfluential and allow political elites to make decisions independently. Thus the tension we are describing lies within the role of citizen.

Norms, Perceptions, and Activity

... Our data suggest that in two broad ways the civic culture maintains the citizen's active-influential role as well as his more passive role: on the one hand, there is in the society a *distribution* of individuals who pursue one or the other of the conflicting citizen goals; on the other hand, certain *inconsistencies in the attitudes of an individual* make it possible for him to pursue these seemingly conflicting goals at the same time. Let us first consider the inconsistencies within the individual.

As our survey showed, there exists a gap between the *actual political behavior* of our respondents, on the one hand, and their *perceptions of their capacities to act* and their *obligations to act*, on the other. Respondents in Britain and the United States manifest high frequencies of what we have called subjective political competence. ... [A] large proportion considers itself able to influence the decisions of the local government, and a substantial, though not quite as large, proportion feels the same way about the activities of the national government. Yet this high estimation of one's competence as an influential citizen is certainly not matched by actual political behavior. In the first place, only a small proportion of those respondents who say they could influence the government report that they have ever attempted such influence. And even if those who think they could influence governmental decisions were to attempt to do so—which is unlikely—they would almost certainly not have the success that they believe they would have. It is clearly an exaggeration when forty per cent of American respondents or twenty-four per cent of the British say that there is some likelihood that an attempt of theirs to influence the national legislature would be successful.

A similar gap exists between the sense of obligation to participate in political life and actual participation. ...

[A] much higher proportion of respondents says that the ordinary man has some obligation to participate in the affairs of his local community than in fact does participate; and again the pattern is clearest in the United States and Britain. As one respondent ... put it, "I'm saying what [one] ought to do, not what I do." ... Fifty-one per cent of the American respondents report that the ordinary man ought to take some active part in the affairs of his community. But when asked what they do in their free time, only about ten per cent of the American respondents mention such activities. ... These two gaps— between a high perception of potential influence and a lower level of actual influence, and between a high frequency of expressed obligation to participate and the actual importance and amount of participation— help explain how a democratic political culture can act to maintain a balance between governmental elite power and governmental elite responsiveness (or its complement, a balance between nonelite activity and influence and nonelite passivity and noninfluence). The comparative infrequency of political participation, its relative lack of importance for the individual, and the objective weakness of the ordinary man allow governmental elites to act. The inactivity of the ordinary man and his inability to influence decisions help provide the power that governmental elites need if they are to make decisions. But this maximizes only one of the contradictory goals of a democratic system. The power of the elites must be kept in check. The citizen's opposite role, as an active and influential enforcer of the responsiveness of elites, is maintained by his strong commitment to the norm of active citizenship, as well as by his perception that he can be an influential citizen. This may be in part a myth, for it involves a set of norms of participation and perceptions of ability to influence that are not quite matched by actual political behavior. Yet the very fact that citizens hold to this myth—that they see themselves as influential and as obligated to take an active role—creates a potentiality of citizen influence and activity. The subjectively competent citizen. . . has not necessarily attempted to influence the government, but he is *more likely* to have made such attempts than is the citizen who does not consider himself competent.* . . .

We have been saying that inconsistencies within attitudes and inconsistencies between attitudes and behavior, rather than the one-sided attitudes of the rationality-activist model, can maintain the tension between citizen activity and citizen passivity. . . . This inconsistency, however, creates no undue strain within the citizen; for politics, as much of our data suggest and as the data from many other studies confirm, is not the uppermost problem in his mind. . . .

That politics has relatively little importance for citizens is an important part of the mechanism by which the set of inconsistent political orientations keeps political elites in check, without checking them so tightly as to make them ineffective. For the balance of inconsistent orientations would be more difficult to maintain if the issues of politics were always considered important by the citizens. If issues arise that individuals consider important, or if some relatively severe dissatisfaction with government occurs, the individual will be moti-

---

*On the importance of the democratic myth, see V. O. Key, Jr., *Public Opinion and American Democracy* (New York: Alfred A. Knopf, Inc., 1961), p. 547.

vated to think about the topic and thus will be under greater pressure
to resolve the inconsistency—to make attitudes and behavior consonant with each other. One way he may do this is to bring his behavior
into line with norms and perceptions by becoming politically active.
Thus the inconsistency between attitudes and behavior acts as a latent
or potential source of political influence and activity.

To say that the civic culture maintains the balance between power
and responsibility suggests a further point about democratic politics.
It suggests why unresolved political issues of great importance eventually create instability in a democratic political system. The balance
between activity and passivity can be maintained only if the issues of
politics are relatively mild. If politics becomes intense, and if it remains
intense because of some salient issue, the inconsistency between attitude and behavior will become unstable. But any relatively permanent
resolution of the inconsistency is likely to have unfortunate consequences. If behavior is brought into line with attitudes, the amount of
attempted control of elites by nonelites will create governmental in-
effectiveness and instability. On the other hand, if attitudes change
to match behavior, the resulting sense of impotence and noninvolvement will have damaging consequences for the democratic quality of
the political system.

However, this does not suggest that all important issues damage
a democratic political system. It is only when issues become intense
and remain intense that the system may be made unstable.* If signifi-

---

*It is important to stress the term *issues* used in this connection. Not all salient
political events are issues, i.e., points of dispute. This model applies best to those
political disputes in which individuals are involved and have relatively specific
demands that they would like satisfied by the government. The content of some
political events may be so distant from the individual that, though he may consider the events important, he is in no position to formulate demands relevant to
them; thus even if the issue is significant, he will exert less pressure on political
elites than he would on other issues. (Warren Miller has found that there is a
closer relationship between the views of constituents and their Congressmen on
such subjects as civil rights and welfare than on foreign policy. The relatively
greater distance of foreign policy issues from the ordinary man might explain this.
See Miller, "Policy Preferences of Congressional Candidates and Constituents,"
paper delivered at the meetings of the American Political Science Association,
September 1961.)

Some political crises that are not issues—i.e., not subjects of disputes among
the citizens of a nation or between the citizens and the elites—may lead to an
increased involvement in political affairs that is not coupled with increased demands for influence over decisions. Wars, for instance, may unite a population
behind the elites and, by triggering off feelings of loyalty, lead to demands for

cant issues arise only sporadically *and* if the government is able to respond to the demands stimulated by these issues, an equilibrium can be maintained between citizen influence and government influence. ... Furthermore, these cycles of citizen involvement, elite response, and citizen withdrawal may tend to reinforce the balance of opposites needed for democracy. Within each cycle, the citizen's perception of his own influence is reinforced; at the same time the system adjusts to new demands and thereby manifests its effectiveness. And the system may become generally more stable through the loyalty engendered by participation and effective performance.† ...

We have so far dealt with the way in which activity and passivity may be balanced within the individual citizen. But this balance is maintained, not merely by the set of attitudes individuals have, but by the distribution of attitudes among different types of political actors in a system: some individuals believe that they are competent and some do not; some individuals are active and some are not. This variation in beliefs and activity among individuals also helps enforce the power-responsiveness balance. ...

The above discussion is based upon our data on the attitudes of ordinary citizens. But if a mechanism such as the one we postulate is to work, the attitudes of elites must complement those of nonelites. The decision maker must believe in the democratic myth—that ordinary citizens ought to participate in politics and that they are in fact influential. If the decision maker accepts this view of the role of the ordinary citizen, his own decisions serve to maintain the balance between governmental power and responsiveness. On the one hand, he is free to act as he thinks best because the ordinary citizen is not pounding on his door with demands for action. He is insulated by the inactivity of the ordinary man. But if he shares the belief in the influence potential of the ordinary man, his freedom to act is limited by the fact that he believes there *will* be pounding on his door if he does not act in ways that are responsive. Furthermore, if he shares the view that the ordinary man ought to participate in decisions, he

---

strong leadership rather than for chances to participate in decisions. This type of situation may have unstabilizing consequences for democracy, although the consequences will be different from those spelled out above. In this case, the stress on loyalty and the demand for strong leadership may lead to a reduction of citizen control over governmental elites.

†For an example of such a cyclical pattern of disinterest-involvement-influence-withdrawal, see William K. Muir, Jr., *Defending the "Hill" Against Metal Houses*, 1955, cited in Dahl, *Who Governs?* (Yale University Press), chap. xvi. See Dahl, chap. xxviii, for a general discussion relevant to our argument.

is under pressure to act responsively because he believes that such citizen influence is legitimate and justified. Though our data cannot demonstrate this, there is reason to believe that political elites share the political culture of the nonelite; that in a society with a civic culture they, as well as nonelites, hold the attitudes associated with it. Elites are, after all, part of the same political system and exposed to many of the same political socialization processes as are nonelites. And studies have shown that political and community leaders, as well as those of higher social status, are more likely than those of lower status to accept the norms of democracy.* . . .

Within the civic culture, then, the individual is not necessarily the rational, active citizen. His pattern of activity is more mixed and tempered. In this way he can combine some measure of competence, involvement, and activity with passivity and noninvolvement. Furthermore, his relationship with the government is not a purely rational one, for it includes adherence—his and the decision maker's—to what we have called the democratic myth of citizen competence. And this myth has significant consequences. For one thing, it is not pure myth: the belief in the influence potential of the average man has some truth to it and does indicate real behavioral potential. And whether true or not, the myth is believed.

The Management of Affect

. . . Participation in politics, this suggests, ought to be neither purely instrumental nor purely affective. The political participant ought to receive both instrumental and emotional gratifications from his par-

---

*Relevant here are our data on the effect of educational differences on the differences in attitudes among respondents. Also relevant is the finding in Samuel Stouffer's *Communism, Conformity, and Civil Liberties* (New York: John Wiley & Sons, 1955), to the effect that community leaders are more tolerant and more accepting of democratic norms than are nonleaders. Several studies of German public opinion support this general finding. See, for instance, Erich Reigrotski, *Soziale Verflechtungen in der Bundesrepublik*, Part 2, and *Basic Orientation and Political Thinking of West German Youth and Their Leaders* (Frankfurt am Main-Bad Godesberg: DIVO Institute, 1956).

Political leaders in democracies must express agreement with the democratic myth in public. Of course, much of this may be lip service. But the requirement that they give public support to this set of beliefs also puts pressure on them to accept the beliefs—unless hypocrisy is a conscious value among political elites. As the studies in cognitive dissonance have shown, the requirement that an individual make a certain kind of public declaration creates pressures to change his private beliefs in that direction.

ticipation. And this balanced involvement in politics again appears to characterize the civic culture in the two more successful democracies.... [I]n the United States and Britain the more the respondent considers himself capable of participating in politics, the more likely he is to receive affective satisfaction from the political system and to evaluate positively the instrumental performance of that system. In contrast, the other three nations show patterns of unbalanced participation....

Consensus and Cleavage

Our data suggest another way in which the political cultures of the more successful democracies are characterized by a balanced type of commitment.... [R]espondents in the United States and Britain more frequently than respondents in the other three nations express pride in their political system and feel satisfaction when voting.

... [A]ttitudes of interpersonal trust and cooperation are more frequent in the United States and Britain than in the other nations. More important, these general social attitudes penetrate into the realm of politics. The role of social trust and cooperativeness as a component of the civic culture cannot be overemphasized. It is, in a sense, a generalized resource that keeps a democratic polity operating. Constitution makers have designed formal structures of politics that attempt to enforce trustworthy behavior, but without these attitudes of trust, such institutions may mean little. Social trust facilitates political cooperation among the citizens in these nations, and without it democratic politics is impossible. It probably also enters into a citizen's relation with political elites. We argued earlier that the maintenance of elite power was essential in a democracy. We would now add that the sense of trust in the political elite—the belief that they are not alien and extractive forces, but part of the same political community—makes citizens willing to turn power over to them....

This brings us to a further balance that must be maintained within a democratic political system: that between consensus and cleavage. Without some meaningfully structured cleavage in society, it is hard to see how democratic politics can operate. If democracy involves at some point a choice among alternatives, the choice must be about something.... Yet if cleavage went too far, "... a democratic society ... would probably be in danger of its existence. The issues of politics would cut so deeply, be so keenly felt, and, especially, be so fully reinforced by other social identifications of the electorate..." as to threaten democracy. There must be what Parsons has called a "limited polarization" of society.* If there is no consensus within society, there can be little potentiality for the peaceful resolution of political differences that is associated with the democratic process. . . .

This balance between consensus and cleavage is managed within the civic culture by a mechanism similar to the one that managed the balance between activity and passivity: that is, an inconsistency between norms and behavior. This is illustrated by the data presented on attitudes toward primary group membership and partisan affiliation. . . . Again, the civic culture allows a balance between apparently contradictory demands through the mixture of a set of norms (that primary groups be nonpartisan) and actual behavior (that primary groups are indeed homogeneous in the partisan sense) that are themselves in contradiction one with the other.

This is but one example of the way in which the civic culture manages cleavage in society. In general, this management of cleavage is accomplished by subordinating conflicts on the political level to some higher, overarching attitudes of solidarity, whether these attitudes be the norms associated with the "rules of the democratic game" or the belief that there exists within the society a supraparty solidarity based on nonpartisan criteria. . . .

In sum, the most striking characteristic of the civic culture . . . is its mixed quality. It is a mixture in the first place of parochial, subject, and citizen orientations. The orientation of the parochial to primary relationships, the passive political orientation of the subject, the activity of the citizen, all merge within the civic culture. The result is a set of political orientations that are managed or balanced. There is political activity, but not so much as to destroy governmental authority; there is involvement and commitment, but they are moderated; there is political cleavage, but it is held in check. Above all, the political orientations that make up the civic culture are closely related to general social and interpersonal orientations. Within the civic culture the norms of interpersonal relationships, of general trust and confidence in one's social environment, penetrate political attitudes and temper them. The mixture of attitudes found in the civic culture . . . "fits" the democratic political system. It is, in a number of ways, particularly appropriate for the mixed political system that is democracy.

---

*T. Parsons, in Burdick and Brodbeck, eds., *American Voting Behavior* (Glencoe, Ill.: The Free Press, 1959), p. 92.

Excerpts from *Korematsu v. United States*, though not psychological writings, are offered as exemplary empirical data. It is from these kinds of observational materials that social scientists develop hypotheses for systematic study. The opinions of the U.S. Supreme Court justices in *Korematsu v. United States* illustrated the ambivalence between authoritarian and democratic components found in individuals and institutions. Corroborated also are the shifts or changes, perhaps predictable, because of the dual presence of democratic and authoritarian components. From an historical perspective neither the direction of past Supreme Court decisions nor the past opinions of these particular justices could have augured the positions enunciated on the detention and relocation of Americans of Japanese descent. *Korematsu v. United States* is an excellent example of the mixture of authoritarian and democratic components in individual **persons** (personality), in judicial decisions (group), in institutional life (public) and in the American context (culture). Perhaps here best of all is the interplay between micro (individual) and macro (group or societal) dimensions made most explicit.

from Korematsu v. United States (1944)*

Fred Toyosaburo Korematsu, Petitioner,
v.
United States of America (323 U.S. 214–248)

Civil Rights, § 1—restrictions against racial groups.

1. All legal restrictions which curtail the civil rights of a single racial group, although not necessarily unconstitutional, are immediately suspect, and must be subject to the most rigid scrutiny by the courts.

War, § 11—exercise of war powers—validity—exclusion of Japanese from West Coast areas.

2. The exclusion of citizens of Japanese extraction from certain

---

*United States Supreme Court Reports, Vol. 89, L. Ed., pp. 194–215, October 1944 term.

areas on the West Coast at the beginning of the war with Japan, as authorized by congressional enactment (Act of March 21, 1942) and Executive Order (9066), was a valid exercise of the war power at the time these laws went into effect, even as applied to a citizen of Japanese extraction whose loyalty to the United States was unquestioned, where at that time invasion by Japan was threatened, every possible precaution against espionage and sabotage was necessary, and it was impossible, in the short time available, to separate the loyal from the disloyal Japanese.

War, § 11—exclusion of Japanese from West Coast areas—conflicting orders.

3. A military order forbidding Japanese to leave a certain area does not conflict with a later order excluding them from such area, so as to preclude a conviction for violation of the latter order, where the operation of the first order was specifically limited in time "until and to the extent that a future proclamation or order should so permit or direct."

Administrative Law, § 58¾ ; War, § 11—validity of military order—right to attack—exclusion and relocation of Japanese.

4. The validity of a conviction of a citizen of Japanese extraction for violation of a military order excluding Japanese from a certain West Coast area, as authorized by the Act of March 21, 1942 (56 Stat. at L 173) and Executive Order No. 9066, is not subject to attack on the ground of the invalidity of other orders requiring Japanese, after departure from the excluded area, to report at assembly centers, subject to evacuation from there to relocation centers, since, although all a part of the same general program of Japanese evacuation and relocation, the classes of orders are separable, involving separate steps in the complete program.

Criminal Law, § 7—separate offenses—evacuation of Japanese.

5. Where, by different military orders authorized by the Act of March 21, 1942 and by Executive Order No. 9066, persons of Japanese extraction are excluded from certain West Coast areas, are ordered to report at assembly centers, and are afterwards evacuated to relocation centers, the violation of each one

of these different classes of orders constitutes a separate offense.

Courts, § 762—confining decision to case at hand.

6. The courts will not go beyond the issues raised in order to decide momentous questions not contained within the framework of the pleadings or the evidence in the case.

War, § 11—exclusion of Japanese from West Coast areas—assembly centers.

7. The exclusion of citizens of Japanese extraction by military orders from certain West Coast areas, as authorized by the Act of March 21, 1942 and Executive Order No. 9066, adopted at the beginning of the war with Japan, is not rendered invalid merely because their evacuation is accomplished by requiring them, under other orders, to report to assembly centers. . . .

Brief for the Petitioner

The statute under which the appellant was convicted and placed on probation is void for uncertainty and for delegating unlimited legislative power to military commanders, courts, and juries to determine what acts shall be deemed to be criminal and punishable. . . .

The military orders commanding his banishment from an area free from martial rule and ordering his imprisonment in a concentration camp, in the absence of crime upon his part and without an accusation of crime being brought against him, and the statute as their enforcement machinery, are void for being repugnant to the provisions of the Fourth, Fifth, Sixth, Eighth and Thirteenth Amendments. . . .

The Congress neither authorized nor approved the program.

As applied to the citizen appellant the statute and the military proclamations and orders to which it gave effect are unconstitutional and void upon the following grounds: . . .

2. For delegating unlimited judicial power to a military commander to function in lieu of courts by enabling him to hold, in the recesses of his own mind, a mock trial of the citizen appellant and other citizens of like stock, in an area free from martial rule and to condemn them to deportation and imprisonment on mere suspicion or hearsay or simply because he harbors prejudice against them because of their Japanese ancestry, in

violation of § 1 of art. 3 of the Constitution. [Citations.]* . . .

5. As depriving him of the following, among other, inalienable rights of national and state citizenship in violation of the due process clause of the Fifth Amendment. The "rights so vital to the maintenance of democratic institutions." [Citations.] . . .

9. As subjecting him to deportation and internment without charging him with crime and without informing him of the nature and cause of any accusation against him and without affording him a fair trial on the question of the necessity and right to banish and intern him, in violation of the Sixth Amendment and the due process clause of the Fifth Amendment. [Citations.] . . .

11. As imposing upon him in an internment camp a condition of slavery and involuntary servitude, imposed not for crime but solely by reason of his type of ancestry, which is forbidden by the Thirteenth Amendment. [Citations.] . . .

The legislative history of the Act of March 21, 1942, shows that Congress specifically intended to authorize orders excluding persons of Japanese ancestry, both American citizens and aliens, from the West Coast military areas. [Citations.] . . .

Congress gave neither to the President nor to military authorities any power so far-reaching, and in the absence of legislation the President has no such power even in time of war. [Citations.] . . .

"Friend of the Court" Brief from States of California, Oregon, and Washington

The President authorized and Congress ratified the exclusion of persons from Pacific Coast military areas with particular reference to persons of Japanese ancestry.

The exclusion of persons from military areas was within the combined war power of the President and Congress. [Citations.] . . .

In time of war, evacuation has been held to be a reasonable method of removing potentially dangerous persons from critical military areas. [Citations.] . . .

The evacuation of all persons of Japanese ancestry from military areas as a group was not, at the time and under the circumstances, a denial of due process. [Citations.] . . .

---

*Wherever the word "Citations" appears in brackets, it refers primarily to appellate court decisions generally supporting the proposition.

Opinion of the Court

Mr. Justice Black Delivered the Opinion of the Court:

It should be noted, to begin with, that all legal restrictions which curtail the civil rights of a single racial group are immediately suspect. That is not to say that all such restrictions are unconstitutional. It is to say that courts must subject them to the most rigid scrutiny. Pressing public necessity may sometimes justify the existence of such restriction; racial antagonism never can. . . . We uphold the exclusion order as of the time it was made and when the petitioner violated it. . . . In doing so, we are not unmindful of the hardships imposed by it upon a large group of American citizens.

. . . Compulsory exclusion of large groups of citizens from their homes, except under circumstances of direst emergency and peril, is inconsistent with our basic governmental institutions. But when under conditions of modern warfare our shores are threatened by hostile forces, the power to protect must be commensurate with the threatened danger. . . .

It is said that we are dealing here with the case of imprisonment of a citizen in a concentration camp solely because of his ancestry, without evidence or inquiry concerning his loyalty and good disposition towards the United States. Our task would be simple, our duty clear, were this a case involving the imprisonment of a loyal citizen in a concentration camp because of racial prejudice. Regardless of the true nature of the assembly and relocation centers—and we deem it unjustifiable to call them concentration camps with all the ugly connotations that term implies—we are dealing specifically with nothing but an exclusion order. To cast this case into outlines of racial prejudice, without reference to the real military dangers which were presented, merely confuses the issue. Korematsu was not excluded from the Military Area because of hostility to him or his race. He *was* excluded because we are at war with the Japanese Empire, because the properly constituted military authorities feared an invasion of our West Coast and felt constrained to take proper security measures, because they decided that the military urgency of the situation demanded that all citizens of Japanese ancestry be segregated from the West Coast temporarily, and finally, because Congress, reposing its confidence in this time of war in our military leaders—as inevitably it must—determined that they should have the power to do just this. There was evidence of disloyalty on the part of some, the military authorities considered that the need for action was great, and time was short. We cannot—by availing ourselves of the calm perspective of hindsight—now say that at that time these actions were unjustified.

Affirmed. . . .

From the Dissenting Opinions

Mr. Justice Roberts:

I dissent, because I think the indisputable facts exhibit a clear violation of Constitutional rights.

This is not a case of keeping people off the streets at night [citations], nor a case of temporary exclusion of a citizen from an area for his own safety or that of the community, nor a case of offering him an opportunity to go temporarily out of an area where his presence might cause danger to himself or to his fellows. On the contrary, it is the case of convicting a citizen as a punishment for not submitting to imprisonment in a concentration camp, based on his ancestry, and solely because of his ancestry, without evidence or inquiry concerning his loyalty and good disposition towards the United States. If this be a correct statement of the facts disclosed by this record, and facts of which we take judicial notice, I need hardly labor the conclusion that constitutional rights have been violated.

The Government's argument, and the opinion of the court, in my judgment, erroneously divide that which is single and indivisible and thus make the case appear as if the petitioner violated a Military Order, sanctioned by Act of Congress, which excluded him from his home, by refusing voluntarily to leave and, so, knowingly and intentionally, defying the order and the Act of Congress. . . .

. . . The obvious purpose of the orders made, taken together, was to drive all citizens of Japanese ancestry into Assembly Centers within the zones of their residence, under pain of criminal prosecution. . . .

. . . We further know that, on March 18, 1942, the President had promulgated Executive Order No. 9102 [7 Fed. Reg. 2165] establishing the War Relocation Authority under which so-called Relocation Centers, a euphemism for concentration camps, were established pursuant to cooperation between the military authorities of the Western Defense Command and the Relocation Authority. . . .

. . . The liberty of every American citizen freely to come and to go must frequently, in the face of sudden danger, be temporarily limited or suspended. The civil authorities must often resort to the expedient of excluding citizens temporarily from a locality. The drawing of fire lines in the case of a conflagration, the removal of persons from the area where a pestilence has broken out, are familiar examples. . . .

But the facts above recited . . . show that the exclusion was but a part of an over-all plan for forceable detention. . . .

These stark realities are met by the suggestion that it is lawful to compel an American citizen to submit to illegal imprisonment. . . .

Mr. Justice Murphy, dissenting:

This exclusion of "all persons of Japanese ancestry, both alien and non-alien," from the Pacific Coast area on a plea of military necessity in the absence of martial law ought not to be approved. Such exclusion goes over "the very brink of constitutional power" and falls into the ugly abyss of racism. . . .

. . . Being an obvious racial discrimination, the order deprives all those within its scope of the equal protection of the laws as guaranteed by the Fifth Amendment. It further deprives these individuals of their constitutional rights to live and work where they will, to establish a home where they choose and to move about freely. In excommunicating them without benefit of hearings, this order also deprives them of all their constitutional rights to procedural due process. Yet no reasonable relation to an "immediate, imminent, and impending" public danger is evident to support this racial restriction which is one of the most sweeping and complete deprivations of constitutional rights in the history of this nation in the absence of martial law. . . .

. . . [T]o infer that examples of individual disloyalty prove group disloyalty and justify discriminatory action against the entire group is to deny that under our system of law individual guilt is the sole basis for deprivation of rights. Moreover, this inference, which is at the very heart of the evacuation orders, has been used in support of the abhorrent and despicable treatment of minority groups by the dictatorial tyrannies which this nation is now pledged to destroy. To give constitutional sanction to that inference in this case, however well-intentioned may have been the military command on the Pacific Coast, is to adopt one of the cruelest of the rationales used by our enemies to destroy the dignity of the individual and to encourage and open the door to discriminatory actions against other minority groups in the passions of tomorrow. . . .

I dissent, therefore, from this legalization of racism. Racial discrimination in any form and in any degree has no justifiable part whatever in our democratic way of life. It is unattractive in any setting but it is utterly revolting among a free people who have embraced the principles set forth in the Constitution of the United States. All residents of this nation are kin in some way by blood or culture to a foreign land. Yet they are primarily and necessarily a part of the new and distinct civilization of the United States. They must accordingly be treated at all times as the heirs of the American experiment and as entitled to all the rights and freedoms guaranteed by the Constitution.

Mr. Justice Jackson, dissenting:

... [T]he "law" which this prisoner is convicted of disregarding is not found in an act of Congress, but in a military order. Neither the Act of Congress nor the Executive Order of the President, nor both together, would afford a basis for this conviction. It rests on the orders of General DeWitt. And it is said that if the military commander had reasonable military grounds for promulgating the orders, they are constitutional and become law, and the Court is required to enforce them. . . . I cannot subscribe to this doctrine. . . .

Much is said of the danger to liberty from the Army program for deporting and detaining these citizens of Japanese extraction. But a judicial construction of the due process clause that will sustain this order is a far more subtle blow to liberty than the promulgation of the order itself. A military order, however unconstitutional, is not apt to last longer than the military emergency. Even during that period a succeeding commander may revoke it all. But once a judicial opinion rationalizes such an order to show that it conforms to the Constitution, or rather rationalizes the Constitution to show that the Constitution sanctions such an order, the Court for all time has validated the principle of racial discrimination in criminal procedure and of transplanting American citizens. The principle then lies about like a loaded weapon ready for the hand of any authority that can bring forward a plausible claim of an urgent need. . . . A military commander may overstep the bounds of constitutionality, and it is an incident. But if we review and approve, that passing incident becomes the doctrine of the Constitution. There it has a generative power of its own, and all that it creates will be in its own image. Nothing better illustrates this danger than does the Court's opinion in this case. . . . [T]he existence of a military power resting on force, so vagrant, so centralized, so necessarily heedless of the individual, is an inherent threat to liberty. . . . The chief restraint upon those who command the physical forces of the country, in the future as in the past, must be their responsibility to the political judgments of their contemporaries and to the moral judgments of history.

The Perspectives of III
History and Politics:
The Thesis as Record

Up to this point we have presented to the reader both
an introductory essay containing our hypothesis and a
major section of current corroborative writings in the field
of the social sciences. We turn now to some primary
sources in actual American philosophical and political
arenas, which again tend to dramatize the recurrence of
the hypothetical theme by tracing the reappearing ambivalence from Puritan lines to the present.

In a society which promises political equality and equal protection before the law the question of civil disobedience becomes one of central concern. The issue is whether to sanction or condemn opposition to and violation of those laws which the democratic processes have evolved. The answer is related to one's view on the tension between those forces which bind society and recognizable characteristics of democracy. It is also related to philosophical considerations about Man and Society, Man and Freedom, Man and Democracy. It is to these questions that the material in this section is addressed.

One of the ironic conditions extant today is that governments of all forms and nationalities vie as competing "democracies." Nations which are "communist" and those which purport to be "democratic" both claim (adopt) democracy. Clearly both perceive the value in the *slogan* of democracy, if nothing more, and perhaps even in the democratic process.

The fact that democratic norms are sought by and claimed in a variety of circumstances attests to their viability but also to their diversity. There is a tendency in the United States toward "democratic ethnocentrism," one form of democracy and one form of government. The conventional image in this society is that of an impartial government dictated by a theoretical neutral concept of democracy. What is often overlooked is that both the theory and the form of democracy have been defined by our basic documents, themselves a product of diverse interests, interpreted by our forefathers, and modified by the weight of decisions at both the national and local levels of government. We must return on occasion to consider the issues which are fundamental not only to considerations of democracy, but to the very nature of society itself.

At least one school of thought suggests that the overriding claim of democracy has been that it maximizes individual utilities and individual powers. In the traditional sense both claims suggest that the liberal society maintains in the greatest degree those conditions conducive to the fulfillment of the individual. The contradiction arises when as a social organization the State moves from utilitarian to pragmatic motives: from the doctrine that actions are to be judged in terms of their utility in promoting the greatest happiness of the greatest number to one whose truth is circumscribed by its practical efficacy. The admitted growing complexity of social institutions and the impersonalized bureaucracy which accompanies mass organization are forces which tend to vitiate the role of the citizen.

The Puritan
Period

4

John Wise,
>	from *A Vindication of the Government of New Eng-
>	land Churches*

John Cotton,
>	from *Limitation of Government*

Beginning with political philosophers such as Thomas Hobbes the issue of the equality of Man is assumed, independent of sectarian interests. For Hobbes and subsequent writers Man is by nature both equal and rational, but the goal of self-preservation is such that he is forced to adopt society to avoid the natural conditions of chaos. In certain respects the position of John Wise closely parallels Hobbesian philosophy, at least concerning the questions of Man's rationality and equality. Wise also saw that Man entered into civil society in order to protect himself, but that inequalities were the consequence. The considerations, however elemental, precede the question of the form of government a state may adopt and address the more crucial issue of the source of authority in the state and the relationship of the citizens to government. Wise concluded that given the inherent equality of Man it was only logical that the equality and ensuing liberty be preserved to a highest degree in the civil (as opposed to the natural) state, and that the form of government most likely would be one in which Man did not surrender his sovereignty—an arrangement whereby man could administer his common affairs in common judgment. Democracy, of which he is writing, becomes "sovereign power lodged in a council consisting of all members," and democratic government results when the people have agreed to determine the limits of the exercise of power.

The point which John Cotton states unequivocally is that Man's spirit is corruptible and that the limits which are to constrain magistrates, for example, are determined by the laws of God.

from *A Vindication of the Government of New-England Churches* (Boston, 1717)*

I shall disclose several Principles of Natural Knowledge; plainly discovering the Law of Nature; or the true sentiments of Natural Reason, with Respect to Man's Being and Government. And in this Essay I shall peculiarly confine the discourse to two heads, *viz.*
1. Of the Natural (in distinction to the Civil) and then,
2. Of the Civil Being of Man. . . .

Man in a State of Natural Being

I shall consider Man in a state of Natural Being, as a Free-Born Subject under the Crown of Heaven, and owing Homage to none but God himself. It is certain Civil Government in General, is a very Admirable Result of Providence, and an Incomparable Benefit to Mankind, yet must needs be acknowledged to be the Effect of Human Free-Compacts and not of Divine Institution; it is the Produce of Mans Reason, of Human and Rational Combinations, and not from any direct Orders of Infinite Wisdom, in any positive Law wherein is drawn up this or that Scheme of Civil Government. Government (says the Lord *Warrington*) is necessary—in that no Society of Men can subsist without it; and that Particular Form of Government is necessary which best suits the Temper and Inclination of a People. Nothing can be God's Ordinance, but what he has particularly Declared to be such; there is no particular Form of Civil Government described in God's Word, neither does Nature prompt it. The Government of the *Jews* was changed five Times. Government is not formed by Nature, as other Births or Productions; If it were, it would be the same in all Countries; because Nature keeps the same Method, in the same thing, in all Climates. If a Commonwealth be changed into a Monarchy, is it Nature that forms, and brings forth the Monarch? Or if a Royal Family

---

*John Wise, 1652-1725. Graduated Harvard 1673; ordained Congregational minister 1682. The important contribution of this early writer was to generalize the democratic principles which inhered in the Congregational policy of church autonomy and to amplify individual reason. The text is from Chapter II of Wise's comprehensive and important defense of democratic Congregationalism, in this, his primary treatise.

be wholly Extinct (as in *Noah's* Case, being not Heir Apparent from Descent from *Adam*) is it Nature that must go to work [with the King Bees, who themselves alone preserve the Royal Race in that Empire] to Breed a Monarch before the People can have a King, or a Government sent over them? And thus we must leave Kings to Resolve which is their best Title to their Crowns, whether Natural Right, or the Constitution of Government settled by Human Compacts, under the Directtion and Conduct of Reason. But to proceed under the head of a State of Natural Being, I shall more distinctly Explain the State of Human Nature in its Original Capacity, as Man is placed on Earth by his Maker, and Clothed with many Investitures, and Immunities which properly belong to Man separately considered. As,

The Prime Immunity in Mans State, is that he is most properly the Subject of the Law of Nature. He is the Favourite Animal on Earth; in that this Part of Gods Image, *viz.* Reason is Congenial with his Nature, wherein by a Law Immutable, Instamped upon his Frame, God has provided a Rule for Men in all their Actions, obliging each one to the performance of that which is Right, not only as to Justice, but likewise as to all other Moral Virtues, the which is nothing but the Dictate of Right Reason founded in the Soul of Man. . . . That which is to be drawn from Mans Reason, flowing from the true Current of that Faculty, when unperverted, may be said to be the Law of Nature; on which account, the Holy Scriptures declare it written on Mens hearts. For being endowed with a Soul, you may know from your self, how, and what you ought to act, Rom. 2. 14. *These having not a Law, are a Law to themselves.* So that the meaning is, when we acknowledge the Law of Nature to be the dictate of Right Reason, we must mean that the Understanding of Man is endowed with such a power, as to be able, from the Contemplation of human Condition to discover a necessity of Living agreeably with this Law: And likewise to find out some Principle, by which the Precepts of it, may be clearly and solidly Demonstrated. The way to discover the Law of Nature in our own state, is by a narrow Watch, and accurate Contemplation of our Natural Condition, and propensions. Others say this is the way to find out the Law of Nature. If a Man any ways doubts, whether what he is going to do to another Man be agreeable to the Law of Nature, then let him suppose himself to be in that other Mans Room; And by this Rule effectually Executed. A Man must be a very dull Scholar to Nature not to make Proficiency in the Knowledge of her Laws. But more particularly in pursuing our Condition for the discovery of the Law of Nature, this is very obvious to view, *viz.*

A Principle of Self-Love, & Self-Preservation, is very predominant in every Mans Being.

A Sociable Disposition.

An Affection or Love to Mankind in General. And to give such Sentiments the force of a Law, we must suppose a God who takes care of all Mankind, and has thus obliged each one, as a Subject of higher Principles of Being, than mere Instincts. For that all Law properly considered, supposes a capable Subject, and a Superior Power; And the Law of God which is Binding, is published by the Dictates of Right Reason as other ways: Therefore says *Plutarch, To follow God and obey Reason is the same thing.* But moreover that God has Established the Law of Nature, as the General Rule of Government, is further Illustrable from the many Sanctions in Providence, and from the Peace and Guilt of Conscience in them that either obey, or violate the Law of Nature. But moreover, the foundation of the Law of Nature with relation to Government, may be thus Discovered. Man is a Creature extremely desirous of his own Preservation; of himself he is plainly Exposed to many Wants, unable to secure his own safety, and Maintenance without the Assistance of his fellows; and he is also able of returning Kindness by the furtherance of mutual Good; But yet Man is often found to be Malicious, Insolent, and easily Provoked, and as powerful in Effecting mischief, as he is ready in designing it. Now that such a Creature may be Preserved, it is necessary that he be Sociable; that is, that he be capable and disposed to unite himself to those of his own species, and to Regulate himself towards them, that they may have no fair Reason to do him harm; but rather incline to promote his Interests, and secure his Rights and Concerns. This then is a Fundamental Law of Nature, that every Man as far as in him lies, do maintain a Sociableness with others, agreeable with the main end and disposition of human Nature in general. For this is very apparent, that Reason and Society render Man the most potent of all Creatures. And Finally, from the Principles of Sociableness it follows as a fundamental Law of Nature, that Man is not so Wedded to his own Interest, but that he can make the Common good the mark of his Aim: And hence he becomes Capacitated to enter into a Civil State by the Law of Nature; for without this property in Nature, *viz.* Sociableness, which is for Cementing of parts, every Government would soon molder and dissolve.

The Second Great Immunity of Man is an Original Liberty Instampt upon his Rational Nature. He that intrudes upon this Liberty, Violates the Law of Nature. In this Discourse I shall waive the Constitution of Mans Moral Turpitude, but shall view him Physically as a

Creature which God has made and furnished essentially with many Ennobling Immunities, which render him the most August Animal in the World, and still, whatever has happened since his Creation, he remains at the upper-end of Nature, and as such is a Creature of a very Noble Character. For as to his Dominion, the whole frame of the Lower Part of the Universe is devoted to his use, and at his Command; and his Liberty under the Conduct of Right Reason, is equal with his trust. Which Liberty may be briefly Considered, Internally as to his Mind, and Externally as to his Person.

The Internal Native Liberty of Mans Nature in general implies, a faculty of Doing or Omitting things according to the Direction of his Judgment. But in a more special meaning, this Liberty does not consist in a loose and ungovernable Freedom, or in an unbounded Licence of Acting. Such Licence is disagreeing with the condition and dignity of Man, and would make Man of a lower and meaner Constitution than Brute Creatures; who will in all their Liberties [be] kept under a better and more Rational Government, by their Instincts. Therefore as *Plutarch* says, *Those Persons only who live in Obedience to Reason, are worthy to be accounted free: They alone live as they Will, who have Learnt what they ought to Will.* So that the true Natural Liberty of Man, such as really and truly agrees to him, must be understood, as he is Guided and Restrained by the Ties of Reason, and Laws of Nature; all the rest is Brutal, if not worse.

Mans External Personal, Natural Liberty, Antecedent to all Human parts, or Alliances must also be considered. And so every Man must be conceived to be perfectly in his own Power and disposal, and not to be controlled by the Authority of any other. And thus every Man, must be acknowledged equal to every Man, since all Subjection and all Command are equally banished on both sides; and considering all Men thus at Liberty, every Man has a Prerogative to Judge for himself, *viz.* What shall be most for his Behoof, Happiness and Well-being.

The Third Capital Immunity belonging to Mans Nature, is an equality amongst Men; Which is not to be denied by the Law of Nature, till Man has Resigned himself with all his Rights for the sake of a Civil State; and then his Personal Liberty and Equality is to be cherished, and preserved to the highest degree, as will consist with all just distinctions amongst Men of Honour, and shall be agreeable with the public Good. For Man has a high valuation of himself, and the passion seems to lay its first foundation (not in Pride, but) really in the high and admirable Frame and Constitution of Human Nature. The Word Man, says my Author, is thought to carry somewhat of Dignity in its sound; and we commonly make use of this as the most proper and prevailing Argument against a rude Insulter, *viz. I am not a Beast or a Dog, but am a Man as well as your self.* Since then Human Nature agrees equally with all persons; and since no one can live a Sociable Life with another that does not own or Respect him as a Man; It follows as a Command of the Law of Nature, that every Man Esteem and treat another as one who is naturally his Equal, or who is Man as well as he. There be many popular, or plausible Reasons that greatly Illustrate this Equality, *viz.* that we all Derive our Being from one stock, the same Common Father of the human Race. On this Consideration *Boethius* checks the pride of the Insulting Nobility. . . .

And also that our Bodies are Composed of matter, frail, brittle, and liable to be destroyed by [a] thousand Accidents; we all owe our Existence to the same Method of propagation. The Noblest Mortal in his Entrance on to the Stage of Life, is not distinguished by any pomp or of passage from the lowest of Mankind; and our Life hastens to the same General Mark: Death observes no Ceremony, but Knocks as loud at the Barriers of the Court, as at the Door of the Cottage. This Equality being admitted, bears a very great force in maintaining Peace and Friendship amongst Men. For that he who would use the Assistance of others, in promoting his own Advantage, ought as freely to be at their service, when they want his help on the like Occasions. . . . That it would be the greatest absurdity to believe, that Nature actually Invests the Wise with a Sovereignty over the weak; or with a Right of forcing them against their Wills; for that no Sovereignty can be Established, unless some Human Deed, or Covenant Precede: Nor does Natural fitness for Government make a Man presently Governor over another; for that as *Ulpian* says, *by a Natural Right all Men are born free;* and Nature having set all Men upon a Level and made them Equals, no Servitude or Subjection can be conceived without Inequality; and this cannot be made without Usurpation or Force in others, or Voluntary Compliance in those who Resign their freedom, and give away their degree of Natural Being. And thus we come.

Man in a Civil State of Being

To consider Man in a Civil State of Being; wherein we shall observe the great difference between a Natural, and Political State, for in the Latter State many Great disproportions appear, or at least many obvious distinctions are soon made amongst Men; which Doctrine is to be laid open under a few heads.

Every Man considered in a Natural State, must be allowed to be Free, and at his own dispose; yet to suit Mans Inclinations to Society;

And in a peculiar manner to gratify the necessity he is in of public Rule and Order, he is Impelled to enter into a Civil Community; and divests himself of his Natural Freedom, and puts himself under Government; which amongst other things Comprehends the Power of Life and Death over Him; together with Authority to Enjoin him some things to which he has an utter Aversion, and to prohibit him other things, for which he may have as strong an Inclination; so that he may be often under this Authority, obliged to Sacrifice his Private, for the Public Good. So that though Man is inclined to Society, yet he is driven to a Combination by great necessity. For that the true and leading Cause of forming Governments, and yielding up Natural Liberty, and throwing Mans Equality into a Common Pile to be new Cast by the Rules of fellowship; was really and truly to guard themselves against the Injuries Men were liable to Interchangeably; for none so Good to Man, as Man, and yet none a greater Enemy. So that,

The first Human Subject and Original of Civil Power is the People. For as they have a Power every Man over himself in a Natural State, so upon a Combination they can and do bequeath this Power unto others; and settle it according as their united discretion shall Determine. For that this is very plain, that when the Subject of Sovereign Power is quite Extinct, that Power returns to the People again. And when they are free, they may set up what species of Government they please; or if they rather incline to it, they may subside into a State of Natural Being, if it be plainly for the best. . . .

The formal Reason of Government is the Will of a Community, yielded up and surrendered to some other Subject, either of one particular Person, or more. . . .

The Forms of a Regular State are three only, which Forms arise from the proper and particular Subject, in which the Supreme Power Resides. As,

A Democracy, which is when the Sovereign Power is Lodged in a Council consisting of all the Members, and where every Member has the Privilege of a Vote. This Form of Government, appears in the greatest part of the World to have been the most Ancient. For that Reason seems to show it to be most probable, that when Men (being Originally in a condition of Natural Freedom and Equality) had thoughts of joining in a Civil Body, would without question be inclined to Administer their common Affairs, by their common Judgment, and so must necessarily to gratify that Inclination establish a Democracy; neither can it be rationally imagined, that Fathers of Families being yet Free and Independent, should in a moment, or little time take off their long delight in governing their own Affairs, & Devolve all upon some single Sovereign Commander; for that it seems to have been thought more Equitable, that what belonged to all, should be managed by all, when all had entered by Compact into one Community. . . .

A democracy is then Erected, when a Number of Free Persons, do Assemble together, in Order to enter into a Covenant for Uniting themselves in a Body: And such a Preparative Assembly hath some appearance already of a Democracy; it is a Democracy in *Embryo* properly in this Respect, that every Man hath the Privilege freely to deliver his Opinion concerning the Common Affairs. Yet he who dissents from the Vote of the Majority, is not in the least obliged by what they determine, till by a second Covenant, a Popular Form be actually Established; for nct before then can we call it a Democratical Government, *viz.* Till the Right of Determining all matters relating to the public Safety, is actually placed in a General Assembly of the whole People; or by their own Compact and Mutual Agreement, Determine themselves the proper Subject for the Exercise of Sovereign Power. And to complete this State, and render it capable to Exert its Power to answer the End of a Civil State: These Conditions are necessary.

1. That a certain Time and Place be Assigned for Assembling.

2. That when the Assembly be Orderly met, as to Time and Place, that then the Vote of the Majority must pass for the Vote of the whole Body.

3. That Magistrates be appointed to Exercise the Authority of the whole for the better dispatch of Business, of every days Occurrence; who also may with more Mature diligence, search into more Important Affairs; and if in case any thing happens of greater Consequence, may report it to the Assembly; and be peculiarly Serviceable in putting all Publick Decrees into Execution. Because a large Body of People is almost useless in Respect of the last Service, and of many others, as to the more Particular Application and Exercise of Power. Therefore it is most agreeable with the Law of Nature, that they Institute their Officers to act in their Name, and Stead.

The Second Species of Regular Government, is an Aristocracy and this is said then to be Constituted when the People, or Assembly United by a first Covenant, and having thereby cast themselves into the first Rudiments of a State; do then by Common Decree, Devolve the Sovereign Power, on a Council consisting of some Select Members; and these having accepted of the Designation, are then properly invested with Sovereign Command; and then an Aristocracy is formed.

The Third Species of a Regular Government, is a Monarchy which is settled when the Sovereign Power is confered on some one worthy Person. It differs from the former, because a Monarch who is best one Person in Natural, as well as in Moral account, & so is furnished with an Immediate Power of Exercising Sovereign Command in all Instances of Government; but the fore named must needs have Particular Time and Place assigned; but the Power and Authority is Equal in each.

An Aristocracy is a dangerous Constitution in the Church of Christ as it possesses the Presbytery of all Church Power: What has been observed sufficiently Evinces it. And not only so but from the Nature of the Constitution, for it has no more Barrier to it, against the Ambitious Insults, and Arbitrary measures of Men, then an absolute Monarchy But to abbreviate; it seems most agreeable with the Light of Nature that if there be any of the Regular Government settled in the Church of God it must needs be.

A Democracy. This is a form of Government, which the Light of Nature does highly value, & often directs to as most agreeable to the Just and Natural Prerogatives of Humane Beings. This was of great account, in the early times of the World. And not only so, but upon the Experience of several Thousand years, after the World had been tumbled, and tost from one Species of Government to another, at a great Expence of Blood and Treasure, many of the wise Nations of the World have sheltered themselves under it again; or at least have blendished, and balanced their Governments with it.

from *Limitation of Government* (1646)*

If there be power given to speak great things, then look for great blasphemies, look for a licentious abuse of it.

This may serve to teach us the danger of allowing to any mortall man an inordinate measure of power to speak great things, to allow to

---

*John Cotton, 1584-1652. Graduated M.A., Emmanuel College, Cambridge 1606; arrived Boston 1633 and was appointed to a position of church (and therefore civil) importance almost immediately. His significance to political theory was his explication of the social compact. Accordingly, the laws which governed Man in society were not natural but distinctly positive, as was the relationship between the rulers and the ruled. From Perry Miller and Thomas H. Johnson, *The Puritans*, (New York: American Book Co., 1938) pp. 212–14.

any man uncontrollableness of speech, you see the desperate danger
of it: Let all the world learn to give mortall men no greater power than
they are content they shall use, for use it they will: and unlesse they
be better taught of God, they will use it ever and anon, it may be make
it the passage of their proceeding to speake what they will: And they
that have liberty to speak great things, you will finde it to be true, they
will speak great blasphemies. No man would think what desperate
deceit and wickedness there is in the hearts of men: And that was the
reason why the Beast did speak such great things, hee might speak,
and no body might controll him: What saith the Lord in *Jer.* 3. 5. *Thou
hast spoken and done evill things as thou couldst.* If a Church or head
of a Church could have done worse, he would have done it: This is
one of the straines of nature, it affects boundlesse liberty, and to runne
to the utmost extent: What ever power he hath received, he hath a
corrupt nature that will improve it in one thing or other; if he have
liberty, he will think why may he not use it. Set up the Pope as Lord
Paramount over Kings and Princes, and they shall know that he hath
power over them, he will take liberty to depose one, and set up another.
Give him power to make Laws, and he will approve, and disprove as
he list; what he approves is Canonicall, what hee disproves is rejected:
Give him that power, and he will so order it at length, he will make
such a State of Religion, that he that so lives and dyes shall never be
saved, and all this springs from the vast power that is given to him,
and from the deep depravation of nature. Hee will open his mouth, *His
tongue is his owne, who is Lord over him,* Psal, 12. 3, 4. It is therefore
most wholsome for Magistrates and Officers in Church and Common-
wealth, never to affect more liberty and authority then will do them
good, and the People good; for what ever transcendant power is
given, will certainly over-run those that give it, and those that receive
it: There is a straine in a mans heart that will sometime or other runne
out to excesse, unlesse the Lord restraine it, but it is not good to venture
it: It is necessary therefore, that all power that is on earth be limited,
Church-power or other: If there be power given to speak great things,
then look for great blasphemies, look for a licentious abuse of it. It is
counted a matter of danger to the State to limit Prerogatives; but it is
a further danger, not to have them limited: They will be like a Tempest,
if they be not limited: A Prince himselfe cannot tell where hee will
confine himselfe, nor can the people tell: But if he have liberty to speak
great things, then he will make and unmake, say and unsay, and undertake such things as are neither for his owne honour, nor for the safety
of the State. It is therefore fit for every man to be studious of the
bounds which the Lord hath set: and for the People, in whom funda-

mentally all power lyes, to give as much power as God in his word gives to men: And it is meet that Magistrates in the Common-wealth, and so Officers in Churches should desire to know the utmost bounds of their own power, and it is safe for both: All intrenchment upon the bounds which God hath not given, they are not enlargements, but burdens and snares; They will certainly lead the spirit of a man out of his way sooner or later. It is wholsome and safe to be dealt withall as God deales with the vast Sea; *Hitherto shalt thou come, but there shalt thou stay thy proud waves:* and therefore if they be but banks of simple sand, they will be good enough to check the vast roaring Sea. And so for Imperiall Monarchies, it is safe to know how far their power extends: and then if it be but banks of sand, which is most slippery, it will serve, as well as any brazen wall. If you pinch the Sea of its liberty, though it be walls of stone or brasse, it will beate them downe: So it is with Magistrates, stint them where God had not stinted them, and if they were walls of brasse, they would beate them downe, and it is meet they should: but give them the liberty God allows, and if it be but a wall of sand it will keep them: As this liquid Ayre in which we breath, God hath set it for the waters of the Clouds to the Earth: It is a Firmament, it is the Clouds, yet it stands firme enough, because it keeps the Climate where they are, it shall stand like walls of brasse: So let there be due bounds set, and I may apply it to Families; it is good for the Wife to acknowledg all power and authority to the Husband, and for the Husband to acknowledg honour to the Wife, but still give them that which God hath given them, and no more nor lesse: Give them the full latitude that God hath given, else you will finde you dig pits, and lay snares, and cumber their spirits, if you give them lesse: there is never peace where full liberty is not given, nor never stable peace where more then full liberty is granted: Let them be duely observed, and give men no more liberty then God doth, nor women, for they will abuse it: The Devill will draw them, and Gods providence leade them thereunto, therefore give them no more then God gives. And so for children; and servants, or any others you are to deale with, give them the liberty and authority you would have them use, and beyond that stretch not the tether, it will not tend to their good nor yours: And also from hence gather, and goe home with this meditation; That certainly here is this distemper in our natures, that we cannot tell how to use liberty, but we shall very readily corrupt our selves: Oh the bottomlesse depth of sandy earth! of a corrupt spirit, that breaks over all bounds, and loves inordinate vastnesse; that is it we ought to be carefull of.

The Constitutional Period 5

Thomas Jefferson,
> from *Proposed Charter for France*
> A letter to Noah Webster
> from *Notes on Virginia*
> A letter to de Meusnier
> A letter to Edward Carrington

Alexander Hamilton,
> *The Federalist,* Nos. 33 and 27

Thomas Jefferson and Alexander Hamilton are two important authors of the Constitutional Period concerned with the problem of translating philosophical concerns into operational forms. Guarantees such as due process and the freedom from false imprisonment, designed to protect the equality and freedom of man, are now proposed. Unfortunately there is concrete evidence of a reprehensible omission in the example of Jefferson at least in that the equality of man is jeopardized by the manner in which the slavery issue is concluded. The responsibility is not Jefferson's alone, however, for the Convention of 1787 which drafted the Constitution was more desirous of compromise among the parties present than of debate on the philosophical question of equality.

Hamilton, writing in *Federalist Papers,* Nos. 33 and 27, addresses the issue of the power of the national government *vis à vis* the states, particularly the supremacy of the national Constitution. Together with Jefferson, Hamilton reinforces the sovereignty of the people, and, by extension, the necessary superiority of national law in a federal system.

from Proposed Charter for France (June 3d, 1789)*

A CHARTER OF RIGHTS, SOLEMNLY
ESTABLISHED BY THE KING AND NATION

1. The States General shall assemble, uncalled, on the first day of November, annually, and shall remain together so long as they shall see cause. They shall regulate their own elections and proceedings, and until they shall ordain otherwise, their elections shall be in the forms observed in the present year, and shall be triennial.

2. The States General alone shall levy money on the nation, and shall appropriate it.

3. Laws shall be made by the States General only, with the consent of the King.

4. No person shall be restrained of his liberty, but by regular process from a court of justice, authorized by a general law. (Except that a Noble may be imprisoned by order of a court of justice, on the prayer of twelve of his nearest relations.) On complaint of an unlawful imprisonment, to any judge whatever, he shall have the prisoner immediately brought before him, and shall discharge him, if his imprisonment be unlawful. The officer in whose custody the prisoner is, shall obey the orders of the judge; and both judge and officer shall be responsible, civilly and criminally, for a failure of duty herein.

5. The military shall be subordinate to the civil authority.

6. Printers shall be liable to legal prosecution for printing and publishing false facts, injurious to the party prosecuting; but they shall be under no other restraint.

7. All pecuniary privileges and exemptions, enjoyed by any description of persons, are abolished.

8. All debts already contracted by the King, are hereby made the debts of the nation; and the faith thereof is pledged for their payment in due time.

Thomas Jefferson, 1743-1826. Attended the College of William and Mary; author, revolutionary leader, and third President of the United States (1801-1809). Jefferson, because of his early influence, is considered the principal philosopher of American democracy. Associated throughout his early career with republican government and the decentralization of political power, upon assuming office Jefferson's practice became one of "peaceable coercion," both nationally and internationally. All Jefferson extracts are from *Basic Writings of Thomas Jefferson*, Philip S. Foner, ed., (New York: John Wiley & Sons, 1944).

9. Eighty millions of livres are now granted to the King, to be raised by loan, and reimbursed by the nation; and the taxes heretofore paid, shall continue to be paid to the end of the present year, and no longer.

10. The States General shall now separate, and meet again on the 1st day of November next.

Done, on behalf of the whole nation, by the King and their representatives in the States General, at Versailles, this————day of June, 1789.

Signed by the King, and by every member individually, and in his presence.

A letter to Noah Webster*
(Philadelphia, December 4, 1790)

. . . that the purposes of society do not require a surrender of all our rights to our ordinary governors: that there are certain portions of right not necessary to enable them to carry on an effective government, and which experience has nevertheless proved they will be constantly encroaching on, if submitted to them: that there are also certain fences which experience has proved peculiarly efficacious against wrong, and rarely obstructive of right, which yet the governing powers have ever shown a disposition to weaken and remove. Of the first kind, for instance, is freedom of religion: of the second, trial by jury, Habeas corpus laws, free presses. These were the settled opinions of all the states, of that of Virginia, of which I was writing, as well as of the others. The others had in consequence delineated these unceded portions of right, and these fences against wrong, which they meant to exempt from the power of their governors, in instruments called declarations of rights and constitutions: and as they did this by Conventions which they appointed for the express purpose of reserving these rights, and of delegating others to their ordinary legislative, executive and judiciary bodies, none of the reserved rights can be touched without resorting to the people to appoint another convention for the express purpose of permitting it. Where the constitutions then have been so

---

*Famous lexicographer and prominent Federalist.

formed by conventions named for this express purpose they are fixed and unalterable but by a convention or other body to be specially authorized. And they have been so formed by, I believe, all the States, except Virginia. That State concurs in all these opinions, but has run into the wonderful error that her constitution, tho made by the ordinary legislature, cannot yet be altered by the ordinary legislature. I had therefore no occasion to prove to them the expediency of a constitution alterable only by a special convention. Accordingly I have not in my notes advocated that opinion, tho it was and is mine, as it was and is theirs. I take that position as admitted by them: and only proceed to adduce arguments to prove that they were mistaken in supposing their constitution could not be altered by the common legislature. Among other arguments I urge that the Convention which formed the constitution had been chosen merely for ordinary legislation; that they had no higher power than every subsequent legislature was to have; that all their acts are consequently repealable by subsequent legislatures; that their own practice at a subsequent session proved they were of this opinion themselves; that the opinion and practice of several subsequent legislatures had been the same, and so conclude "that their constitution is alterable by the common legislature." Yet these arguments urged to prove that their constitution *is* alterable, you cite as if urged to prove that it *ought not to be* alterable, and you combat them on that ground. An argument which is good to prove one thing, may become ridiculous when exhibited as intended to prove another thing. I will beg the favor of you to look over again the passage in my *Notes,* and am persuaded you will be sensible that you have misapprehended the object of my arguments, and therefore have combatted them on a ground for which they were not intended. My only object in this is the rectification of your own opinion of me, which I repeat that I respect too much to neglect. I have certainly no view of entering into the contest whether it be expedient to delegate unlimited powers to our ordinary governors? My opinion is against that expediency; but my occupations do not permit me to undertake to vindicate all my opinions, nor have they importance enough to merit it. It cannot, however, but weaken my confidence in them when I find them opposed to yours, there being no one who respects the latter more than Sir your most obed‍ᵗ and most humble serv‍ᵗ.

from Notes on Virginia,
Query XIV (1781)

To change the rules of descent, so as that the lands of any person dying intestate shall be divisible equally among all his children, or other representatives, in equal degree.

To make slaves distributable among the next of kin, as other movables.

To have all public expences, whether of the general treasury, or of a parish or county, (as for the maintenance of the poor, building bridges, courthouses, &c.,) supplied by assessments on the citizens, in proportion to their property.

To hire undertakers for keeping the public roads in repair, and indemnify individuals through whose lands new roads shall be opened.

To define with precision the rules whereby aliens should become citizens, and citizens make themselves aliens.

To establish religious freedom on the broadest bottom.

To emancipate all slaves born after passing the act. The bill reported by the revisers does not itself contain this proposition; but an amendment containing it was prepared, to be offered to the legislature whenever the bill should be taken up, and further directing, that they should continue with their parents to a certain age, then be brought up, at the public expence, to tillage, arts, or sciences, according to their geniusses, till the females should be eighteen, and the males twenty-one years of age, when they should be colonized to such place as the circumstances of the time should render most proper, sending them out with arms, implements of household and of the handicraft arts, seeds, pairs of the useful domestic animals, &c. to declare them a free and independant people, and extend to them our alliance and protection, till they shall have acquired strength; and to send vessels at the same time to other parts of the world for an equal number of white inhabitants; to induce whom to migrate hither, proper encouragements were to be proposed. It will probably be asked, Why not retain and incorporate the blacks into the state, and thus save the expence of supplying by importation of white settlers, the vacancies they will leave? Deep rooted prejudices entertained by the whites; ten thousand recollections, by the blacks, of the injuries they have sustained; new provocations; the real distinctions which nature has made; and many other circumstances will divide us into parties, and produce convulsions, which will probably never end but in the extermination of our or the other race.

Answers to Questions Propounded by
M. de Meusnier (January 24, 1786)

It has been said, too, that our governments, both federal and particular, want energy; that it is difficult to restrain both individuals and States from committing wrong. This is true, and it is an inconvenience. On the other hand, that energy which absolute governments derive from an armed force, which is the effect of the bayonet constantly held at the breast of every citizen, and which resembles very much the stillness of the grave, must be admitted also to have its inconveniences. We weigh the two together, and like best to submit to the former. Compare the number of wrongs committed with impunity by citizens among us with those committed by the sovereign in other countries, and the last will be found most numerous, most oppressive on the mind, and most degrading of the dignity of man.

A Letter to Edward Carrington*
(Paris, January 16, 1787)

DEAR SIR,— ... The tumults in America,† I expected would have produced in Europe an unfavorable opinion of our political state. But it has not. On the contrary, the small effect of these tumults seems to have given more confidence in the firmness of our governments. The interposition of the people themselves on the side of government has had a great effect on the opinion here. I am persuaded myself that the good sense of the people will always be found to be the best army. They may be led astray for a moment, but will soon correct themselves.

---

*Prominent Virginian who was a member of the Continental Congress.

†The reference is to Shays' Rebellion, an uprising of debt-ridden farmers in Western Massachusetts in September, 1786.

The people are the only censors of their governors: and even their errors will tend to keep these to the true principles of their institution. To punish these errors too severely would be to suppress the only safeguard of the public liberty. The way to prevent these irregular interpositions of the people is to give them full information of their affairs thro' the channel of the public papers, and to contrive that these papers should penetrate the whole mass of the people. The basis of our governments being the opinion of the people, the very first object should be to keep that right; and were it left to me to decide whether we should have a government without newspapers or newspapers without a government, I should not hesitate a moment to prefer the latter. But I should mean that every man should receive those papers and be capable of reading them. I am convinced that those societies (as the Indians) which live without government enjoy in their general mass an infinitely greater degree of happiness than those who live under the European governments. Among the former, public opinion is in the place of law, and restrains morals as powerfully as laws ever did anywhere. Among the latter, under pretence of governing they have divided their nations into two classes, wolves and sheep. I do not exaggerate. This is a true picture of Europe. Cherish therefore the spirit of our people, and keep alive their attention. Do not be too severe upon their errors, but reclaim them by enlightening them. If once they become inattentive to the public affairs, you and I, and Congress and Assemblies, judges and governors shall all become wolves. It seems to be the law of our general nature, in spite of individual exceptions; and experience declares that man is the only animal which devours his own kind, for I can apply no milder term of the governments of Europe, and to the general prey of the rich on the poor. The want of news has led me into disquisition instead of narration, forgetting you have every day enough of that. I shall be happy to hear from you sometimes, only observing that whatever passes thro' the post is read, and that when you write what should be read by myself only, you must be so good as to confide your letter to some passenger or officer of the packet. I will ask your permission to write to you sometimes, and to assure you of the esteem and respect with which I have honour to be Dear Sir your most obedient and most humble servt.

The Federalist No. 33 (January 3, 1788)*

To the People of the State of New York:
The residue of the argument against the provisions of the Constitution in respect to taxation is ingrafted upon the following clause.† The last clause of the eighth section of the first article of the plan under consideration authorizes the national legislature "to make all laws which shall be *necessary* and *proper* for carrying into execution *the powers* by that Constitution vested in the government of the United States, or in any department or officer thereof"; and the second clause of the sixth article declares, "that the Constitution and the laws of the United States made *in pursuance thereof* and the treaties made by their authority shall be the *supreme law* of the land, any thing in the constitution or laws of any State to the contrary notwithstanding."

These two clauses have been the source of much virulent invective and petulant declamation against the proposed Constitution. They have been held up to the people in all the exaggerated colors of misrepresentation as the pernicious engines by which their local governments were to be destroyed and their liberties exterminated; as the hideous monster whose devouring jaws would spare neither sex nor age, nor high nor low, nor sacred nor profane; and yet, strange as it may appear, after all this clamor, to those who may not have happened to contemplate them in the same light, it may be affirmed with perfect confidence that the constitutional operation of the intended government would be precisely the same, if these clauses were entirely obliterated, as if they were repeated in every article. They are only declaratory of a truth which would have resulted by necessary and unavoidable implication from the very act of constituting a federal government, and vesting it with certain specified powers. This is so clear a proposition, that moderation itself can scarcely listen to the railings which have been so copiously vented against this part of the plan, without emotions that disturb its equanimity.

What is a power, but the ability or faculty of doing a thing? What

---

*Alexander Hamilton, 1757-1804. Attended King's College (Columbia University); Revolutionary soldier; author and Secretary of the Treasury in the Washington Administration. One of the original proponents of the Constitutional Convention of 1787, and through his writings (*The Federalists*, 1788) its most important advocate. Hamilton's experiences led him to a brilliant defense of the strong central government thesis which the Constitution intimated.

†This was the point at which No. 31 of the original newspaper essays was divided, and this opening sentence appeared first in the McLean edition of 1788.

is the ability to do a thing, but the power of employing the *means* necessary to its execution? What is a LEGISLATIVE power, but a power of making LAWS? What are the *means* to execute a LEGISLATIVE power, but LAWS? What is the power of laying and collecting taxes, but a *legislative power,* or a power of *making laws,* to lay and collect taxes? What are the proper means of executing such a power, but *necessary* and *proper* laws?

This simple train of inquiry furnishes us at once with a test by which to judge of the true nature of the clause complained of. It conducts us to this palpable truth, that a power to lay and collect taxes must be a power to pass all laws *necessary* and *proper* for the execution of that power; and what does the unfortunate and calumniated provision in question do more than declare the same truth, to wit, that the national legislature, to whom the power of laying and collecting taxes had been previously given, might, in the execution of that power, pass all laws *necessary* and *proper* to carry it into effect? I have applied these observations thus particularly to the power of taxation, because it is the immediate subject under consideration, and because it is the most important of the authorities proposed to be conferred upon the Union. But the same process will lead to the same result, in relation to all other powers declared in the Constitution. And it is *expressly* to execute these powers that the sweeping clause, as it has been affectedly called, authorizes the national legislation to pass all *necessary* and *proper* laws. If there is any thing exceptionable, it must be sought for in the specific powers upon which this general declaration is predicated. The declaration itself, though it may be chargeable with tautology or redundancy, is at least perfectly harmless.

But SUSPICION may ask, Why then was it introduced? The answer is, that it could only have been done for greater caution, and to guard against all cavilling refinements in those who might hereafter feel a disposition to curtail and evade the legitimate authorities of the Union. The Convention probably foresaw, what it has been a principal aim of these papers to inculcate, that the danger which most threatens our political welfare is that the State governments will finally sap the foundations of the Union; and might therefore think it necessary, in so cardinal a point, to leave nothing to construction. Whatever may have been the inducement to it, the wisdom of the precaution is evident from the cry which has been raised against it; as that very cry betrays a disposition to question the great and essential truth which it is manifestly the object of that provision to declare.

But it may be again asked, Who is to judge of the *necessity* and *propriety* of the laws to be passed for executing the powers of the

Union? I answer, first that this question arises as well and as fully upon the simple grant of those powers as upon the declaratory clause; and I answer, in the second place, that the national government, like every other, must judge, in the first instance, of the proper exercise of its powers, and its constituents in the last. If the federal government should overpass the just bounds of its authority and make a tyrannical use of its powers, the people, whose creature it is, must appeal to the standard they have formed, and take such measures to redress the injury done to the Constitution as the exigency may suggest and prudence justify. The propriety of a law, in a constitutional light, must always be determined by the nature of the powers upon which it is founded. Suppose, by some forced constructions of its authority (which, indeed, cannot easily be imagined), the Federal legislature should attempt to vary the law of descent in any State, would it not be evident that, in making such an attempt, it had exceeded its jurisdiction, and infringed upon that of the State? Suppose, again, that upon the pretence of an interference with its revenues, it should undertake to abrogate a land-tax imposed by the authority of a State; would it not be equally evident that this was an invasion of that concurrent jurisdiction in respect to this species of tax, which its Constitution plainly supposes to exist in the State governments? If there ever should be a doubt on this head, the credit of it will be entirely due to those reasoners who, in the impudent zeal of their animosity to the plan of the convention, have labored to envelop it in a cloud calculated to obscure the plainest and simplest truths.

But it is said that the laws of the Union are to be the *supreme law* of the land. But what inference can be drawn from this, or what would they amount to, if they were not to be supreme? It is evident they would amount to nothing. A LAW, by the very meaning of the term, includes supremacy. It is a rule which those to whom it is prescribed are bound to observe. This results from every political association. If individuals enter into a state of society, the laws of that society must be the supreme regulator of their conduct. If a number of political societies enter into a larger political society, the laws which the latter may enact, pursuant to the powers intrusted to it by its constitution, must necessarily be supreme over those societies, and the individuals of whom they are composed. It would otherwise be a mere treaty, dependent on the good faith of the parties, and not a government, which is only another word for POLITICAL POWER AND SUPREMACY. But it will not follow from this doctrine that acts of the larger society which are *not pursuant* to its constitutional powers, but which are invasions of the residuary authorities of the smaller societies, will become the supreme law of the land. These will be merely acts of usurpation, and will deserve to be treated as such. Hence we perceive that the clause which declares the supremacy of the laws of the Union, like the one we have just before considered, only declares a truth, which flows immediately and necessarily from the institution of a federal government. It will not, I presume, have escaped observation, that it *expressly* confines this supremacy to laws made *pursuant to the Constitution;* which I mention merely as an instance of caution in the convention; since that limitation would have been to be understood, though it had not been expressed.

Though a law, therefore, laying a tax for the use of the United States would be supreme in its nature, and could not legally be opposed or controlled, yet a law for abrogating or preventing the collection of a tax laid by the authority of the State (unless upon imports and exports), would not be the supreme law of the land, but a usurpation of power not granted by the Constitution. As far as an improper accumulation of taxes on the same object might tend to render the collection difficult or precarious, this would be a mutual inconvenience, not arising from a superiority or defect of power on either side, but from an injudicious exercise of power by one or the other, in a manner equally disadvantageous to both. It is to be hoped and presumed, however, that mutual interest would dictate a concert in this respect which would avoid any material inconvenience. The inference from the whole is, that the individual States would, under the proposed Constitution, retain an independent and uncontrollable authority to raise revenue to any extent of which they may stand in need, by every kind of taxation, except duties on imports and exports. It will be shown in the next paper that this CONCURRENT JURISDICTION in the article of taxation was the only admissible substitute for an entire subordination, in respect to this branch of power, of the State authority to that of the Union. —PUBLIUS

The Federalist No. 27 (December 25, 1787)

To the People of the State of New York:
It has been urged, in different shapes, that a Constitution of the kind proposed by the convention cannot operate without the aid of a mili-

tary force to execute its laws. This, however, like most other things that have been alleged on that side, rests on mere general assertion, unsupported by any precise or intelligible designation of the reasons upon which it is founded. As far as I have been able to divine the latent meaning of the objectors, it seems to originate in a presupposition that the people will be disinclined to the exercise of federal authority in any matter of an internal nature. Waiving any exception that might be taken to the inaccuracy or inexplicitness of the distinction between internal and external, let us inquire what ground there is to presuppose that disinclination of the people. Unless we presume at the same time that the powers of the general government will be worse administered than those of the State government, there seems to be no room for the presumption of ill-will, disaffection, or opposition in the people. I believe it may be laid down as a general rule that their confidence in and obedience to a government will commonly be proportioned to the goodness or badness of its administration. It must be admitted that there are exceptions to this rule; but these exceptions depend so entirely on accidental causes, that they cannot be considered as having any relation to the intrinsic merits or demerits of a constitution. These can only be judged of by general principles and maxims.

Various reasons have been suggested, in the course of these papers, to induce a probability that the general government will be better administered than the particular governments: the principal of which reasons are that the extension of the spheres of election will present a greater option, or latitude of choice, to the people; that through the medium of the State legislatures—which are select bodies of men, and which are to appoint the members of the national Senate—there is reason to expect that this branch will generally be composed with peculiar care and judgment; that these circumstances promise greater knowledge and more extensive information in the national councils, and that they will be less apt to be tainted by the spirit of faction, and more out of the reach of those occasional ill-humors, or temporary prejudices and propensities, which, in smaller societies, frequently contaminate the public councils, beget injustice and oppression of a part of the community, and engender schemes which, though they gratify a momentary inclination or desire, terminate in general distress, dissatisfaction, and disgust. Several additional reasons of considerable force, to fortify that probability, will occur when we come to survey, with a more critical eye, the interior structure of the edifice which we are invited to erect. It will be sufficient here to remark, that until satisfactory reasons can be assigned to justify an opinion, that the federal government is likely to be administered in such a manner as to render its odious or contemptible to the people, there can be no reasonable foundation for the supposition that the laws of the Union will meet with any greater obstruction from them, or will stand in need of any other methods to enforce their execution, than the laws of the particular members.

The hope of impunity is a strong incitement to sedition; the dread of punishment, a proportionably strong discouragement to it. Will not the government of the Union, which, if possessed of a due degree of power, can call to its aid the collective resources of the whole Confederacy, be more likely to repress the *former* sentiment and to inspire the *latter,* than that of a single State, which can only command the resources within itself? A turbulent faction in a State may easily suppose itself able to contend with the friends to the government in that State; but it can hardly be so infatuated as to imagine itself a match for the combined efforts of the Union. If this reflection be just, there is less danger of resistance from irregular combinations of individuals to the authority of the Confederacy than to that of a single member.

I will, in this place, hazard an observation, which will not be the less just because to some it may appear new; which is, that the more the operations of the national authority are intermingled in the ordinary exercise of government, the more the citizens are accustomed to meet with it in the common occurrences of their political life, the more it is familiarized to their sight and to their feelings, the further it enters into those objects which touch the most sensible chords and put in motion the most active springs of the human heart, the greater will be the probability that it will conciliate the respect and attachment of the community. Man is very much a creature of habit. A thing that rarely strikes his senses will generally have but little influence upon his mind. A government continually at a distance and out of sight can hardly be expected to interest the sensations of the people. The inference is, that the authority of the Union, and the affections of the citizens towards it, will be strengthened, rather than weakened, by its extension to what are called matters of internal concern; and will have less occasion to recur to force, in proportion to the familiarity and comprehensiveness of its agency. The more it circulates through those channels and currents in which the passions of mankind naturally flow, the less will it require the aid of the violent and perilous expedients of compulsion.

One thing, at all events, must be evident, that a government like the one proposed would bid much fairer to avoid the necessity of using force, than that species of league contended for by most of its opponents; the authority of which should only operate upon the States in their political or collective capacities. It has been shown that in such a

Confederacy there can be no sanction for the laws but force; that frequent delinquencies in the members are the natural offspring of the very frame of the government; and that as often as these happen, they can only be redressed, if at all, by war and violence.

The plan reported by the convention, by extending the authority of the federal head to the individual citizens of the several States, will enable the government to employ the ordinary magistracy of each, in the execution of its laws. It is easy to perceive that this will tend to destroy, in the common apprehension, all distinction between the sources from which they might proceed; and will give the federal government the same advantage for securing a due obedience to its authority which is enjoyed by the government of each State, in addition to the influence on public opinion which will result from the important consideration of its having power to call to its assistance and support the resources of the whole Union. It merits particular attention in this place, that the laws of the Confederacy, as to the *enumerated* and *legitimate* objects of its jurisdiction, will become the SUPREME LAW of the land; to the observance of which all officers, legislative, executive, and judicial, in each State, will be bound by the sanctity of an oath. Thus the legislatures, courts, and magistrates, of the respective members, will be incorporated into the operations of the national government *as far as its just and constitutional authority extends;* and will be rendered auxiliary to the enforcement of its laws. Any man who will pursue, by his own reflections, the consequences of this situation, will perceive that there is good ground to calculate upon a regular and peaceable execution of the laws of the Union, if its powers are administered with a common share of prudence. If we will arbitrarily suppose the contrary, we may deduce any inferences we please from the supposition; for it is certainly possible, by an injudicious exercise of the authorities of the best government that ever was, or ever can be instituted, to provoke and precipitate the people into the wildest excesses. But though the adversaries of the proposed Constitution should presume that the national rulers would be insensible to the motives of public good, or to the obligations of duty, I would still ask them how the interests of ambition, or the views of encroachment, can be promoted by such a conduct?

—PUBLIUS

The Jacksonian Period

6

Orestes Brownson,
        Notes on "The Democratic Principle"
        The Laboring Classes
        Democracy and Liberty

James Fenimore Cooper,
        from *The American Democrat*

The following chapter, "The Jacksonian Period," is a reaffirmation of the democratic equality envisioned by earlier authors. The arguments now become those of form and content. For authors such as Orestes Brownson, democracy is redefined as a goal, as a principle which strives toward the moral, physical, and intellectual freedom of the people. James Cooper recognizes the need for government but suggests that democracy is only less imperfect than other forms.

Notes on "The Democratic Principle" (1873)*

. . . We hold that whatever constitutional or organic provisions may be adopted, the stronger interest of a country, in the absence of all recognition of the law of nations, limiting and defining the rights and powers of the nation, will govern the country, whether the interest and pursuits of the numerical majority or not; or at least dictate the policy of its government. . . .

The Laboring Classes (1840)†

Now the great work for this age and the coming is to raise up the laborer, and to realize in our own social arrangements, and in the actual condition of all men, that equality between man and man, which God has established between the rights of one and those of another. In other words, our business is to emancipate the proletaries, as the past has emancipated the slaves. This is our work. There must be no class of our fellow men doomed to toil through life as mere workmen at wages. If wages are tolerated it must be, in the case of the individual operative, only under such conditions that by the time he is of a proper age to settle in life, he shall have accumulated enough to be an independent laborer on his own capital,—on his own farm or in his own shop. Here is our work. How is it to be done?

Reformers in general answer this question, or what they deem its equivalent, in a manner which we cannot but regard as very unsatisfactory. They would have all men wise, good, and happy; but in order to make them so, they tell us that we want not external changes, but internal; and therefore instead of declaiming against society and seek-

---

Orestes Augustus Brownson, 1803–1876. Attended Norwich Academy; ordained Universalist minister but was converted to Catholicism in 1844. An editor for most of his adult life, his major political treatise was published in 1865, *The American Republic; Its Constitution, Tendencies and Destiny*. The most consistent issue with which Brownson was concerned was the tension between social classes—and particularly the condition of what he referred to as the wage slave— the working class. This selection from *Selected Essays*, Russell Kirk, ed., *Quarterly Review*, April, 1873.

†Orestes Brownson, (from *Boston Quarterly*, July, 1840), reprinted in *The Brownson Reader*, Alvin S. Ryan, ed.

ing to disturb existing social arrangements, we should confine ourselves to the individual reason and conscience; seek merely to lead the
individual to repentance, and to reformation of life; make the individual
a practical, a truly religious man, and all evils will either disappear, or
be sanctified to the spiritual growth of the soul. . . .

For our part, we yield to none in our reverence for science and
religion; but we confess that we look not for the regeneration of the
race from priests and pedagogues. They have had a fair trial. They
cannot construct the temple of God. They cannot conceive its plan, and
they know not how to build. They daub with untempered mortar, and
the walls they erect tumble down if so much as a fox attempt to go up
thereon. In a word, they always league with the people's masters, and
seek to reform without disturbing the social arrangements which
render reform necessary. They would change the consequents without
changing the antecedents, secure to men the rewards of holiness, while
they continue their allegiance to the devil. We have no faith in priests
and pedagogues. They merely cry peace, peace, and that too when there
is no peace, and can be none. . . .

But what shall government do? Its first doing must be an *undoing*.
There has been thus far quite too much government, as well as government of the wrong kind. The first act of government we want is a still
further limitation of itself. It must begin by circumscribing within
narrower limits its powers. And then it must proceed to repeal all laws
which bear against the laboring classes, and then to enact such laws
as are necessary to enable them to maintain their equality. We have no
faith in those systems of elevating the working classes, which propose
to elevate them without calling in the aid of the government. We must
have government, and legislation expressly directed to this end.

Democracy and Liberty (1843)*

The great end with all men in their religious, their political, and
their individual actions, is FREEDOM. The perfection of our nature is in
being able "to look into the perfect law of liberty," for liberty is only

---

*Orestes Brownson, (from *Democratic Review*, April, 1843), reprinted in *The
Brownson Reader, ibid.*

another name for power. The measure of my ability is always the exact measure of my freedom. The glory of humanity is in proportion to its freedom. Hence, humanity always applauds him who labors in right-down earnest to advance the cause of freedom. . . .

Democracy, in our judgment, has been wrongly defined to be a *form* of government; it should be understood of the *end*, rather than of the *means*, and be regarded as a principle rather than a form. The end we are to aim at, is the freedom and progress of all men, especially of the poorest and most numerous class. He is a democrat who goes for the highest moral, intellectual, and physical elevation of the great mass of the people, especially of the laboring population, in distinction from a special devotion to the interests and pleasures of the wealthier, more refined, or more distinguished few. But the means by which this elevation is to be obtained, are not necessarily the institution of the purely democratic form of government. . . .

from *The American Democrat* (1838)*

Political systems ought to be, and usually are, framed on certain great and governing principles. These principles cannot be perverted, or lost sight of, without perverting, or rendering nugatory the system itself; and, under a popular government, in an age like this, far more is to be apprehended from indirect attacks on the institutions, than from those which are direct. It is usual to excuse these departures from the right on the plea of human propensities, but human institutions are framed expressly to curb such propensities, and no truth is more salutary than that which is contained in the homely saying, that "law makers should not be law breakers." . . .

We do not adopt the popular polity because it is perfect, but be-

---

*James Fenimore Cooper, 1789-1851. Attended Yale University; midshipman 1808-1811; prolific author of popular titles. Two important political contributions were *Notions of the Americans* (1828), and *The American Democrat* (1838). It is interesting that while Cooper was essentially defending the position of a landowning class against the growing influence of a mercantilist class, he argued for the extension of suffrage and was opposed to the property requirements for voting then extant, the "stake in society" principle. This selection from *The American Democrat*, 1838 (New York: Alfred A. Knopf, 1931).

cause it is less imperfect than any other. As man, by his nature, is liable to err, it is vain to expect an infallible whole that is composed of fallible parts. The government that emanates from a single will, supposing that will to be pure, enlightened, impartial, just and consistent, would be the best in the world, were it attainable for men. Such is the government of the universe, the result of which is perfect harmony. . . .

Aristocracies have a facility in combining measures for their interests that is not enjoyed by democracies. The power being in the hands of a few, these few can act with a despatch and energy, which, though unequaled by those of a monarchy, commonly have the material advantage of better agents. In an aristocracy, influence among the aristocrats themselves depending chiefly on the manly qualities, history shows us that the public agents are usually more chosen for their services than in a monarchy, where the favor of the prince is the chief requisite for success; it may therefore be assumed that the higher qualities of those who fill the public trusts, in an aristocracy, more than neutralize the greater concentration of a monarchy, and render it the most efficient form of government, for the purposes of conquest and foreign policy, that is known. Aristocracy has an absorbing quality, if such a term may be used, by which the active and daring of conquered territories, are induced to join the conquerors, in order to share in the advantages of the system. . . .

No expedients can equalize the temporal lots of men; for without civilization and government, the strong would oppress the weak, and, with them, an inducement to exertion must be left, by bestowing rewards on talents, industry and success. All that the best institutions, then, can achieve, is to remove useless obstacles, and to permit merit to be the artisan of its own fortune, without always degrading demerit to the place it ought naturally to fill. . . .

The terms liberty, equality, right and justice, used in a political sense, are merely terms of convention, and of comparative excellence, there being no such thing, in practice, as either these qualities being carried out purely, according to the abstract notions of theories.

The Turn of the Century 7

Woodrow Wilson,
> The Liberation of a People's Vital Energies

Richard T. Ely,
> Social Aspects of Christianity

William Graham Sumner,
> Liberty and Responsibility
> Advancing Social and Political Organizations in the United States
> Democracy and Modern Problems
> Republican Government

The government remains the focus of reformers and those anxious to preserve the freedom of the masses. No longer do we find spokesmen who challenge the need for social organization or rationalize the human condition beyond what exists. Woodrow Wilson sees freedom guaranteed in a mechanistic adjustment of human activities (government) and human energies (goals). During this same period authors such as Richard Ely propose that the system of moral values lies not in the individual, but in society. Writing near the end of the last century, it is William Sumner who synthesizes the philosophical strains of the American experience when he advocates liberty—the opportunity for Man to actualize his identity—as the greatest civil good, and civil liberty as a matter of law and institutions. The increasingly differentiated society leads to more complex political forms and consequently to a republic whose aim becomes not equality, but civil liberty. According to Sumner, democracy which teaches political dogma is the enemy of the constitutional republic.

The Liberation of a People's
Vital Energies (1913)*

What is liberty? You say of the locomotive that it runs free. What do you mean? You mean that its parts are so assembled and adjusted that friction is reduced to a minimum, and that it has perfect adjustment. . . . Human freedom consists in perfect adjustments of human interests and human activities and human energies.

Now, the adjustments necessary between individuals, between individuals and the complex institutions amidst which they live, and between those institutions and the government, are infinitely more intricate to-day than ever before. . . . Life has become complex; there are many more elements, more parts, to it than ever before. And, therefore, it is harder to keep everything adjusted,—and harder to find out where the trouble lies when the machine gets out of order.

You know that one of the interesting things that Mr. Jefferson said in those early days of simplicity which marked the beginnings of our government was that the best government consisted in as little governing as possible. And there is still a sense in which that is true. It is still intolerable for the government to interfere with our individual activities except where it necessary to interfere with them in order to free them. But I feel confident that if Jefferson were living in our day he would see what we see: that the individual is caught in a great confused nexus of all sorts of complicated circumstances, and that to let him alone is to leave him helpless as against the obstacles with which he has to contend, and that, therefore, law in our day must come to the assistance of the individual. It must come to his assistance to see that he gets fair play; that is all, but that is much. Without the watchful interference, the resolute interference, of the government, there can be no fair play between individuals and such powerful institutions as the trusts. Freedom to-day is something more than being let alone. The program of a government of freedom must in these days be positive, not negative merely. . . .

I believe in human liberty as I believe in the wine of life. There is no salvation for men in the pitiful condescensions of industrial masters.

---

*Woodrow T. Wilson, 1856-1924. Graduated Princeton University 1889; political scientist; 28th President of the United States (1913-1921). That government should be sensitive to the voices of public opinion was central to Wilson's philosophy. He became, during his first campaign for office, the leading spokesman of American liberalism. Not a radical in any sense of the term, Wilson sought to return equality to the common man. This selection from "The New Freedom" (1913), in A. T. Mason, *Free Government in the Making*, (3d Ed.; New York: Oxford University Press, 1965).

Guardians have no place in a land of freemen. Prosperity guaranteed by trustees has no prospect of endurance. Monopoly means the atrophy of enterprise. If monopoly persists, monopoly will always sit at the helm of the government. I do not expect to see monopoly restrain itself. If there are men in this country big enough to own the government of the United States, they are going to own it; what we have to determine now is whether we are big enough, whether we are men enough, whether we are free enough, to take possession again of the government which is our own.

I do not believe that America is securely great because she has great men in her now. America is great in proportion as she can make sure of having great men in the next generation. She is rich in her unborn children; rich, that is to say, if those unborn children see the sun in a day of opportunity, see the sun when they are free to exercise their energies as they will. If they open their eyes in a land where there is no special privilege, then we shall come into a new era of American greatness and American liberty; but if they open their eyes in a country where they must be employees or nothing, if they open their eyes in a land of merely regulated monopoly, where all the conditions of industry are determined by small groups of men, then they will see an America such as the founders of this Republic would have wept to think of. . . .

Since their day the meaning of liberty has deepened. But it has not ceased to be a fundamental demand of the human spirit, a fundamental necessity for the life of the soul. And the day is at hand when it shall be realized on this consecrated soil,—a New Freedom,—a Liberty widened and deepened to match the broadened life of man in modern America. . . .

Social Aspects of Christianity (1889)*

It may be well . . . to point out the fact that the ethical conception of political economy harmonizes with recent tendencies in ethics. The

---

*Richard T. Ely, 1854-1943. Graduated Columbia University 1876; teacher and economist; a founder of the American Economic Association in 1885. Although educated in economics Ely was a man of strong religious convictions. This did not deter him, however, from criticizing classical economics or from preaching socialism, an economic philosophy not widely popular in this country then or now. This selection from *Social Aspects of Christianity* (New York: Thomas Y. Crowell and Company, 1889).

older ethical systems may, I think, be called individual. The perfection
of the individual, or the worthiness of the individual, to use another
expression, was the end proposed. Moral excellence of a single person
was considered as something which might exist by itself, and need not
bear any relation to one's fellows. Men were treated as units, and not
as members of a body. The new tendency of which I speak, however,
proceeds from the assumption that society is an organism, and that the
individual is a part of a larger whole. Rudolph von Ihering develops
this idea in the first two volumes of his *Zweck im Recht.* The source of
ethics he finds in society; the end of ethics likewise is discovered in
society; and from society, according to this theory, is derived the ethical
motive power which resides in the human will. Social ethics thus replaces individual ethics.

Liberty and Responsibility (1889)*

... I have now arrived at the point where the true idea of liberty, as
the greatest civil good, can be brought forward. The link between
liberty and responsibility can be established and upheld only by law;
for this reason, civil liberty, the only real liberty which is possible or
conceivable on earth, is a matter of law and institutions. It is not meta-
physical at all. Civil liberty is really a great induction from all the
experience of mankind in the use of civil institutions; it must be defined,
not in terms drawn from metaphysics, but in terms drawn from history
and law. It is not an abstract conception; it is a series of concrete facts.
These facts go to constitute a status—the status of a freeman in a
modern jural state. It is a product of institutions; it is embodied in
institutions; it is guaranteed by institutions. It is not a matter of resolu-

---

William Graham Sumner, 1840-1910. Graduated Yale University 1863; ordained
priest 1869, Protestant Episcopal Church; Yale professor beginning 1872 and for
the remainder of his life. A copious writer in the fields of education and the social
sciences, he is most widely known as the primary American exponent of social
Darwinism. Applied to politics, social Darwinism becomes "laissez-faire" or limited government. This selection from *The Independent* (November 21, 1889), in
Sumner Today, Maurice R. Davie, ed. (New Haven: Yale University Press, 1940).

tions, or "declarations," as they seemed to think in the last century. It is unfriendly to dogmatism. It pertains to what a man shall do, have, and be. It is unfriendly to all personal control, to officialism, to administrative philanthropy and administrative wisdom, as much as to bureaucratic despotism or monarchical absolutism. It is hostile to all absolutism, and people who are well-trained in the traditions of civil liberty are quick to detect absolutism in all its new forms. Those who have lost the traditions of civil liberty accept phrases.

Advancing Social and Political
Organization in America (1896)*

. . . Thus the whole of this country, until the beginning of the eighteenth century, presented the picture of the loosest and most scattered human society which is consistent with civilization at all, and there were not lacking phenomena of a positive decline of civilization and gravitation towards the life of the Indians. Political organization scarcely existed and civil organization was but slight. Later generations have condemned and ridiculed the religious bigotry of the colonists with its attendant religious persecution and the political ostracism of all but the ruling sect; but if this strong religious sympathy had not existed, what associative principle would they have had to hold them together and build up a civil society?

I have said that the picture presented by the settlements in this country until the beginning of the eighteenth century was that of little groups of farmers scattered along the coast and rivers, forming towns under the loosest possible organization. Names such as Massachusetts, Connecticut, were used then to cover areas very great as compared with the amount of land under cultivation. Those names had very little meaning to the people of that time, for life and its interests were bounded by the town. Only in the eighteenth century can we see the

---

*William Graham Sumner, in *Essays of William Graham Sumner*, Vol. II, Albert Galloway Keller and Maurice R. Davie, eds. (New Haven: Yale University Press, 1934).

horizon extend so that the province grows to be the real civil unit and grows into a real commonwealth; the process was slow, however, and for the most part unwilling. In the nineteenth century the conception of the national and civil unit has expanded so that our sense of nationality cleaves to the Union as a great confederated state. This advance in the feeling of the people as to what the country to which they belong is, and what that is which is the object of patriotism, is one of the interesting developments of our history. The merging of the town into the state and of the state into the United States has been brought about by the increase of population, the filling up of the country, the multiplication of interests reaching out all over it and grappling the people together. The bonds are those of kin, of industry and commerce, of religion through the various denominations and churches, of common pursuits in education, science, and art, and of associations for various purposes of culture or pleasure. This is what we mean by the advancing social organization. It unites us into a whole; it forms us into a society; it gives us sentiments of association and co-operation. Our states, instead of being separate bodies united only by neighborhood and alliance, are formed into one body with nerves running through it; and it is by virtue of these nerves, that is, of the lines of common feeling and interest which I have mentioned, that a touch at one point brings out a reaction from the whole.

There are other causes which are always at work in the contrary direction. They are the forces of discord and divergent interest. In a state of seventy million people scattered over a continent the forces of disruption are always at work. The great social organization all the time tends to promote a great political organization; as the interests multiply and become complex, there is a call for federal legislation in order to get uniformity, *e.g.*, as to marriage, divorce, bankruptcy. The laws also get extensions from use and new application, the effects of which in a few years amaze us by their magnitude and importance, as, for example, the Interstate Commerce Law. Now all this extension, systematization, and uniformity-making produces symmetry, order, and elegance, but it goes with the old terror of our statesmen—consolidation. It is making of us a great empire. Few people, even of those who have lived through it, seem to notice the great change which has come over our federal system since the Civil War. The most important alteration is that in the feeling of the people about what sort of a government there is at Washington—what it is and what it can do. . . .

Democracy and Modern Problems (1889)*

Renunciation is not agreeable to any body or person, but I have expressed the opinion that democracy ought to renounce; that its prosperity and success depend upon renunciation. This needs some explanation and illustration.

In another form the same idea has often been enunciated. If we want a free government we must be content to forego a great many fine things which other civil forms might get for us. A "free government," under the democratic republican form, first of all renounces all the ceremonial and pageantry of the aristocratic or monarchical form; that is of little importance, although perhaps we assume too easily that the poetic and imaginative element is absent from a democratic community. But a democratic republic will never be neat, trim, and regular in its methods, or in the external appearance which it presents; it will certainly lack severity and promptitude of operation. A great many things are sure to be left at loose ends; in a word, there is sure to be little discipline. There is a lounging air, a lack of formality, an exaggerated horror of red tape, a neglect of regularity.

Beyond this, however, and more important, is the fact that there are important functions which older forms of the state have been accustomed to perform, which the democratic republic cannot well perform: it cannot make war without great waste and expense, both of life and money; it cannot do any work which requires high and strict organization, and do it well—if it tries to do work of that kind, it does it only at great expense, and under great waste. Germany is the best drilled and disciplined state of modern times, while the United States is the leading example of a democratic republic. The judgments of these two countries about each other, and their influence on each other, are among the most remarkable facts in modern life. The judgments of Germans generally on the United States are those of the men accustomed to an administrative system which works accurately and promptly, also pedantically and cheaply, on a system which is inaccurate and unprompt, and is not cheap; they are accustomed to respect state action, to believe in it, and to rely upon it; with a population trained to respond at the tap of the drum, uneducated to individual initiative, and with a bureaucracy of long tradition and intense training, the state may present itself as an entity of a different sort,

---

*William Graham Sumner, *The Independent* (March 28, 1889), in Keller & Davie, *op. cit.*

and an agent of different power from the American State. The question then is, whether we can draw any inferences as to state functions from Germany, or whether we should be willing to see the American State undergo those changes which it would have to undergo in order to fit it to undertake all the functions which are undertaken by the German State.

This question needs only to be stated to answer itself. The especial changes which the American State would have to undergo would be to weaken democracy and to strengthen bureaucracy. These are the two changes which would be the most impossible of all which could be attempted. It is much more probable that democracy will sweep away all the bulrushes in the shape of "monarchical institutions" which are being built up against it, and, seizing upon the military organization and the state socialistic institutions as at once its prey and its instrumentalities, will triumph over everything else, in Germany as well as elsewhere.

If we turn back, then, to the free democratic state as the state of the present and future, the one which is alone possible for us and which must go on to meet and work out its destiny, then I think it will appear that its civil service is its weakest point. The recent history of the French Republic, joined with our own, has gone far to show that a republican system with party government is drawn toward the abuse of the civil service by forces which it is folly to underestimate. One must shut one's eyes to facts if one would deny that the sentiments "I am a Democrat," "this is a Republican Administration," strike a responsive chord in the hearts of the masses, where denunciations of the corruption of the civil service, or of wasteful expenditures of public money, fall on dull ears. These watchwords, however, are only the doctrines: "To the victor belong the spoils," and "Woe to the vanquished," in a little less cynical and shocking form, and they mean that, in the modern democratic state, parties fight each other for control of the state, which they rule, having won it, like a conquered territory. If this state, then, has state-socialistic functions, it is sure to produce the worst exploitation of man by man which has ever existed; to live under it, and not be in it, would be to suffer a tyranny such as no one has experienced yet.

Republican Government (1889)*

I beg leave here to emphasize the distinction between a democracy and a republic because the people of the United States, living in a democratic republic, almost universally confuse the two elements of their system. Each, however, must stand or fall by itself. Louis Napoleon gave the French democracy, under his own despotism; France is now called a republic although MacMahon was never voted for on a popular vote. If the principle of equality is what we aim at we can probably get it—we can all be equally slaves together. If we want majority rule, we can have it—the majority can pass a *plébiscite* conferring permanent power on a despot. A republic is quite another thing. It is a form of self-government, and its first aim is not equality but civil liberty. It keeps the people active in public functions and public duties; it requires their activity at stated periods when the power of the state has to be re-conferred on new agents. It breaks the continuity of power to guard against its abuse, and it abhors as much the irresponsible power of the many as of the one. It surrounds the individual with safeguards by its permanent constitutional provisions, and by no means leaves the individual or the state a prey to the determination of a numerical majority. In our system the guarantees to liberty and the practical machinery of self-government all come from the constitutional republic; the dangers chiefly from democracy. Democracy teaches dogmas of absolute and sweeping application, while, in truth, there are no absolute doctrines in politics. . . .

---

*William Graham Sumner, in Keller & Davie, *op. cit.*

Current Attitudes

8

In this final section we find some contradictions manifest in contemporary society, a product of the dualism which inheres in political theory, a tension between those who maintain the supremacy of positive law over natural right, of forms over ends.

The opening essay by Walter Lippmann admits the need for equalized acting and consenting powers as a necessary condition for the existence of society. The Free Speech Movement (FSM), the "Port Huron Statement" and the poetry of Pam Edwards are more visceral reactions to mass society and dehumanization with the concomitant losses of those liberties guaranteed. Society, accordingly, has stepped away from the liberal tradition, but some actions of the New Left manifest those same authoritarian predilections which are deplored in totalitarian societies generally. The right of individual dissent is obviated by the goals of the organization; consensus democracy is a contradiction. On the other hand, the question of who determines what are the limits of dissent is a searching problem. Carl Oglesby and Michael Harrington, spokesmen for differing facets of the New Left, give voice to sharply opposing viewpoints on how best to achieve the new America they both seek.

In their contributions Stanmeyer and Van Dusen have perhaps taken too literally De Tocqueville's admonition that "the influence of the lawyers in public business must increase in proportion to the power of the people"; however, they speak at least for the "silent majority," when they observe that the equal rights and equal opportunity upon which this country is predicated can exist only under the law. One caveat should be remembered: the existence of institutions of representation and courts of law, important though they may be, is not a sufficient condition to insure liberty and equality in the framework presented.

We close the section with a recent address given by Senator Margaret Chase Smith of Maine, on the occasion of the twentieth anniversary of her noteworthy speech denouncing the evils of McCarthyism. In the speech reprinted here, the Senator warns the nation of the possible perils resulting from the extremism of the New Left, particularly its campus militants. Also included is a retort to the speech from the editorial page of *The New Yorker*.

The Derangement of Powers (1955)*

The Governors and the Governed

When I describe the malady of democratic states as a derangement in the relation between the mass of the people and the government, I am, of course, implying that there is a sound relationship and that we should be able to know what it is. We must now examine this assumption. We are looking into the relation between, on the one hand, the governing or executive power, and, on the other hand, the elected assembly and the voters in the constitutencies. The best place to begin is in the simple beginnings of our constitutional development—in the medieval English Parliament—before the essential functions and their relations had become complicated by their later development.

No relationship, sound or unsound, could exist until the functions of execution and representation had become differentiated. In primitive societies they are not differentiated. Under the Norman and Angevin rulers the differentiation had not yet occurred. These rulers "judged and legislated as well as administered."[†] But by the thirteenth century the differentiation is already visible, and the essential relation in which we are interested can be recognized. There is a writ issued under Henry III in 1254, summoning Parliament. The sheriff of each county is ordered to "cause to come before the King's Council two good and discreet Knights of the Shire, whom the men of the county shall have chosen for this purpose in the stead of all and of each of them, to consider along with knights of other shires what aid they will grant the King."[‡]

Let us note the dualism. There is the government, which means the

---

*Walter Lippmann, 1889-   . Graduated Harvard University 1910. Writer and occasional political advisor. Among the more well-known works of the author are: *A Preface to Politics* (1913); *Public Opinion* (1922); and *Essays in the Public Philosophy* (1955). A central theme with which Lippmann has been concerned is the need for order in democratic society. According to Lippmann, the public philosophy is the overriding claim of society from which order is created. It is a philosophy which is discovered by any rational mind. This selection from *The Public Philosophy* (Boston: Little, Brown and Company, 1955), copyright 1955, by Walter Lippmann.

[†]A. F. Pollard, *The Evolution of Parliament* (London: Longmans, Green & Co., 1926), p. 240.

[‡]*Encyclopedia Britannica* (1952), Vol. 19, p. 164, article "Representation."

King and his Council of prelates and peers. Then there are the Knights of the Shires, representing the men of the counties. They are to meet, and the King will ask the Knights what aid they will grant to him. This is the basic relationship. The government can act. Because it can act, it decides what action should be taken, and it proposes the measures; it then asks the representatives of those who must supply the money and the men for the means to carry out its decisions. The governed, through their representatives, the two Knights of the Shire from each county, give or withhold their consent.

From the tension and the balance of the two powers—that of the ruler and that of the ruled—there evolved the written and the unwritten contracts of the constitution. The grant of aid by the ruled must be preceded by the ruler's redress of their grievances. The government will be refused the means of governing if it does not listen to the petitions, if it does not inform, if it does not consult, if it cannot win the consent of, those who have been elected as the representatives of the governed.

The executive is the active power in the state, the asking and the proposing power. The representative assembly is the consenting power, the petitioning, the approving and the criticizing, the accepting and the refusing power. The two powers are necessary if there is to be order and freedom. But each must be true to its own nature, each limiting and complementing the other. The government must be able to govern and the citizens must be represented in order that they shall not be oppressed. The health of the system depends upon the relationship of the two powers. If either absorbs or destroys the functions of the other power, the constitution is deranged.

There is here a relationship between governors and governed which is, I would contend, rooted in the nature of things. At the risk of reasoning by analogy, I would suggest that this duality of function within a political society has a certain resemblance to that of the two sexes. In the act of reproduction each sex has an unalterable physiological function. If this function is devitalized or is confused with the function of the other sex, the result is sterility and disorder.

FSM's Joy to U.C.—Free Speech Carols (1964)*

I

Oski dolls, Pompom girls, U.C. all the
    way.
Oh, what fun it is to have your mind
    reduced to clay.
Civil rights, politics, just get in the way.
Questioning authority when you should
    obey.

Sleeping on the lawn
In a double sleeping bag
Doesn't get things done—
Freedom is a drag.

Junk your principles
Don't stand up and fight
You won't get democracy
If you yell all night.

II

U. C. Administration
Your clumsy punchcard mind
Has put your back against the wall
And tied you in a bind.

Paul Jacobs, born in New York City in 1918 and educated in New York public schools. A frequent contributor to many magazines, Mr. Jacobs is the author of *Is Curly Jewish?* and the *State of the Unions*. Mr. Jacobs has served on the staff of the Center for the Study of Democratic Institutions, and was associated with the Center for the Study of Law and Society at the University of California.

Saul Landau was an editor of *Studies on the Left* (1959-1967) and a staff reporter for *Ramparts* magazine.

This selection from "The Free Speech Movement" in Paul Jacobs and Saul Landau, *The New Radicals* (New York: Vintage Books, 1966).

"In the spirit of farce and of Christmas, these songs were written and sung. We of the FSM are serious, but we hope we are still able to laugh at ourselves, as well as those who would restrict our Constitutional freedoms."
Those lines from the liner notes of the record Joy to U.C.—Free Speech Carols describe part of the University of California at Berkeley Free Speech Movement which received very little attention: its humor. The lyrics to the carols were written by members of the FSM and recorded by The Free Speech Five Plus Four.

Yet in the darkness shineth
An Oakland Cop's flashlight
To strengthen all your arguments
And prove your cause is right.

III. It belongs to the University

On the first of semester
The dean said to me:
   It belongs to the University
On the second of semester
The dean said to me:
   No bumper stickers, it belongs . . .
3rd Don't ask for members
4th Don't collect money
5th NO civil rights
6th NO organizing
7th NO mounting action
8th NO demonstrations
9th You'll be suspended
10th We'll call out troopers
11th Maybe we'll bargain
12th Our word is law

The Port Huron Statement (1962)*

. . . We regard *men* as infinitely precious and possessed of unful-
filled capacities for reason, freedom, and love. In affirming these principles we are aware of countering perhaps the dominant conceptions
of man in the twentieth century: that he is a thing to be manipulated,
and that he is inherently incapable of directing his own affairs. We

---

*From "The Free Speech Movement" in Paul Jacobs and Saul Landau, *The New
Radicals* (New York: Vintage Books, 1966). Of the many new organizations
constituting the "Radical Left", one of the first in time was the Students for a
Democratic Society (SDS). Born originally in 1960 as an integral part of the
League for Industrial Democracy, it broke off in 1962 and formed a separatist
group whose policies and ideology were set forth in The Port Huron Statement.
The bulk of the statement is generally attributed to Tom Hayden, and is essentially a critique of middle-class intellectual (read "Liberal") politics in America,
containing, as well, a series of guidelines for a new radical politics.

oppose the depersonalization that reduces human beings to the status of things—if anything, the brutalities of the twentieth century teach that means and ends are intimately related, that vague appeals to "posterity" cannot justify the mutilations of the present. We oppose, too, the doctrine of human incompetence because it rests essentially on the modern fact that men have been "competently" manipulated into incompetence—we see little reason why men cannot meet with increasing skill the complexities and responsibilities of their situation, if society is organized not for minority, but for majority, participation in decision-making.

Men have unrealized potential for self-cultivation, self-direction, self-understanding, and creativity. It is this potential that we regard as crucial and to which we appeal, not to the human potentiality for violence, unreason, and submission to authority. The goal of man and society should be human independence: a concern not with image of popularity but with finding a meaning in life that is personally authentic; a quality of mind not compulsively driven by a sense of powerlessness, nor one which unthinkingly adopts status values, nor one which represses all threats to its habits, but one which has full, spontaneous access to present and past experiences, one which easily unites the fragmented parts of personal history, one which openly faces problems which are troubling and unresolved; one with an intuitive awareness of possibilities, an active sense of curiosity, an ability and willingness to learn.

This kind of independence does not mean egotistic individualism—the object is not to have one's way so much as it is to have a way that is one's own. Nor do we deify man—we merely have faith in his potential.

Human relationships should involve fraternity and honesty. Human interdependence is contemporary fact; human brotherhood must be willed, however, as a condition of future survival and as the most appropriate form of social relations. Personal links between man and man are needed, especially to go beyond the partial and fragmentary bonds of function that bind men only as worker to worker, employer to employer, teacher to student, American to Russian. . . .

We would replace power rooted in possession, privilege, or circumstance by power and uniqueness rooted in love, reflectiveness, reason, and creativity. As a *social system* we seek the establishment of a democracy of individual participation, governed by two central aims: that the individual share in those social decisions determining the quality and direction of his life; that society be organized to encourage independence in men and provide the media for their common participation.

Untitled Poem*

Whole land masses
wretching to rid their sanitary countries
of the Revolutionary Mind
Adamant against the Truth spliced
before their scurrying eyes
Grasping shredded social standards
tattered patches of Reason
schedules, dockets, degrees, and condolences
Goose-stepping to the drum and drone of
mutilated mankind.

Mind masticating mouthpieces of hate
puppeted parleying:
nasal notations, anal analyses
redundant reiterations of objectivity.

Objectivity! I will go Mad
before I tame this tongue
to monkey mime.

Looming on their darkness
screeching mouth spitting
thorn torn and bleeding
hollering my sacraments
to their trained ears—barking
at the foreign feel of Truth.

A straight-jacketed caterpillar—
my nation moaned for metamorphoses
Cocooned crying to that democratic mirage
long ago led us
then spit a greasy moat at our feet
that sprouted billion throated vines
of thorn and thistle
and swallowed the drawbridge—
the toll being twice as high

---

*By Pam Edwards, from an unknown Bay Area, California, newspaper.

Revelations of Revolution:
that startled mad joy of day
tossing its meadow mane
leaping green and golden spilling
from the sun
When from concentration camps of chrysallis
     characterizations
the Wings of Freedom rising
                         naked to the noon.

The New Left and the Old Law (1969)*

The arrogance of their pretensions . . . provokes and challenges us to
an inquiry into their foundation. . . . With them defects in wisdom are to
be supplied by the plentitude of force.

—EDMUND BURKE, *Reflections on
the Revolution in France*

Were Edmund Burke alive today, he might consider writing an
American sequel to his book on the French Revolution. For he would
find disturbing parallels between the mad passion in revolutionary
France to destroy concrete values in the name of abstract freedoms and
the rhetoric and techniques of some of our "New Left." He would
wonder why a man who virtually embodies civility and highminded-
ness, George Kennan, should feel constrained to undertake a criticism
of attitudes and conduct which history shows nihilistic and which even
a decade ago would have been beneath serious consideration.[1]

But it may be that history does repeat itself. Certain it is that what
a decade ago was perhaps a chip of ice afloat in a vast ocean has grown
into a sizable iceberg. Although the New Left represents only a tiny
minority of college students and young adults,[2] it is nonetheless true,

William A. Stanmeyer is an associate professor of law at the Georgetown University Law Center. He received his A.B. degree from Xavier University in 1958,
an M.A. in philosophy from Loyola University of Chicago in 1962 and a J.D.
from DePaul University Law School in 1966. He practiced law in Chicago and
taught courses in social philosophy at Loyola before joining the Georgetown
faculty. This selection from *American Bar Association Journal*, Vol. 55 (April
1969), p. 319.

as Mr. Kennan writes, that "tendencies that represent the obsession of only a few may not be without partial appeal . . . to many others." Besides, it is not merely a matter of gross numbers; a militant minority can override the wishes of almost any disorganized majority.[3]

Some lawyers may wonder why a discussion of the rhetoric, tactics and goals of the New Left is relevant to them. The link is law and what we call the rule of law. In the final analysis, we are dealing with the guarantees and highest products of civilization itself—freedom, order and respect for the rights of others—and with an attack—however haphazard, misguided and, one may hope, foredoomed to fail—on those ultimates. We lawyers have society itself as our client. We should attend to legal—and illegal—challenges to that society. The violent wing of the New Left is such a challenge.

The Columbia Attacks Signal a New Strategy

On April 23-30, 1968, student radicals seized and occupied five Columbia University buildings, barred faculty and students from their offices and classrooms, held a dean hostage, made photocopies of the university president's files and committed uncounted acts of property damage—at last triggering a police confrontation engaging nearly 1,000 officers at a price of more than one hundred injured persons. For the nonmilitant students the aftermath was high priced as well: cancellation or postponement of the spring classes for most of the school.[4]

That New Left leaders welcome this disruption is clear from comments such as these from Tom Hayden, one of the founders of Students for a Democratic Society, who took an active part in the Columbia disorders:

> Columbia opened a new tactical stage in the resistance movement which began last fall: from the overnight occupation of buildings to permanent occupation; from mill-ins to the creation of revolutionary committees; from symbolic civil disobedience to barricaded resistance. Not only are these tactics already being duplicated on other campuses, but they are sure to be surpassed by even more militant tactics.
>
> In the future it is conceivable that students will threaten destruction of buildings as a last deterrent to police attacks. [Other tactics might be] raids on the offices of professors doing weapons research. . . .[5]

Besides the well-publicized Columbia take-over, students and other young adults have been busy and imaginative in their crusade to disrupt —and "radically transform"—society through purposeful lawbreaking. Other veiled hints from persons sharing the New Left's vision have urged: arson in schools,[6] burning or blowing up of Government property,[7] dumping and setting garbage afire at subway exits,[8] promoting guerrilla warfare in American cities,[9] techniques of using Molotov cocktails and "thermite bombs"[10] and actual sabotage.[11]

The "Movement": Who Are They?

This partial litany of criminality is adduced to show how serious a threat is the violent wing of the New Left to a society that has committed itself to the rule of law and eschews, as both morally unacceptable and practically counterproductive, the resort to violence to achieve social change. But of itself the litany says nothing about the origins, élan or world view of the violent left or the New Left in general.

It would be a mistake to categorize the antisocial conduct of the radical left in any one of the familiar pigeonholes. It is not a collegiate reaction to tasting the heady wine of freedom, a modern equivalent to goldfish swallowing or spring panty raids. Nor is its criminal aspect induced primarily by protest against subhuman conditions for minority groups. It is not a loose organization of juveniles with perfervid, TV-fed imaginations playing a rough version of cops and robbers. At the level of college disruptions like Columbia's, it is not simply student dissenters trying to reform an archaic and unrepresentative decision-making process. Nor can the New Left be characterized simplistically as a different, amorphous, Communist "front" group: "If we are to understand the New Left, we must think of it in the complex terms in which it exists. To write it off as a purely Communist stimulated movement is both unfair and untrue."[12] What, then, is it?

The New Left includes drop-outs, students and (usually young) teachers who are "alienated" by the hollowness of affluence as they have experienced it; activists sincerely concerned with the sluggishness of civil rights progress; Marxists, existentialists, pacifists, anarchists, draft protesters, dissenters; disciples of C. Wright Mills (*The Power Elite*) and Herbert Marcuse (*One Dimensional Man*). United in their hatred of the "establishment," the "military-industrial complex," or "corporate liberalism," their kaleidoscopic movement reflects now the image of Socrates, now Genghis Khan, sometimes Rousseau and, now and again, Lenin. In his book on the student left, Mr. Kennan aptly called them "rebels without a program."

Variegated and decentralized, the New Left cannot be pigeonholed. Indeed, until its recent propensity toward violence erupted, it could not be subjected to blanket criticism. Disagreement, yes; condemnation, no. Even now—after Berkeley, Columbia and the spreading anarchy on other college campuses—it would be unfair to condemn the radical student movement as a whole because of the violence and criminality of some. The "New Left in general" and the "violent New Left" are related as a whole to one of its parts. The distinction is the difference between dissent and resistance.[13]

But the partisans of resistance—as opposed to "mere" dissent—are growing in numbers. They rationalize their lawlessness by the convenient device of blaming or questioning the law itself. Tom Hayden told the National Commission on the Causes and Prevention of Violence on October 23, 1968: ". . . The activists [found] that . . . the channels merely existed to pacify protest, that the police will be called to enforce an order which, because it is without justice, *is itself unconstitutional.*" He added: "Regardless of police violence or repression, the movement will not go away, but will accelerate, *using any tactics* that seem suitable to stop the Vietnam aggression and begin the process of social change at home. As long as the United States . . . [is] enforcing an unjust order, *it has no right—legal or moral—*to lecture protestors about the tactics which we employ." Their self-conscious goal is to "build a movement of people who have broken with American society *through resistance to authority and law.*"[14]

A New Type of Person: the Ideological Criminal

The violent New Left, those who would instigate guerrilla warfare, who condone or encourage bombings and arson, who premeditate the seizure of private property or forcefully prevent legitimate business or government activities, whose heroes are Che, Mao and Lenin—this violent New Left is unique in American experience. It produces a type of person who can only be called the ideological criminal.* Lawyers, police, public officials—indeed, all of us who realize that the values of a free society are jeopardized by inaction in the face of an epidemic of political crimes—had better study his mentality.

The ideological criminal violates the law for a political purpose. Unlike the traditional lawbreaker, he does not seek any immediate

---

*This shorthand phrase, although technically somewhat imprecise, is useful in characterizing a person whose disrespect for or willingness to break the laws arises from a political-ideological world view. This should not be taken to suggest any prejudgment of a person because of his ideas. Our concern is conduct that is criminal, not the ideas.

return for himself. If he attacks a bank, say, the prime purpose is not to steal money for himself but to destroy or disrupt a symbol of the "power structure." If he holds a dean hostage, it is not for ransom but to discomfort a representative of a despised cog—the university—in the "military-industrial complex."

The ideological criminal seeks maximum publicity for his actions but often does not care whether he attains his alleged goal. This doubly untraditional conduct is explained by the ideologue's duality of purpose: he really has two targets—the "establishment" and the uncommitted onlookers. Thus, in most cases of campus violence, to grant his initial demands does not bring peace. He simply escalates them beyond reason, in order to make a political—as opposed to academic —point. He hopes to trigger a physical "confrontation" that will "radicalize" sympathetic bystanders who are often drawn into the melee, physically injured or shaken up, and so forced to "take sides"—against the "establishment," of course, which harmed them.

The ideological criminal is driven by a vision. The traditional lawbreaker has little time for theory, for his view of the world is largely circumscribed by his immediate experience and structured by the urgency of satisfying immediate needs. But the ideologue starts with a theory of existing social conditions, commits himself to the destruction of political and social evils (as he sees and defines them) and tacks on, in his thinking, the assumption—unverified—that his destructive action will somehow "bring about a better world."

The ideological criminal is part of the "movement." Unlike the traditional lawbreaker, who acted as a loner or as part of small gangs, the criminal ideologue feels a comradeship with his fellow missionaries of a new order throughout the country and even the world. The traditional lawbreaker has little concern for others of his class and draws slight comfort from their successes. The ideological criminal, on the contrary, "does his thing" only after calculating the possible effects on the movement as a whole, and he draws strength from news of success a thousand miles away.

The ideological criminal is self-righteous. He asserts that he follows a higher law. He claims that the present laws of society "lack legitimacy," either because he had no hand in their passage, as if every law from city ordinances prohibiting spontaneous parades to the national draft law should be subject to some kind of popular referendum, or because the law's purpose is to "oppress" some "exploited class" whose plight he has suddenly discovered and bold champion he now is. Some go further and find a moral duty to violate laws that support and express the allegedly corrupted values of a society which must be "rad-

ically restructured," for they vaguely grasp the function of law as a
bulwark of civilization: Breach the wall at enough places and you cap-
ture the city within. Like Moses descending the mountain, the ideologue
has a new law to give. Woe betide those recalcitrant souls who would
contest his authority or resist his mandate.

The ideological criminal has blind confidence in the constructive
power of tearing things down. He is fond of oxymoronic phrases like
"creative destruction" and "repressive tolerance." Confused by mis-
understood slogans drawn from Marx and Lenin, he romantically
opines that "Old societies pregnant with the new can give birth only
when violence is the midwife," or that "Dialectical thinking reveals that
an intrinsically evil society can be smashed only by means which that
society believes evil." Less arcanely, he may assert that "The System
is so bad now that maybe if it's destroyed something good will take its
place."

Blissfully ignorant of the incredible efforts men have put forth
to build political economies that provide a people with abundant material goods and the orderly freedom with which to enjoy them, he
blandly spouts hatred for an economy that lavishes on him more
comforts than earlier societies bestowed on their kings. Endowed with
a social conscience far more acute than that of ordinary mortals and
armed with a "radical analysis" from learned texts by social critics who
themselves never personally experienced the inner workings of the
system they pillory, he sallies forth to "tear down this rotten system"
—although he could not write one page on what will replace it.

But for all his arrogance, the ideological criminal is in many ways
—if one prescinds from his deeds and such superficialities as the way
he usually dresses—an appealing person. Although not very wise, he
often is very intelligent. Although disrespectful of those who disagree
with him, he is frequently most generous, even profligate, in spending
his time, energy and very substance on the causes that engage him.
He is committed—and willing to "go to the barricades" to live that
commitment. His long suit is sincerity.

Nonetheless, he is a threat to law and the values law protects.

Ideological Criminal Destroys Law and Values

It is ironic that today's criminal ideologue spent his nursery days
fighting for "free speech." But in the five years from Berkeley to Columbia a bizarre about-face has occurred: Today's ideologue, whatever
lip service he gives to his early rhetoric, fights against free speech.

College teachers must call off classes, universities terminate research projects, professors discontinue scholarly writing, government officials refuse speaking engagements, Presidential candidates shout down hecklers or yield the rostrum to them—all because the "protesters" disagree. In the ideologue's value scheme, there is no room for others to dissent from his dissent. The First Amendment protection of robust, hearty public discussion is mangled beyond recognition; it becomes a cloak for conduct destroying the very values it would protect. In the name of "free speech" we are all to remain silent—except the ideologue.

A strong case can be made that civilization is—or at least cannot do without—procedural due process. Evidence acquired through unlawful search, involuntary confessions, verdicts by nonimpartial judges and a hundred other shortcuts can at times actually produce a just result. But long ago civilized men realized that these methods will do more harm than good. They knew that procedural safeguards are necessary to achieve justice in the long run, even if in a given case the procedures seem to block the rightful result. They understood that even a rightful end does not legitimatize an unfair means, that "Insistence upon procedural standards . . . is not a technicality," that, as Justice Fortas says, "Constitutional procedure is the heart, conscience and soul of a civilized community." They saw that the chief distinction between a civilization and a jungle is that civilization proscribes certain means to an end. This is as true for the political process as it is for the legal process.

But for the violent New Left, anything goes. There is "no time" to talk; going through proper channels only dissipates the energy of the movement. The ideologue wants due process only when *he* is arrested —otherwise, his response to those who preach civility is "Up against the wall!"*

The implications for the future of the rule of law ought to be obvious. . . .

Nothing in this article should be taken as a blanket defense of the *status quo* or a denial that many American institutions have not come to grips with pressing social problems. Nor do I assert that we who occupy leadership positions have nothing to learn from our student critics.

---

*Mark Rudd, leader of the Columbia student rebellion, quoted in *The National Guardian*, May 11, 1968, explaining his *Kampf* in a letter to Columbia's former president, Grayson Kirk: "Your power is directly threatened, since we will have to destroy that power before we take over. . . . We will have to destroy at times, even violently, in order to end your power and your system. . . ." He adds that this is not nihilism, since it is all for the goals of justice, freedom and socialism.

But while accepting dissent, we must take a stand against "resistance." Some methods of expressing "dissent" are criminal anarchy and cannot be tolerated in a civilized society. However cosmic the evil that is the pretext for violence, violent shortcuts only worsen the problem they purport to solve and crush in a moment the values men struggled a lifetime to create. These truths the violent New Left cannot—or will not—understand.

We must separate the violent ideologues from their misguided followers and deflect the students of good will into more positive outlets for their energies. They must discover the alternatives to destruction. The violent New Left is a phenomenon traditional law enforcement methods alone cannot contain. Although police, courts and jails may prevent anarchy, they do not win over the anarchist's followers. Maintenance of public order is a necessary first step, but it is ultimately insufficient unless someone initiates energetic programs by leadership groups to channel the left's explosiveness into productive outlets and open student minds to the vital necessity of political due process.

This is—or should be—where the legal profession comes in.

FOOTNOTES

1. George Kennan, *Democracy and the Student Left* (1968).

2. This is the conclusion of writers of differing views. In addition to Mr. Kennan, see the favorable view of Newfield, *A Prophetic Minority: The American New Left* (1966), and the unfavorable view of Luce, *The New Left* (1966).

3. Address by Lewis F. Powell, Jr., before the American Association of State Colleges and Universities, November 11, 1968. See also "Report from the Barricades—Rebellion at Columbia," *New Republic*, May 11, 1968.

4. *Crisis at Columbia, Report of the Fact-Finding Commission Appointed to Investigate the Disturbances at Columbia University in April and May 1968* xv (Vintage paperback ed. 1968). See "Campus or Battleground? Columbia Is a Warning to All Americans," *Barron's*, May 20, 1968, p. 1.

5. *Ramparts*, June 15, 1968.

6. Widener, *Student Subversion* 34 (1968), quoting from a 1965 pamphlet by Mark Kleiman, "High School Reform: Towards a Student Movement."

7. *U.S. News & World Report*, May 20, 1968, quoting from an S.D.S. leaflet: ". . . [I]s there anyone who doubts that a small home-made incendiary device with a timing mechanism planted in a broom closet at the Oakland induction center would result in fire and smoke and damage to the entire building, thus making it unusable for weeks and months?"

8. Widener, *Subcellar Student Subversion*, U.S.A. March 1, 1968.

9. The New York *Times*, May 7, 1967, quoting Gregory Calvert, former national S.D.S. secretary: "We are working to build a guerrilla force in an urban environment. We are actively organizing sedition."

10. "The Story of Crime in the U.S.," by J. Edgar Hoover, *U.S. News & World Report*, October 7, 1968, p. 64.

11. Brownfield, *The New Left* 101 (1968). This is a memorandum prepared for the Senate Committee on the Judiciary, 90th Congress, 2d Session.

12. *Ibid.*, p. 67.

13. "Ten Days in April," *Barron's*, March 11, 1968, quoting from a "Movement" position paper: "In the last year or so, the Movement has come from dissent to resistance."

14. "SDS Theory: The New Working Class Concept—Students Would Set Up Cadre of Radical Organizers," by J. A. Smith, *The National Guardian*, April 22, 1967. Emphasis supplied here and in Hayden statement.

Trapped in a System*

... We are here again to protest again a growing war. Since it is a very bad war, we acquire the habit of thinking that it must be caused by very bad men. But we only conceal reality, I think, by denouncing on such grounds the menacing coalition of industrial and military power, or the brutality of the blitzkrieg we are waging against Vietnam, or the ominous signs around us that heresy may soon no longer be permitted. We must simply observe, and quite plainly say that this coalition, this blitzkrieg, and this demand for acquiescence are creatures, all of them, of a Government that since 1932 has considered itself to be fundamentally *liberal*.

The original commitment in Vietnam was made by President Truman, a mainstream liberal. It was seconded by President Eisenhower, a moderate liberal. It was intensified by the late President Kennedy, a flaming liberal. Think of the men who now engineer that war—those who study the maps, give the commands, push the buttons, and tally the dead: Bundy, McNamara, Rusk, Lodge, Goldberg, the President himself.

They are not moral monsters.

They are all honorable men.

They are all liberals.

But so, I'm sure, are many of us who are here today in protest. To understand the war, then, it seems necessary to take a closer look at this American liberalism. Maybe we are in for some surprises. Maybe we have here two quite different liberalisms: one authentically humanist; the other not so human at all.

Carl Oglesby was an early leader of Students for a Democratic Society. He co-authored the book *Containment and Change: Two Dissenting Views of American Society* in 1967, and in 1969 edited *The New Left Reader*. Mr. Oglesby's speeches, articles, and essays have appeared in *Saturday Review, Ramparts, The Nation,* and *The Center Magazine.*

The speech reproduced here was delivered when Mr. Oglesby was president of the SDS, at the October 27, 1965, antiwar march in Washington. It has become a classic in the New Left because of its open indictment of corporate liberalism. In its various reprintings, the speech has been entitled either "Trapped in a System" or "Let Us Shape the Future." Reprinted from *The New Left: A Documentary History,* Massimo Teodori, ed. (New York: The Bobbs-Merrill Co., Inc., 1970), pp. 182–188. Reprinted by permission of Carl Oglesby.

Not long ago, I considered myself a liberal. And if someone had asked me what I meant by that, I'd perhaps have quoted Thomas Jefferson or Thomas Paine, who first made plain our nation's unprovisional commitment to human rights. But what do you think would happen if these two heroes could sit down now for a chat with President Johnson and McGeorge Bundy?

They would surely talk of the Vietnam war. Our dead revolutionaries would soon wonder why their country was fighting against what appeared to be a revolution. The living liberals would hotly deny that it is one: there are troops coming in from outside, the rebels get arms from other countries, most of the people are not on their side, and they practice terror against their own. Therefore, *not* a revolution.

What would our dead revolutionaries answer? They might say: "What fools and bandits, sirs, you make then of us. Outside help? Do you remember Lafayette? Or the 3,000 British freighters the French navy sunk for our side? Or the arms and men we got from France and Spain? And what's this about terror? Did you never hear what we did to our own loyalists? Or about the thousands of rich American Tories who fled for their lives to Canada? And as for popular support, do you not know that we had less than one-third of our people with us? That, in fact, the colony of New York recruited more troops for the British than for the revolution? Should we give it all back?"

Revolutions do not take place in velvet boxes. They never have. It is only the poets who make them lovely. What the National Liberation Front is fighting in Vietnam is a complex and vicious war. This war is also a revolution, as honest a revolution as you can find anywhere in history. And this is a fact which all our intricate official denials will never change. . . .

. . . We have become a nation of young, bright-eyed, hard-hearted, slim-waisted, bullet-headed makeout artists. A nation—may I say it?—of beardless liberals.

You say I am being hard? Only think.

This country, with its thirty-some years of liberalism, can send 200,000 young men to Vietnam to kill and die in the most dubious of wars, but it cannot get 100 voter registrars to go into Mississippi.

What do you make of it?

The financial burden of the war obliges us to cut millions from an already pathetic War on Poverty budget. But in almost the same breath, Congress appropriates $140 million for the Lockheed and Boeing companies to compete with each other on the supersonic transport project—that Disneyland creation that will cost us all about $2 billion before it's done.

What do you make of it?

Many of us have been earnestly resisting for some years now the idea of putting atomic weapons into West German hands, an action that would perpetuate the division of Europe and thus the Cold War. Now just this week we find out that, with the meagerest of security systems, West Germany has had nuclear weapons in her hands for the past six years.

What do you make of it?

Some will make of it that I overdraw the matter. Many will ask: What about the other side? To be sure, there is the bitter ugliness of Czechoslovakia, Poland, those infamous Russian tanks in the streets of Budapest. But my anger only rises to hear some say that sorrow cancels sorrow, or that *this* one's shame deposits in *that one's* account the right to shamefulness.

And others will make of it that I sound mighty anti-American. To these, I say: Don't blame *me* for *that!* Blame those who mouthed my liberal values and broke my American heart. . . .

Let's stare our situation coldly in the face. All of us are born to the colossus of history, our American corporate system—in many ways, an awesome organism. There is one fact that describes it: With about 5% of the world's people, we consume about half the world's goods. We take a richness that is in good part not our own, and we put it in our pockets, our garages, our split-levels, our bellies, and our futures.

On the *face* of it, it is a crime that so few should have so much at the expense of so many. Where is the moral imagination so abused as to call this just? Perhaps many of us feel a bit uneasy in our sleep. We are not, after all, a cruel people. And perhaps we don't really need this super-dominance that deforms others. But what can we do? The investments are made. The financial ties are established. The plants abroad are built. Our system *exists*. One is swept up into it. How intolerable—to be born moral, but addicted to a stolen and maybe surplus luxury. Our goodness threatens to become counterfeit before our eyes—unless we change. But change threatens us with uncertainty —at least.

Our problem, then, is to justify this system and give its theft another name—to make kind and moral what is neither, to perform some alchemy with language that will make this injustice seem to be a most magnanimous gift.

A hard problem. But the Western democracies, in the heyday of their colonial expansion, produced a hero worthy of the task.

Its name was free enterprise, and its partner was an *illiberal liberalism* that said to the poor and the dispossessed: What we acquire of your resources we repay in civilization. The white man's burden. But this was too poetic. So a much more hard-headed theory was produced. This theory said that colonial status is in fact a *boon* to the colonized. We give them technology and bring them into modern times.

But this deceived no one but ourselves. We were delighted with this new theory. The poor saw in it merely an admission that their claims were irrefutable. They stood up to us, without gratitude. We were shocked—but also confused, for the poor seemed again to be right. How long is it going to be the case, we pondered, that the poor will be right and the rich will be wrong?

Liberalism faced a crisis. In the face of the collapse of the European empires, how could it continue to hold together our twin need for richness and righteousness? How can we continue to sack the ports of Asia and still dream of Jesus?

The challenge was met with a most ingenious solution: the ideology of anti-Communism. This was the bind: we cannot call revolution bad, because we started that way ourselves, and because it is all too easy to see why the dispossessed should rebel. So we will call revolution *Communism*. And we will reserve for ourselves the right to say what Communism means. We take note of revolution's enormities, wrenching them where necessary from their historical context and often exaggerating them, and say: Behold, Communism is a bloodbath. We take note of those reactionaries who stole the revolution, and say: Behold, Communism is a betrayal of the people. We take note of the revolution's needs to consolidate itself, and say: Behold, Communism is a tyranny.

It has been all these things, and it will be these things again, and we will never be at a loss for those tales of atrocity that comfort us so in our self-righteousness. Nuns will be raped and bureaucrats will be disembowelled. Indeed, revolution is a fury. For it is a letting loose of outrages pent up sometimes over centuries. But the more brutal and longer-lasting the suppression of this energy, all the more ferocious will be its explosive release.

Far from helping Americans deal with this truth, the anti-Communist ideology merely tries to disguise it so that things may stay the way they are. Thus, it depicts our presence in other lands not as a coercion, but a protection. It allows us even to say that the napalm in Vietnam is only another aspect of our humanitarian love—like those exorcisms in the Middle Ages that so often killed the patient. So we say to the Vietnamese peasant, the Cuban intellectual, the Peruvian worker: "You are better dead than Red. If it hurts or if you don't understand why—sorry about that."

This is the action of *corporate liberalism*. It performs for the corporate state a function quite like what the Church once performed for the feudal state. It seeks to justify its burdens and protect it from change. As the Church exaggerated this office in the Inquisition, so with liberalism in the McCarthy time—which, if it was a reactionary phenomenon, was still made possible by our anti-Communist corporate liberalism.

Let me then speak directly to humanist liberals. If my facts are wrong, I will soon be corrected. But if they are right, then you may face a crisis of conscience. Corporatism or humanism: which? For it has come to that. Will you let your dreams be used? Will you be a grudging apologist for the corporate state? Or will you help try to change it—not in the name of this or that blueprint or "ism," but in the name of simple human decency and democracy and the vision that wise and brave men saw in the time of our own Revolution?

And if your commitment to human value is unconditonal, then disabuse yourselves of the notion that statements will bring change, if only the right statements can be written, or that interviews with the mighty will bring change if only the mighty can be reached, or that marches will bring change if only we can make them massive enough, or that policy proposals will bring change if only we can make them responsible enough.

We are dealing now with a colossus that does not want to be changed. It will not change itself. It will not cooperate with those who want to change it. Those allies of ours in the Government—are they really our allies? If they *are*, then they don't need advice, they need *constituencies;* they don't need study groups, they need a *movement*. And if they are *not*, then all the more reason for building that movement with a most relentless conviction.

There are people in this country today who are trying to build that movement, who aim at nothing less than a humanist reformation. And the humanist liberals must understand that it is this movement with which their own best hopes are most in tune. We radicals know the same history that you liberals know, and we can understand your occasional cynicism, exasperation, and even distrust. But we ask you to put these aside and help us risk a leap. Help us find enough time for the enormous work that needs doing here. Help us build. Help us shake the future in the name of plain human hope.

For a First Party*

[The government of the United States has] . . . raised up the hopes of the Negroes, the poor and their middle-class sympathizers and then dashed them down. The militant blacks and the radical young concluded that the entire society was therefore dishonest and that they would have nothing to do with the traditional reform movement. Having thus cut themselves off from the majority of the people, they had forfeited the possibility of a democratic perspective even though some of them—the young radicals—spoke in the name of ultra-democracy. It is necessary to sympathize with the emotions at work in all of this and impossible to approve of the logic which they inspired. The objections to a theory of radical, minority change are both practical and moral.

Black America shares traits with the Third World countries in the days of white rule—but there is one crucial difference. In the colonies, the nationalist movement embraced, or represented the aspirations of, 80 or 90 percent of the people. Their struggle against white imperialism had a mass base and a democratic legitimacy. In the United States, Negroes are a minority of between 12 and 15 percent. . . .

But even if one adopts the integrated perspective of the young radicals and seeks to unite both black and white leftouts, the fundamental problem remains. The poor constitute, at the highest estimate, somewhere between 20 and 25 percent of the people, and that figure includes the majority of Negroes. There is no census of the alienated, but even if they could be recruited to activism, they hardly represent

---

*Michael Harrington, born in 1928, first came to the attention of most Americans with the publication of his book *The Other America*. This work, and the one that followed, *The Accidental Century*, mark him as one of the leading voices of a newer socialist philosophy and movement. Mr. Harrington has been active in both the Socialist Party and the League for Industrial Democracy. From Michael Harrington, *Toward a Democratic Left* (New York: The Macmillan Co., 1968) pp. 270-271, 290-297. Copyright by Michael Harrington, 1968.

another quarter or third of the population. Moreover, poverty demoralizes people at least as much as it incites them to rebel. That is why there is a lower level of political participation in the other America than anywhere else in the country. But in the New Left vision, a minority of participatory democrats are supposed to govern the corrupt majority of the nation.

And it is important to have a proper respect for that white power structure which the Negro militants excoriate. It will savagely repress violence if it becomes convinced that such a tactic is necessary, and it cannot be dislodged nonviolently except by a politically organized majority. . . .

Thus, on grounds of both practicality and democratic principle, nothing less than a new political majority will be able to make the sweeping changes which America needs. . . .

From Marx to Mills, the Left has regarded the middle class as a stratum of hypocritical, vacillating rear-guarders. There was often sound reason for this contempt. But now it is possible that a new class is coming into being. It is not the old middle class of small-property owners and entrepreneurs, nor the new middle class of managers. It is composed of scientists, technicians, teachers and professionals in the public sector of the society. By education and work experience it is predisposed toward planning. It could be an ally of the poor and the organized workers—or their sophisticated enemy. In other words, an unprecedented social and political variable seems to be taking shape in America.

There have always been both conscience and cotton wings in American politics, and even upper-class reformers, like the Abolitionists. It is now possible—not assured, but possible—that the economy is creating a social structure which vastly enlarges the conscience constituency. If this is indeed the case, it is one of the most optimistic facts the democratic Left can find.

So the daily concerns of working people and the poor must merge with the values of the college-educated and religiously inspired in a new majority party.

There are many ways in which this is an undramatic, and even tedious, strategy. It would be much more emotionally satisfying if there were some majoritarian proletariat with internal cohesion and solidarity seeking to find its own mighty voice. There isn't. So one is forced to the politics of coalition not because it is an ideal instrument to make sweeping changes but because it is the only way available to American society for the foreseeable future. Given this perspective, there is no point in papering over the difficulties in the proposal. For, as in any coalition, there will be tensions and even open conflicts among its various constituent elements.

Non-economic issues will be a particular source of internal antagonism on the democratic Left. When it comes to civil liberties, aesthetics, capital punishment and the like, profound differences divide the poor and the workers from the middle-class liberals and radicals. In general, the more educated a group, the greater is its sensitivity to "ethical" questions in politics. People whose work and/or neighborhood are rough do not, for instance, instinctively defend the speaking rights of a hated opponent. There are powerful impulses toward solidarity and brotherhood among people who have been denied a decent education, but they do not ordinarily extend to strangers and certainly not to enemies. It was one of the great triumphs of the Negro religious spirit in the civil-rights movement that, for a while, it inspired masses to non-violent struggle and an exception to this rule.

But even more important, in terms of the strategy of the democratic Left, there are potential conflicts in the area of foreign policy. On disarmament, as on civil liberties, almost all of the polls describe a decline in positive sentiment as one descends the educational scale. For this reason, a mass party of the democratic Left cannot be initially organized in response to the international issues where there is a maximum potential for discord among its various constituencies. It will develop first out of domestic stirrings and crises. This emphatically does not mean that the peace activists should become quiescent and cite sociology as an excuse for doing nothing. It is just that they should not expect that a new party will accept their views at the outset.

But there is hope in the long run. If a movement arises which challenges corporate power within the United States, its members could come to question the myths of free enterprise on a global scale. The civil-rights movement is again a hopeful precursor. Negroes in the ghettos of the Sixties were much more concerned about the issue of war and peace than the white poor. One reason was, of course, that the solidarity of color extended to the Third World. But another was the fact that, in creating their own movement in this country, they became much more sensitive to struggles going on in distant places. If the empire of oil can be defeated at home in the Seventies, the new majority may well understand that it is necessary to defeat it abroad as well.

In the fall of 1967 this possibility became actual in the San Francisco election. Some peace activists had placed a purist resolution on Vietnam on the ballot. By demanding that the voters choose between an either-or of immediate withdrawal or Lyndon Johnson's policy, they forced many opponents of the Vietnam tragedy, even including some pacifists, into attitudes of opposition, boycott or qualified support. But even though a marvelous opportunity to repudiate Washington's policy was thus lost, the response of the poor people in areas where community organization had taken place was most instructive. For contrary to sociological expectation, it was these neighborhoods and not those of the middle class which returned the highest percentages against the war. For the people in them had understood the relationship between the retreat from social goals and the escalation of the killing in Southeast Asia. If there were a vital movement of the democratic Left on the national level which was first rallied into existence by domestic concerns, it might well make the same kind of connections between the injustices structured into the American system at home and those which we export abroad.

These possibilities clearly concern over-all strategy and not the problems of immediate action. There is a certain necessary vagueness since it is impossible to second-guess the next twenty years. Yet there are some specifics that can be outlined.

At the present writing, the main arena in which the struggle for a new majority party is taking place is the Democratic Party. It claims the allegiance of the overwhelming bulk of the organized reform forces, largely because it was the instrumentality of the last two effective majorities in American history, the Rooseveltian coalition of 1932-1938 and the Johnson consensus of 1964-1965. It is also the supreme national example of an unprincipled, and now impossible, compromise. In the Congress of 1967 and 1968, the leading foes of the social programs of the Democratic President were the Southern Democratic committee chairman. And so long as a liberal victory on the Presidential line thus strengthens Congressional reaction, there is not the least possibility of confronting the issues analyzed in this book.

At this time, then, the best strategy for the democratic Left is to seek to win the Democratic Party in such a way as to exclude its Right wing permanently. Whether this situation will persist into the future is, it must be emphasized, a tactical, not a moral, question. It is an unhappy, but compelling, fact of American life that membership in a political party does not constitute a commitment either to its program or leadership, and it is precisely the aim of the democratic Left to overturn this tradition. However, this unfortunate reality cannot be transformed by pretending that it does not exist. Therefore, as long as major party politics, with all their lack of principle, offer the best point of departure for basic change, that is where one must work.

So the democratic Left does not work in the Democratic Party in order to maintain that institution but to transform it. The lack of political principle which it finds there is most certainly an indictment of the American party system generally *and* a dynamic contradiction which can be used to challenge that system. There is obvious danger when those committed to a new morality thus maneuver on the basis of the old hypocrisies. Yet, as the New Politics Conference in Chicago in the summer of 1967 so cruelly demonstrated, a relatively small coalition of enthusiasts, black-power militants, idealists and Communist machine politicians cannot create a nationwide movement by fiat. More poignantly, the ethical anarchism of the hippies in recent years often led them to underestimate how hostile to love the society can be, and the result in some cases was drug addiction or even death.

It would be neater, and more ethically appealing, if American politics allowed the Left to make a total break with the past and start a party of its own. And indeed such a strategy might be required. But if it is, the moment will be signaled by the actual disaffection of great masses of people from the Democratic Party. Such a vast shift in political habits cannot be sermonized into existence, a point which middle-class activists with their philosophic loyalties and motives do not always understand. Before raising the banner of a new party, in short, there must be some reasonable expectation that significant forces will join it. That could happen in the next twenty years; it is not presently imminent; and the dispute over whether it is indeed approaching will turn upon fact and not morality.

It sounds radical to take an intransigent position. It is radical to go among the people as they actually are and work with them to create a new majority party. For apocalypses are easy to proclaim but the structural reform of the most powerful nation in history is much more difficult and not so dramatic.

But there will almost certainly be disputes within the democratic Left on these tactical questions. The various social groupings involved have different attitudes and passions and, moreover, there are often grounds for honest difference in the complexities of the moment. Yet, however vigorous the internal debates of the democratic Left may be, the various partisans must remember that their unity is the only eventual hope.

As the 1968 elections approached, many of the potential partisans of the democratic Left had almost totally lost sight of this point. The trade-unionists, with some exceptions, viewed President Johnson as a man of domestic social accomplishment and certainly the best realistic candidate from the wage workers' point of view. There were some in the labor leadership who were ideological hawks, but most supported the Administration in Vietnam because they approved of what it was doing in the United States. On the other hand, the overwhelming majority of the middle-class liberals, reformers, religious activists and college students were passionately opposed to Mr. Johnson because of his policies in Southeast Asia. As a result, the advocates of social change often fought more bitterly among themselves than with their enemies on the Right.

There is no easy resolution to this split. It will almost certainly last as long as the tragic military intervention in Vietnam and while it persists America will continue to retreat from its most fundamental commitments both at home and abroad. And yet both sides in this fratricidal dispute must be reminded over and over of the electoral mathematics of the United States. The middle class, even with its qualitatively new dimensions, is not a majority; neither is the labor movement; and black America is 12 or 13 percent of the nation. To obtain the massive popular suport required for radical transformations in the very structures of American life requires that these movements once again come together in a coalition. And in debating the profound tactical differences which in the late Sixties exist, no one can ever forget that this eventual unity is the only possible road to democratic change.

Yet the coming coalition, this chapter should have made plain, cannot be patterned on the old, New Deal model. The Left must go beyond Franklin Roosevelt in political strategy as well as in social and economic program. The Dixiecrats must be excluded, the progressive Southerners included; the Negroes are going to organize and speak for themselves and not be voted by white politicians; the middle class (or perhaps new class) elements will have a much greater weight than in the Rooseveltian coalition, for they are much more important now; and there is realistic hope for the renewal of labor's domestic social idealism. And even though practically every one of these groups is quarreling with every other as the Sixties come to an end, they will either come together or else America has no hope.

But with all these problems it is realistic to work toward a majority party of the democratic Left. The country is not fated, as so many academics claim, to a mindless politics which never poses basic issues. The majority is not so corrupt, as some black militants and young radicals argue, that nothing can be done save to shake the pillars and bring the roof down on the whole decadent scene. For there is even a possibility within American society of actually building a political movement equal to the monumental tasks we have so casually defined for ourselves.

There can be a first party.

Civil Disobedience:
Destroyer of Democracy (1969)*

As Charles E. Wyzanski, Chief Judge of the United States District Court in Boston, wrote in the February, 1968, *Atlantic:* "Disobedience is a long step from dissent. Civil disobedience involves a deliberate and punishable breach of legal duty." Protesters might prefer a different definition. They would rather say that civil disobedience is the peaceable resistance of conscience.

The philosophy of civil disobedience was not developed in our American democracy, but in the very first democracy of Athens. It was expressed by the poet Sophocles and the philosopher Socrates. In Sophocles's tragedy, Antigone chose to obey her conscience and violate the state edict against providing burial for her brother, who had been decreed a traitor. When the dictator Creon found out that Antigone had buried her fallen brother, he confronted her and reminded her that there was a mandatory death penalty for this deliberate disobedience of the state law. Antigone nobly replied, "Nor did I think your orders were so strong that you, a mortal man, could overrun the gods' unwritten and unfailing laws."

Conscience motivated Antigone. She was not testing the validity of the law in the hope that eventually she would be sustained. Appealing to the judgment of the community, she explained her action to the chorus. She was not secret and surreptitious—the interment of her brother was open and public. She was not violent; she did not trespass

---

Lewis H. Van Dusen, Jr., practices law in Philadelphia and has been active in the organized Bar, serving as Chancellor of the Philadelphia Bar Association in 1968. He holds a B.A. degree from Princeton University and a B.C.L. degree from Oxford University, where he attended New College as a Rhodes Scholar. He also attended the Harvard Law School. From *American Bar Association Journal*, Vol. 55 (Feb. 1969), p. 123.

on another citizen's rights. And finally, she accepted without resistance the death sentence—the penalty for violation. By voluntarily accepting the law's sanctions, she was not a revolutionary denying the authority of the state. Antigone's behavior exemplifies the classic case of civil disobedience.

Socrates believed that reason could dictate a conscientious disobedience of state law, but he also believed that he had to accept the legal sanctions of the state. In Plato's *Crito*, Socrates from his hanging basket accepted the death penalty for his teaching of religion to youth contrary to state laws.

The sage of Walden, Henry David Thoreau, took this philosophy of nonviolence and developed it into a strategy for solving society's injustices. First enunciating it in protest against the Mexican War, he then turned it to use against slavery. For refusing to pay taxes that would help pay the enforcers of the fugitive slave law, he went to prison. In Thoreau's words, "If the alternative is to keep all just men in prison or to give up slavery, the state will not hesitate which to choose."

Sixty years later, Gandhi took Thoreau's civil disobedience as his strategy to wrest Indian independence from England. The famous salt march against a British imperial tax is his best-known example of protest.

But the conscientious law breaking of Socrates, Gandhi and Thoreau is to be distinguished from the conscientious law testing of Martin Luther King, Jr., who was not a civil disobedient. The civil disobedient withholds taxes or violates state laws knowing he is legally wrong, but believing he is morally right. While he wrapped himself in the mantle of Gandhi and Thoreau, Dr. King led his followers in violation of state laws he believed were contrary to the Federal Constitution. But since Supreme Court decisions in the end generally upheld his many actions, he should not be considered a true civil disobedient.

The civil disobedience of Antigone is like that of the pacifist who withholds paying the percentage of his taxes that goes to the Defense Department, or the Quaker who travels against State Department regulations to Hanoi to distribute medical supplies, or the Vietnam war protester who tears up his draft card. This civil disobedient has been nonviolent in his defiance of the law; he has been unfurtive in his violation; he has been submissive to the penalties of the law. He has neither evaded the law nor interfered with another's rights. He has been neither a rioter nor a revolutionary. The thrust of his cause has not been the might of coercion but the martyrdom of conscience.

Was the Boston Tea Party Civil Disobedience?

Those who justify violence and radical action as being in the tradition of our Revolution show a misunderstanding of the philosophy of democracy.

James Farmer, former head of the Congress of Racial Equality, in defense of the mass action confrontation method, has told of a famous organized demonstration that took place in opposition to political and economic discrimination. The protesters beat back and scattered the law enforcers and then proceeded to loot and destroy private property. Mr. Farmer then said he was talking about the Boston Tea Party and implied that violence as a method for redress of grievances was an American tradition and a legacy of our revolutionary heritage. While it is true that there is no more sacred document than our Declaration of Independence, Jefferson's "inherent right of rebellion" was predicated on the tyrannical denial of democratic means. If there is no popular assembly to provide an adjustment of ills, and if there is no court system to dispose of injustices, then there is, indeed, a right to rebel.

The seventeenth century's John Locke, the philosophical father of the Declaration of Independence, wrote in his *Second Treatise on Civil Government:* "Wherever law ends, tyranny begins . . . and the people are absolved from any further obedience. Governments are dissolved from within when the legislative [chamber] is altered. When the government [becomes] . . . arbitrary disposers of lives, liberties and fortunes of the people, such revolutions happen . . . ."

But there are some sophisticated proponents of the revolutionary redress of grievances who say that the test of the need for radical action is not the unavailability of democratic institutions but the ineffectuality of those institutions to remove blatant social inequalities. If social injustice exists, they say, concerned disobedience is required against the constituted government, whether it be totalitarian or democratic in structure.

Of course, only the most bigoted chauvinist would claim that America is without some glaring faults. But there has never been a utopian society on earth and there never will be unless human nature is remade. Since inequities will mar even the best-framed democracies, the injustice rationale would allow a free right of civil resistance to be available always as a shortcut alternative to the democratic way of petition, debate and assembly. The lesson of history is that civil insurgency spawns far more injustices than it removes. The Jeffersons, Washingtons and Adamses resisted tyranny with the aim of promoting the procedures of democracy. They would never have resisted a democratic government with the risk of promoting the techniques of tyranny.

Legitimate Pressures and Illegitimate Results

There are many civil rights leaders who show impatience with the process of democracy. They rely on the sit-in, boycott or mass picketing to gain speedier solutions to the problems that face every citizen. But we must realize that the legitimate pressures that won concessions in the past can easily escalate into the illegitimate power plays that might extort demands in the future. The victories of these civil rights leaders must not shake our confidence in the democratic procedures, as the pressures of demonstration are desirable only if they take place within the limits allowed by law. Civil rights gains should continue to be won by the persuasion of Congress and other legislative bodies and by the decision of courts. Any illegal entreaty for the rights of some can be an injury to the rights of others, for mass demonstrations often trigger violence.

Those who advocate taking the law into their own hands should reflect that when they are disobeying what they consider to be an immoral law, they are deciding on a possibly immoral course. Their answer is that the process for democratic relief is too slow, that only mass confrontation can bring immediate action, and that any injuries are the inevitable cost of the pursuit of justice. Their answer is, simply put, that the end justifies the means. It is this justification of any form of demonstration as a form of dissent that threatens to destroy a society built on the rule of law.

Our Bill of Rights guarantees wide opportunities to use mass meetings, public parades and organized demonstrations to stimulate sentiment, to dramatize issues and to cause change. The Washington freedom march of 1963 was such a call for action. But the rights of free expression cannot be mere force cloaked in the garb of free speech. As the courts have decreed in labor cases, free assembly does not mean mass picketing or sit-down strikes. These rights are subject to limitations of time and place so as to secure the rights of others. When militant students storm a college president's office to achieve demands, when certain groups plan rush-hour car stalling to protest discrimination in employment, these are not dissent, but a denial of rights to others. Neither is it the lawful use of mass protest, but rather the unlawful use of mob power.

Justice Black, one of the foremost advocates and defenders of the right of protest and dissent, has said:

... Experience demonstrates that it is not a far step from what to many seems to be the earnest, honest, patriotic, kind-spirited multitude of today, to the fanatical, threatening, lawless mob of tomorrow. And the crowds that press in the streets for noble goals today can be supplanted tomorrow by street mobs pressuring the courts for precisely opposite ends.[1]

Society must censure those demonstrators who would trespass on the public peace, as it must condemn those rioters whose pillage would destroy the public peace. But more ambivalent is society's posture toward the civil disobedient. Unlike the rioter, the true civil disobedient commits no violence. Unlike the mob demonstrator, he commits no trespass on others' rights. The civil disobedient, while deliberately violating a law, shows an oblique respect for the law by voluntarily submitting to its sanctions. He neither resists arrest nor evades punishment. Thus, he breaches the law but not the peace.

But civil disobedience, whatever the ethical rationalization, is still an assault on our democratic society, an affront to our legal order and an attack on our constitutional government. To indulge civil disobedience is to invite anarchy, and the permissive arbitrariness of anarchy is hardly less tolerable than the repressive arbitrariness of tyranny. Too often the license of liberty is followed by the loss of liberty, because into the desert of anarchy comes the man on horseback, a Mussolini or a Hitler.

Violations of Law Subvert Democracy

Law violations, even for ends recognized as laudable, are not only assaults on the rule of law, but subversions of the democratic process. The disobedient act of conscience does not ennoble democracy; it erodes it.

First, it courts violence, and even the most careful and limited use of nonviolent acts of disobedience may help sow the dragon-teeth of civil riot. Civil disobedience is the progenitor of disorder, and disorder is the sire of violence.

Second, the concept of civil disobedience does not invite principles of general applicability. If the children of light are morally privileged to resist particular laws on grounds of conscience, so are the children of darkness. Former Deputy Attorney General Burke Marshall said: "If the decision to break the law really turned on individual conscience, it is hard to see in law how [the civil rights leader] is better off than former Governor Ross Barnett of Mississippi who also believed deeply in his cause and was willing to go to jail."[2]

Third, even the most noble act of civil disobedience assaults the rule of law. Although limited as to method, motive and objective, it has the effect of inducing others to engage in different forms of law breaking characterized by methods unsanctioned and condemned by classic theories of law violation. Unfortunately, the most patent lesson of civil disobedience is not so much nonviolence of action as defiance of authority.

Finally, the greatest danger in condoning civil disobedience as a permissible strategy for hastening change is that it undermines our democratic processes. To adopt the techniques of civil disobedience is to assume that representative government does not work. To resist the decisions of courts and the laws of elected assemblies is to say that democracy has failed.

There is no man who is above the law, and there is no man who has a right to break the law. Civil disobedience is not above the law, but against the law. When the civil disobedient disobeys one law, he invariably subverts all law. When the civil disobedient says that he is above the law, he is saying that democracy is beneath him. His disobedience shows a distrust for the democratic system. He is merely saying that since democracy does not work, why should he help make it work. Thoreau expressed well the civil disobedient's disdain for democracy:

> As for adopting the ways which the state has provided for remedying the evil, I know not of such ways. They take too much time and a man's life will be gone. I have other affairs to attend to. I came into this world not chiefly to make this a good place to live in, but to live in it, be it good or bad.[3]

Thoreau's position is not only morally irresponsible but politically reprehensible. When citizens in a democracy are called on to make a profession of faith, the civil disobedients offer only a confession of failure. Tragically, when civil disobedients for lack of faith abstain from democratic involvement, they help attain their own gloomy prediction. They help create the social and political basis for their own despair. By foreseeing failure, they help forge it. If citizens rely on antidemocratic means of protest, they will help bring about the undemocratic result of an authoritarian or anarchic state.

How far demonstrations properly can be employed to produce political and social change is a pressing question, particularly in view of the provocations accompanying the National Democratic Convention in Chicago last August and the reaction of the police to them. A line must be drawn by the judiciary between the demands of those who seek absolute order, which can lead only to a dictatorship, and those who seek absolute freedom, which can lead only to anarchy. The line, wherever it is drawn by our courts, should be respected on the college campus, on the streets and elsewhere.

Undue provocation will inevitably result in overreaction, human emotions being what they are. Violence will follow. This cycle undermines the very democracy it is designed to preserve. The lesson of the past is that democracies will fall if violence, including the intentional provocations that will lead to violence, replaces democratic procedures, as in Athens, Rome and the Weimar Republic. This lesson must be constantly explained by the legal profession.

We should heed the words of William James:

> Democracy is still upon its trial. The civic genius of our people is its only bulwark and . . . neither battleships nor public libraries nor great newspapers nor booming stocks: neither mechanical invention nor political adroitness, nor churches nor universities nor civil service examinations can save us from degeneration if the inner mystery be lost.
>
> That mystery, at once the secret and the glory of our English-speaking race, consists of nothing but two habits. . . . [O]ne of them is habit of trained and disciplined good temper towards the opposite party when it fairly wins its innings. The other is that of fierce and merciless resentment toward every man or set of men who break the public peace.[4]

FOOTNOTES

1. Justice Hugo Black dissenting in *Cox* v. *Louisiana*, 379 U.S. 536, 575, 584 (1965).

2. Burke Marshall, "The Protest Movement and the Law," *Virginia Law Review*, Vol. 51 (1965), p. 785.

3. Henry David Thoreau, "Essay on Civil Disobedience," in Meltzer, ed., *People, Principles and Politics* (1963).

4. Henry James, *Pragmatism*, pp. 127–128 (1907).

Declaration of Conscience—
Twenty Years Later (1970)*

Mr. President, 20 years ago on this June 1 date at this same desk I spoke about the then serious national condition with a statement known as the "Declaration of Conscience." We had a national sickness then from which we recovered. We have a national sickness now from which I pray we will recover.

I would like to recall portions of that statement today because they have application now 20 years later.

I said of the then national condition:

It is a national feeling of fear and frustration that could result in national suicide and the end of everything that we Americans hold dear.

Surely that is the situation today.

I said then:

I speak as briefly as possible because too much harm has already been done with irresponsible words of bitterness and selfish political opportunism.

That is not the only situation today, but it is even worse for irresponsible words have exploded into trespass, violence, arson, and killings.

I said then:

I think that it is high time for the United States Senate and its Members to do some soul searching—for us to weigh our consciences—on the manner in which we are performing our duty to the people of the United States—on the manner in which we are using or abusing our individual powers and privileges.

That applies today. But I would add this to it—expanded application to the people themselves, whether they be students or construction workers, whether they be on or off campus.

I said then:

Those of us who shout the loudest about Americanism in making character assassinations are all too frequently those who, by our own words and acts, ignore some of the basic principles of Americanism—

    The right to criticize;

---

*Margaret Chase Smith was born in Maine in 1897. After a brief career as a teacher and newspaperwoman, she went to the House of Representatives in 1940. She was re-elected four times before her election to the Senate, where she has served since 1948. She was the first woman representative from Maine, and the first woman to be placed in nomination for the presidency (Republican Party, 1964) by a major American political party. Reprinted from *The Congressional Record of the Congress* of the United States, June 1, 1970.

The right to hold unpopular beliefs;
The right to protest;
The right to independent thought.

That applies today—and it includes the right to dissent against the dissenters.

I said then:

The American people are sick and tired of being afraid to speak their minds lest they be politically smeared. . . . Freedom of speech is not what it used to be in America. It has been so abused by some that it is not exercised by others.

That applies today to both sides. It is typified by the girl student at Colby College who wrote me:

I am striking with my heart against the fighting in Cambodia but I am intimidated by those who scream protests and clench their fists and cannot listen to people who oppose their views.

I said then:

Today our country is being psychologically divided by the confusion and the suspicions that are bred in the United States Senate to spread like cancerous tentacles of "know nothing, suspect everything" attitudes.

That applies today—but it must be expanded to the people themselves. Twenty years ago it was the anti-intellectuals who were most guilty of "know nothing" attitudes. Today too many of the militant intellectuals are equally as guilty of "hear nothing" attitudes of refusing to listen while demanding communication.

I said then:

I don't like the way the Senate has been made a rendezvous for villification, for selfish political gain at the sacrifice of individual reputations and national unity.

That applies today. But I would add that equally I do not like the way the campus has been made a rendezvous for obscenity, for trespass, for violence, for arson, and for killing.

I said then:

I am not proud of the way we smear outsiders from the Floor of the Senate and hide behind the cloak of congressional immunity and still place ourselves beyond criticism on the Floor of the Senate.

Today I would add to that—I am not proud of the way in which too many militants resort to the illegalities of trespass, violence, and arson and, in doing so, claim for themselves a special immunity from the law with the allegation that such acts are justified because they have a political connotation with a professed cause.

I then said:

As a United States Senator, I am not proud of the way in which the Senate has been made a publicity platform for irresponsible sensationalism.

Today I would add that I am not proud of the way in which our national television networks and campuses have been made publicity platforms for irresponsible sensationalism—nor am I proud of the countercriticism against the networks and the campuses that has gone beyond the bound of reasonableness and propriety and fanned, instead of drenching, the fires of division.

I have admired much of the candid and justified defense of our Government in reply to the news media and the militant dissenters— but some of the defense has been too extreme and unfair and too repetitive and thus impaired the effectiveness of the previous admirable and justified defense.

I said 20 years ago:

As an American, I am shocked at the way Republicans and Democrats alike are playing directly into the Communist design of "confuse, divide and conquer."

Today I am shocked at the way too many Americans are so doing.

I spoke as I did 20 years ago because of what I considered to be the great threat from the radical right—the threat of a government of repression.

I speak today because of what I consider to be the great threat from the radical left that advocates and practices violence and defiance of the law—again, the threat of the ultimate result of a reaction of repression.

The President denies that we are in a revolution. There are many who would disagree with such appraisal. Anarchy may seem nearer to many of us than it really is.

But of one thing I am sure. The excessiveness of overreactions on both sides is a clear and present danger to American democracy.

That danger is ultimately from the political right even though it is initially spawned by the antidemocratic arrogance and nihilism from the political extreme left.

Extremism bent upon polarization of our people is increasingly forcing upon the American people the narrow choice between anarchy and repression.

And make no mistake about it, if that narrow choice has to be made, the American people, even if with reluctance and misgiving, will choose repression.

For an overwhelming majority of Americans believe that:

Trespass is trespass—whether on the campus or off.

Violence is violence—whether on the campus or off.

Arson is arson—whether on the campus or off.

Killing is killing—whether on the campus or off.

The campus cannot degenerate into a privileged sanctuary for obscentity, trespass, violence, arson and killing with special immunity for participants in such acts.

Criminal acts, active or by negligence, cannot be condoned or excused because of panic, whether the offender be a policeman, a National Guardsman, a student, or one of us in this legislative body.

Ironically, the excesses of dissent on the extreme left can result in repression of dissent. For repression is preferable to anarchy and nihilism to most Americans.

Yet, excesses on the extreme right, such as those 20 years ago, can mute our national conscience.

As was the case 20 years ago when the Senate was silenced and politically intimidated by one of its Members, so today many Americans are intimidated and made mute by the emotional violence of the extreme left. Constructive discussion on the subject is becoming increasingly difficult of attainment.

It is time that the great center of our people, those who reject the violence and unreasonableness of both the extreme right and the extreme left, searched their consciences, mustered their moral and physical courage, shed their intimidated silence, and declared their consciences.

It is time that with dignity, firmness and friendliness, they reason with, rather than capitulate to, the extremists on both sides—at all levels—and caution that their patience ends at the border of violence and anarchy that threatens our American democracy.

Notes and Comment (1970)*

Since the beginning of the Cold War, this country has had an extraordinarily difficult time preserving its sense of proportion in matters that concern the political left. Even when the influence of the left has been virtually negligible, men like Senator Joseph McCarthy have been

---

*This response to Senator Margaret Chase Smith's Senate speech of June 1, 1970, appeared in the "Talk of the Town" column of *The New Yorker*, Vol. XLVI, No. 19, June 27, 1970. Reprinted by permission; ©1970 *The New Yorker Magazine*, Inc.

able to create an atmosphere of panic and suspicion among large parts of the public by falsely claiming the existence of leftist conspiracies in high places. In recent years, the problem has been complicated by the appearance of a small, disorganized, but indubitably real and active extreme-left-wing movement, which, although it has almost no support in the nation as a whole, has been able, through the actions of some of its more militant members, to do real damage to the functioning of many universities. The current Administration's response to this new danger has been to exploit and exaggerate it by creating the impression that just about anyone who questions the Administration's war policies is an extremist, and in so doing it has created a threat to the freedom of the nation as a whole which is vastly greater than any threat that the extreme left could ever have posed in the first place. This campaign has put university administrators, who must actually deal with the dangers of disruption, in a very difficult position. At the time the campaign was launched, many of them had already had to face the awful choice of suffering the occupation of university buildings, the destruction of university property, and the disruption of classes or calling in police and National Guardsmen who were likely to use a degree of force that might bring about serious injuries—perhaps even death—and would almost certainly aggravate the crisis rather than solve it. Now, in addition to the task of opposing the real dangers that threaten their universities, the administrators, because of the inflamed state of public opinion, have been burdened with the task of opposing the circulation of unreal fears that have been spread publicly by political leaders. In recent weeks, some of the most distinguished and respected voices in the country have spoken on the question of campus disruptions. In their remarks, they have met the problem of disruption within the universities head on, but they have met less forcefully the problem of the spreading public misinformation outside the universities, and we fear that some of the statements they have made about the nature of the radical left have been inaccurate in a way that will further inflame the public, rather than reassure it. Senator Margaret Chase Smith, who was one of the few senators who had the courage to speak out against McCarthy's campaign of intimidation, and whose voice carries tremendous weight in matters that concern our freedom, has likened the disruptive activities of today's radical groups to McCarthyism. In a recent speech to the Senate, she said, "I spoke as I did twenty years ago because of what I considered to be the great threat from the radical right—the threat of government repression. I speak today because of what I consider to be the great threat from the radical left that advocates and practices violence and defiance of the law—again the threat of the ultimate result of a reaction of repression. .... The Senate was silenced and politically intimidated by one of its own members; so today many Americans are intimidated and made mute by the emotional violence of the extreme left." President Nathan Pusey, of Harvard, another of those who opposed McCarthy in the nineteen-fifties, has added his voice to that of Senator Smith, saying, "Now, less than twenty years later, our campuses are experiencing a not dissimilar period of torment, whiplashed as they are by a resurgence of his [McCarthy's] hateful technique. Again people are looking for scapegoats. But this time the attack comes not from the outside but from within, from extremist splinter groups of the New Left." President Pusey also likened both McCarthy and the New Left to Hitler and the Nazis, on the ground that all of them relied on the tactic of telling "the big lie" in order to gain support. The *Times*, too, has likened the American left to the Nazi movement, saying in a recent editorial that "it is not surprising that the new breed of campus revolutionaries intent on destroying all freedom except their own are now turning to what they call 'trashing'—the setting of fires, hurling of rocks, smashing of windows—ominously reminiscent of the shattered storefronts with which the Nazis sought to intimidate their political opponents of a generation ago."

On the whole, the comparison between today's radical left and McCarthyism and Nazism is a confusing one—and anything that adds to the already vast current confusion is dangerous. It is true that none of these groups have respected democratic freedoms, but in almost every other respect the differences between today's radical left and the two other movements seem to us immense. (Most of the comparisons that have lately been made—by all sides, including the radical-left side—between Germany in the nineteen-thirties and forties and America in the nineteen-sixties and seventies have been confusing. The Vietcong are not the Nazis. Americans are not the Nazis. Ho Chi Minh was not Hitler. Nixon is not Hitler. The radical students are not the Hitler Youth.) What is perhaps most striking is the disproportion between the danger posed by today's left and the dangers that were posed by McCarthyism and by Nazism. McCarthy had widespread public support, and he had access, as a United States Senator, to the enormous power of the government. Today, the extreme left has almost no support in the general public and no chance of winning access to state power, whether through revolution or through electoral politics. McCarthy, because of his power, succeeded in frightening scores of politicians as well as millions of citizens into silence, and even greatly respected public figures like Senator Smith could oppose him only at

great political risk to themselves. Today, there is not even one politi-
cian who is so afraid of the extreme left that he does not dare to denounce it; in fact, the nation's politicians have denounced the left
almost unanimously and have found it very advantageous politically
to do so. McCarthy was able to prevent people from speaking out anywhere, at any time—to silence them completely. The left today is able
to prevent people from speaking at certain times, from certain platforms, but it cannot prevent them from speaking at some other time
or in some other place. In this society, although groups with anti-
democratic tendencies who work outside the government can have a
damaging effect on American political life and can mount dangerous
attacks on certain institutions, such as the universities, it is only
groups who have the backing of state power, or might be able to
gain access to state power, who can pose a mortal threat to American
democracy.

Senator Smith, after levelling her most strongly worded denunci-
ation at the left, went on to recognize these crucial distinctions when
she pointed out that, ultimately, it would be not the extreme left but
the government that, in the name of opposing the left, would actually
impose repression. In other words, the left is important because it
could provide the government with a pretext for intimidating the public, not because it could do the intimidating itself. McCarthy, on the
other hand, was able to intimidate the public through his own efforts.
And this, of course, suggests that the analogy should be not between
McCarthyism and the left but between McCarthyism and government
attempts—and potential attempts—to intimidate citizens into silence.

We know from the McCarthy period that the fear of an imaginary
danger from the left can inflame a large section of the population with
anti-democratic passions just as surely as any real danger from the left.
Comparisons like the ones that have recently been drawn, which tend
to make the left seem more powerful and dangerous than it is, may
build up still further the public's already exaggerated fear of the left
and thus serve to create public supports for repressive tendencies in
the government. Moreover, these comparisons have been drawn at a
time when, as a result of the invasion of Cambodia, the minority of
students who are inclined to violence has been swamped in a gigantic
outpouring of sentiment and energy on the part of students who are
dedicated to nonviolent political activity. Thus, oddly, the comparisons have come just when the influence of the extreme-left groups is
the weakest it has been in several years. Indeed, one of the few hopeful signs of the moment is that on many campuses—perhaps on most—
students have been able to break away from their futile and destruc-

tive but peculiarly fascinating internal grappling and, together with faculties and administrators, turn their energies outward. It would be a tragic irony if, at just the moment when the power of the extreme left is fading, an artificial intensification of the fear of the extreme left were to provoke the repression we all hope to avoid.

Bibliography

Arendt, H., *The Origins of Totalitarianism* (2d Ed.; New York: Meridian, 1958).

Barker, E. N., "Authoritarianism of the Political Right, Center, and Left," *Journal of Social Issues*, Vol. 19-2 (April 1963), pp. 63-74.

Christie, R., and J. Garcia, "Subcultural Variation in Authoritarian Personality," *Journal of Abnormal and Social Psychology*, Vol. 46-4 (1951), pp. 457-69.

Christie, R., and M. Jahoda, eds., *Studies in the Scope and Method of "The Authoritarian Personality"* (Glencoe, Ill.: The Free Press, 1954).

Frenkel-Brunswik, E., "Intolerance of Ambiguity as an Emotional and Perceptual Variable," *Journal of Personality*, Vol. 18 (1949), pp. 108-43.

Fromm, E., *Escape from Freedom* (New York: Rinehart, 1941).

Greenstein, F., "Personality and Political Socialization: The Theories of Authoritarian and Democratic Character," *Annals of the American Academy of Political and Social Science*, Vol. 361 (1965), pp. 81-95.

Greenstein, F. I., ed., "Personality and Politics: Theoretical and Methodological Issues," *Journal of Social Issues*, Vol. 24-3 (1968).

Greenstein, F. I., "Harold D. Lasswell's Concept of Democratic Character," *Journal of Politics*, Vol. 30-3 (Aug. 1968), pp. 696-709.

Harned, L., "Authoritarian Attitudes and Party Activity," *Public Opinion Quarterly*, No. 3 (Fall 1961), pp. 393-99.

Haythorn, W., A. Couch, D. Haefner, P. Langham, and L. Carter, "The Effects of Varying Combinations of Authoritarian and Equalitarian Leaders and Followers," *Journal of Abnormal and Social Psychology*, Vol. 53 (1956), pp. 210–19.

Hennessy, B., "Politicals and Apoliticals: Some Measurements of Personality Traits," *Midwest Journal of Political Science*, Vol. 3 (Nov. 1959), pp. 336-55.

Kirscht, J. P., and R. C. Dillehay, *Dimensions of Authoritarianism: A Review of Research and Theory* (Lexington: University of Kentucky Press, 1967).

Lane, Robert, *Political Life* (Glencoe, Ill.: The Free Press, 1959).

Levinson, D. J., "Authoritarian Personality and Foreign Policy," *Journal of Conflict Resolution*, Vol. 1-1 (March 1957), pp. 37-47.

Lipset, S. M., "Three Decades of the Radical Right: Coughlinites, McCarthyites, and Birchers (1962)," in D. Bell, ed., *The Radical Right* (Garden City, N.Y.: Anchor Books, 1964).

Milgram, S., "Behavioral Study of Obedience," *Journal of Abnormal and Social Psychology*, Vol. 67-4 (1963), pp. 371-78.

Milgram, S., "Some Conditions of Obedience and Disobedience to Authority," *Human Relations*, Vol. 18 (1965), pp. 57-76.

Miller, P., and T. H. Johnson, eds., *The Puritans* (New York: American Book Co., 1938).

Miller, P., *Roger Williams: His Contribution to the American Tradition* (Indianapolis: Bobbs-Merrill, 1953).

Newcomb, T. M., K. E. Koenig, R. Flacks, and D. P. Warwick, *Persistence and Change* (New York: John Wiley & Sons, 1967).

Newmann, F. M., "Adolescents' Acceptance of Authority: A Methodological Study," *Harvard Educational Review*, Vol. 35-3 (Summer, 1965).

Prothro, E. T., and L. Melikian, "The California Public Opinion Scale in an Authoritarian Culture," *Public Opinion Quarterly*, Vol. 17 (1953), pp. 353-62.

Rostow, E. V., "The Japanese American Cases—A Disaster," *Yale Law Journal*, Vol. 54-3 (1945), pp. 489-533.

Sanford, N., "Developmental Status of the Entering Freshmen," in N. Sanford, ed., *The American College* (New York: John Wiley & Sons, Inc., 1962).

Schiff, L. F., "The Obedient Rebels: A Study of College Conversions to Conservatism," *Journal of Social Issues*, Vol. 20-4 (Oct. 1964), pp. 74-95.

Sellin, T., and R. D. Lambert, eds., "Political Socialization: Its Role in the Political Process," *Annals of the American Academy of Political and Social Science*, September, 1965.

Smith, M. B., J. S. Bruner, and R. W. White, *Opinions and Personality* (New York: John Wiley & Sons, 1958).

Smith, M. B., "An Analysis of Two Measures of 'Authoritarianism' Among Peace Corps Teachers," *Journal of Personality*, Vol. 33-4 (Dec. 1965), pp. 513-35.

Smith, T. V., *The Ethics of Compromise and the Art of Containment* (Boston: Starr King, 1956).

Spitz, D., "Power and Personality: The Appeal to the 'Right Man' in Democratic States," *American Political Science Review*, Vol. 52-1 (March 1958), pp. 84-97.

Stern, G. G., "Environments for Learning," in N. Sanford, ed., *The American College* (New York: John Wiley & Sons, 1962), pp. 690-730.

Stewart, D., and T. Hoult, "A Social-Psychological Theory of the Authoritarian Personality," *American Journal of Sociology*, Vol. 65-3 (1959), p. 274.

Tapp, J., *A Cross-Cultural Study of American and Swiss Stereopathic and Non-Stereopathic Personalities.* (Unpublished doctoral dissertation, Syracuse University, 1963).

Westie, F. R., "The American Dilemma: An Empirical Test," *American Sociological Review*, Vol. 30-4 (Aug. 1965), pp. 527–38.